# The Geography of Belonging

## A Love Story

"*The Geography of Belonging* is a gorgeous adventure of the heart and spirit, across cultural and species lines. This is a riveting and unusual love story of persons and of place told in sensuous, muscular prose."

Erin Robinsong, author of *Rag Cosmology*

"There is precious little left right now, of the magic that arises from relating to extraordinary animals in healthy wild settings. *The Geography of Belonging* is, in part, a realistic fresh-from-the-field portrait of an increasingly grim situation regarding the greatest of land mammals and the ecosystems they inhabit."

Douglas Chadwick, author of *Fate of the Elephant*
and National Geographic contributor

"Absolutely no doubt about this, Oriane Lee Johnston is a gifted writer. Her memoir reveals, with anguished directness at times, the longing for identity after a dramatic life-shift. The reader applauds her, is intimidated by and in awe of her courage, her openness to experience, and her many very real gifts of character. This is a lovely, deeply touching and above all, a serious book about the possibilities in life that many of us close ourselves off to, far too soon."

Sharon Butala, author of *Perfection of the Morning. This Strange Visible Air* and many award-winning best-sellers

"Oriane Lee's writing, about the seasons of life and death, and the frailty juxtaposed to the strength and endurance in the safari horse, is one of the best epitaphs to the horse I have ever read."

Karl Van Lauren, DVM,
southern Africa's prominent veterinarian

"Beginning with a dark horse dream, a respect for all layers of consciousness continues through every page of *The Geography of Belonging*. In that luminous space, we see that we already know what a land asks of us – to remember."

Odette Auger, Indigenous journalist.<br>Sagamok Anishnawbekwe, living in the Salish Sea.

"*The Geography of Belonging* is gripping, complex and very moving; flowing gracefully from the personal to the political/cultural and back again, in a voice that is sensitive, intelligent, and alive with the details of life. Oriane Lee writes beautifully, her spirit infuses the page, drawing the reader's sympathies and keeping us engaged all the way. This is a worthy book and one that deserves to be widely read. The philosophical asides are economical and poignant and invite the reader to consider the heart of the ethical dilemma of a white woman with a black man in an African country alongside the injustices of post-colonial Zimbabwe itself. If you care about what it means to be human in an increasingly inhumane world, and how to live an awakened life in an imperfect world, you will love this book."

Mark Matousek, author of *Sex Death Enlightenment:*<br>*A True Story*, and *Ethical Wisdom: The Search for a Moral life*

"Having been born in Southern Africa, I love *The Geography of Belonging*, travelling in my imagination with Oriane Lee Johnston on her amazing journey with Zimbabwe. She opens us to many questions about class, race, nature and the courage to follow love beyond our comfort level in order to discover the heart of another culture. The *svikiro*, a spiritual medium of the Shona people, said to her: "To see our traditional ways kept alive with your interest and your writing. That is what you can give us." Oriane Lee has indeed given that gift to all of us."

Ann Mortifee, author of *In Love with the Mystery*. Composer of<br>*Into the Heart of the Sangoma*

# The Geography of Belonging

## A Love Story

### Oriane Lee Johnston

Salmonberry
ARTS & PUBLISHING

Library and Archives in Canada Cataloguing in Publication

ISBN 978-1-7771492-0-8 (paperback)
ISBN 978-1-7771492-1-5 (ebook)

Permissions:
Excerpt from *The Fate of the Elephant* by Douglas Chadwick reprinted by permission of the author.
Excerpt from *Nine Gates* by Jane Hirshfield. Copyright © 1997 by Jane Hirshfield. Used by permission of Harper Collins Publishers.
"Just Sit There", from the Penguin publication *The Subject Tonight is Love: 60 Wild and Sweet Poems of Hafiz* by Daniel Ladinsky, copyright 1996 and used with permission.
"Pale Sunlight, Pale the Wall", version of Rumi, included by permission of Coleman Barks.

Published by Salmonberry Arts & Publishing
www.salmonberry.ca

Credits:
Cover Design by Saki Mafundikwa
Interior Design by SpicaBookDesign
Printed and bound in Canada

# Contents

*Horses come in the night. Into my dreams in the dark hours.*

*In a vast sun-filled field, I lie down in the middle of the grassland and begin to stretch my arms and legs, spiraling my torso, twirling my hands and feet.*

*All at once, I sense, something, coming, through the trees on the far side of the vlei. A dark form materializes.*

*An immense, gleaming, black horse thunder-gallops toward me. I press into the ground, terrorized, in the split-second of being trampled, to death.*

*But the trustworthy beauty leaps over me. Underbelly arcing above, as if I am a river.*

*He does this again and again, thundering and leaping, thundering and leaping, until my fright dissolves in the sound of his hooves, the sheen of his body, the pureness of his power.*

# PART ONE

HWANGE WILDERNESS. ZIMBABWE

# Baptism in the Wild

Bloomer, the young park ranger, packs a modest Cobra smg 8 mm in his saddle holster.

"I am here to protect you." He grins at me, hand on the firearm.

James Varden, safari head guide, has a Colt Python handgun and a Winchester rifle—one for loud noise, one for business. Stephen Hambani, Shona horseman and tracker, carries a braided bullwhip. Noise only.

Nine humans ride single file on horseback in the African bush; day four in a seven-day wildlife safari into the wilderness of Hwange National Park, Zimbabwe. We're on a thirty-three-kilometre ride to our next camping site, Jambili Pan, setting out just after sunrise to arrive before nightfall.

James leads on his strong buckskin gelding Munhondo, whose thick black mane and tail shine in the early light. I'm on the dark bay, Manini, who is wide-girthed and comfortable, assigned to me for his steadfastness. In front of me, Theresa Warth rides the grey mare Bhura, as she does each day in this position, a reassuring familiarity by now. The lively Theresa is about fifty and though Swiss-born, she is most at home in the bushveld, having married a Zimbabwean and lived in this country all her adult life.

A stroke of luck, in response to my desire to see wildlife up-close, that one space remained open in this safari planned for her relatives' visit from Switzerland. Though I haven't met Theresa or the Vardens before I feel like one of the family. James'

Australian-born wife and safari co-director, Janine, has expertly matched each of us with our mounts. The horses are specially trained for riding in the wilderness and for encounters with the animals of Africa. In stories round the campfire I hear how their sensitivity alerts the tracker, and the rider, to the presence of wildlife. And how their instinct to flee from predators is replaced by trust in the rider's leadership.

We travel not on footpaths made by humans or trails etched by horses but on red dirt tracks trodden by generations of elephants through the thick bush. We come across the elephants time and again, always stopping to make way for their traversing. Most captivating is their bath time at the watering holes—our horses motionless and hyper-alert, riders beaming or teary, profoundly touched by the pachyderm families at play.

But, at the moment, we're tracking fresh lion spoor: paw prints, a dropping of dung, and here, on our left, a big patch of flattened grass. Silently we ride on. Stephen, in front now, leans out of the saddle as he looks at the ground and then scans the bush. James rides alongside the rest of us and Bloomer follows close in the rear. My stomach is tight, gripped by an unfamiliar vigilance. Anticipation builds with the morning heat. Crossing open grassland, we curve toward a watering hole. Brush obscures the far side.

Nearing the water's edge Stephen's hand goes up. Stop. Be still.

Softly I hear from behind, "Look for a patch of yellow in the green brush across the pond."

James rides Munhondo round to the side of the watering hole and points. There she is—one lioness. I can see the shape of her head, the tawny blonde of her fur, the flex of her ears, the curve of her muzzle—and her what-I-imagine-are-amber eyes fixed in our direction. She lies perfectly still, the rest of her body just visible in the shadow of the brush.

James beckons us in his direction. He abruptly stops and points again. Another opening in the scrub brush. Another patch

*The Geography of Belonging*

of yellow. Mama number two. There will be cubs with her and a big male in the vicinity.

"*Shumba*," Stephen says beside me, steadying my horse. Lion.

Unable to look away, I barely fumble my camera out of the saddlebag. The only sound is my thumping heart and the others' whispered ohhh's and ahhhh's.

Something shifts. I sense it, subtle and intense. We are no longer observers, but the observed. And by a predator, not only of humans, but, more certainly, of our horses, prey.

The lion mother rises from the ground, opens her jaw—I can see her teeth—and stretches her front paw and shoulder, as if to take a step forward.

In the corner of my eye, a flash of green shirt. Janine, beside me.

"Go! Now!" she commands, and streaks ahead.

Instinctively I urge Manini forward with my legs, fast. I'm on Bhura's tail, eyes glued to Theresa. All our horses gallop at once toward an opening in the bordering trees. Fast. Manini is huge and thrusts a powerful forward impulsion. This is no time to tense up or fall off and every shred of awareness in my body attunes to the purpose of staying in the saddle. Nine horses lined head to tail, one lightning wave of motion, race through the dense underbrush.

What distance brings us out of range of lion curiosity?

Breathless, exhilarated with long hard riding, we stop for a moment in a small clearing of grass, horses snorting and blowing. The uncontrollable trembling of my legs is about to shake the stirrups off my boots.

A voice beside me shouts, "Let's go!"

I look ahead and Manini bolts forward; a second long sprint steps up the pace of the first. I fleetingly register a slash of thorn-bush that rips my shirt, a streak of bright blood on my forearm.

At last, the urgency eases off when the thick bush recedes, delivering us into an open sunlit grassland. We rein in our horses near the watering hole. I bend forward, utterly spent, wrap my arms around Manini's neck, slip my feet out of the stirrups and let my whole weight rest on him. When he lowers his head to drink, I slide sideways, slowly, down his wither. Stephen appears and takes the reins as I flop onto the grass, lie flat out, close my eyes and yield the intense vibration in my body to the dark earth.

A rustle of grass. Bloomer's face appears grinning above me, brilliant white teeth against the blue sky.

"That was a real good encounter!"

Bush-whacking we call it in the forests of west coast Canada. Here in Zimbabwe, it's bundu-bashing. After an extended lunch and chill-out time, James, with compass and GPS in hand, resumes command for the duration of the day. There are bushes with prickles, bushes with thorns and branches with spikes. Mostly the horses navigate around them; still, I'm glad for the protection of my riding helmet, unglamorous as it looks beside the wide-brimmed safari hats the others wear.

The afternoon heat is inescapable; my shirt sticks to the sweat dripping under my breasts. I peeled my bra off behind a tree at the last pause on the trail and stuffed it in the saddlebag. Faint with hunger, water bottle empty, I'm mildly concerned but voice nothing. My back aches and my ankles are painfully stiff. I wedge my left hand, palm upward, under the front of the saddle for extra leverage and anchoring. How on earth will I keep going through the escalating afternoon?

Desperation clears my thoughts. Get a grip. It's simply sensation, this physical discomfort. Enough time sitting on a meditation cushion through hours of knee pain, finally alleviated on arising, assures me now that this too shall pass. A purposeful breath exhaled in a slow stream brings my attention to Manini's ears, flexed backward toward me. He is with me. A flood of relief dissolves my isolation, and I notice the rhythmic rock of his unwavering forward stride, supporting me no matter what. I have only to feel my seat against the firmness of the saddle, my lower legs against Manini's belly, put my hand in his mane and grip his neck. I hope no one behind or ahead of me stops right now. These are private tears, of gratitude for what is right with the world. I feel the other riders, our human herd, as kindred spirits on the land.

And then it comes. The rain. African rain. Huge voluptuous drops saturate everything. Soaking wet warmth to the bone. Holy water, baptism in the wild.

Helmet off, head bare to the elements, I hold the wet-heavy braid of my hair across my mouth, slowly suck in the gifted water. The cloud sky lifts its hem from the blue horizon. A wide ribbon of pure light appears. Everything on earth glistens.

We're dry, both horses and humans, by the time Jambili Pan spreads before us flushed with the glow of late afternoon. We fan out over the landscape, each in our own world after the cloister of rain and bush.

Something curious on the other side of the watering hole. Manini and I step up lightly beside James, and I wonder aloud whether those zebras would flee if we came close. James nudges Munhondo toward the striped herd, and I follow alongside. I'm intrigued by everything, big and small, every motion, every colour, every call and response. I feel not separate out here but assimilated into this pulsing landscape, as if I know it from the inside. The zebras carry on grazing, swishing their tails and eyeing us as if we're not strangers, just newcomers today in the vast expanse of African horizon.

On the day before we escape the lions, three of us keep watch on the horses while they graze tethered to overhead long lines strung between the msasa trees. Standing between Stephen and his friend, the farrier, I'm a bit awestruck to be working alongside them. Joseph Chiwashira, the farrier, is head of the equestrian department of the Zimbabwe National Police in Harare. He runs the horse breeding and training program for the force's mounted patrols, having apprenticed in the Queen's stables in England. A cuddly bear kind of man, he is married with four adolescent boys.

"Coming on safari, into the wilderness," he says, "takes me far away from the pressing responsibilities of my job in the city."

A story unfolds about the tragic illness and death of his twin brother in Botswana last year. When Joseph returned to work in Harare, he found comfort in his favourite horse at the police stable. She followed him everywhere, keeping close and tender contact, relieving his grief. As he says her name, Jasmine, his eyes grow soft.

"Horses are our friends, our brothers and sisters, their spirit is with us."

After a long silence, I venture to say, "I came, to lie on the earth of Africa."

I can't help myself now and go on about Buddhist meditation practice, of lying on the earth and melting into it, though I stop short of the tantric breathing that brings earth energy up into the body. I tell Joseph that I've brought an offering for this land, for the spirits of this place and this herd of horses.

"A gift of thanks, a little spirit medicine bundle, made of plants from the forest where I live in Canada. It's not clear what to do with it."

Joseph tells me that cultural ceremonies are the centre of Shona family and community life and how they coexist with his Christian faith.

He turns to Stephen and says, "I am very sure when my friend left his home as a young man, his family had a big ceremony asking the Ancestors to protect him. It is our Shona way."

Then he looks at me.

"You know, to lie on the earth is a blessing!" He gestures to the space between us, "Here, please lie down!"

I accept his invitation, and lie down in the tall grass, hands on my belly. The warm ground seems to receive my body. Gravity, a meditation teacher once said, is the love of the earth, holding us close to her. The two men stand above, their backs to the sun. As they quietly talk, a long-tangled knot inside me—that fear of doing something wrong—loosens its grip. My mind seems to fall open, spacious as the sky. Am I dehydrated, or over-tired—or am I simply radically alive? This is not formal practice in a meditation hall; this is life in the raw wild of the earthly world.

In Mozambique, I collected a little vial of Indian Ocean to take home. When I stand again beside the two men, I ask Joseph, "May I scoop a tiny bit of red earth from Zimbabwe, from the spot where the elephants roll and rub? To take home as a gift to the land where I live."

"Yes," he says, "that is a most respectful thing to do. But we'll do it outside the boundary of the park."

Joseph's encouragement of my earth meditation in his own place of origin dissolves a lifelong inhibition in me. Growing up within the confines of a strictly secular family, I have carried an unknown grief from not naming the divine.

"Let's cool down horses in the water." Stephen says.

He boosts me effortlessly onto Manini and sitting bareback I feel much more at home than in the English saddle and stirrups, that I used for the first time ever in Mozambique. My right ankle is swollen and bruised from falling off a horse there. I lift my foot and lean over to pull up the hem of my pant leg to show Stephen the injury, apologizing for needing help to mount and dismount.

Stephen says, "Oh, sorry for that," takes my hand and places it on the back of his neck as he stands beside Manini.

His skin is hot and smooth and I feel his strong pulse under my palm. His attentiveness, his presence on the ground beside me, feels infinitely reassuring—someone, some one man, has got my back, out here in the wild. A second later he twists his head abruptly, I hear and feel a very weird snap.

"Serious, fall off a horse, training him for show jumping competition."

"And now, out on safari," I laugh, "you are coaching us in the fine art of hurdling fallen trees in the bush."

When Stephen hands me the lead rope, Manini heads straight for the watering hole and keeps going until my knees, and his belly, are underwater. I slide sideways off his back, floating into the velvet pool. I'm still holding his lead rope when Manini sinks down and rolls over, horse-groaning with pleasure. The two horsemen stand on the sandy verge, laughing at the showers of horseplay. As the setting sun gilds the landscape and the sky turns deeper blue, we guide the horses away from the watering hole and I ride back to camp, damp-dry and completely unwound.

It's time, I think, to present the medicine bundle I brought from Canada, to release the gratitude it holds for this welcome to Africa. Joseph counsels that I burn the offering in a fire. He'll return to Umtchibi Main Camp in the morning while the rest of us will make the daylong ride to Jambili Pan, me never imagining an encounter with lions.

Walking to dinner I pass Bloomer by the cooking fire. He's cleaning his weapon and looks up.

"How did Zimbabwe find you?" he asks.

# The Beginning

Five months earlier.

The autumn sun hovers golden through the morning mist, silhouetting the herd of horses grazing over the hillside on Vancouver Island. Inside the farmhouse, the cinnamon fragrance of pumpkin pie fills the kitchen; today is a milestone birthday, my sixtieth.

This time last year found me sitting through a three-week silent meditation retreat. Fervently hoping, contrary to all theory of non-attachment, for an opening in the dark forest of my life. Too much change in too short a time: the ending of a long relationship that had run dry in its last years; the loss of home and belonging that came with that, more traumatic than I imagined when my former partner severed communication after we parted company.

It was painful to visit my stepdaughter and grandchildren alone, left out of family gatherings after so many years with her father. On top of that, the responsibilities of active mothering dissolved, as my adult son made his own life, away in the city. All of this on the heels of completing a sixteen-year tenure as program director for Hollyhock retreat centre on Cortes Island. How would I survive the long hours of night with no bookends to hold me?

After leaving that family home, I came to stay at the farm, welcomed by my friend and eight horses, including a black Arab stallion, a rescue, and a white Friesen mare, whose name means reliever of sorrow. Longing for some internal place of refuge as well, I found a new meditation practice, in the Tibetan Buddhist somatic lineage, "Meditating With The Body." The foundation practice is called "Earth Descent." Lie down and melt deep into the earth, then sit up and breathe the earth's energy upward into the body.

I remember one night last winter, waking up in the dark with that metallic taste of unrelenting anxiety, the jaws of an excavator bearing down on my solar plexus. Howling loneliness. I couldn't find a home inside myself, or anywhere. I got out of bed, groped for my down coat, picked up a flashlight, went out to the barn, and lay down on a bale of hay. Feeling the stability of the hay bale against my back, horses quiet in their stalls, I folded my trust into the new meditation practice. It felt like the only ground I had.

I found horses, or they found me, not as a horse-crazy young girl, but in mid-life—and scared of them, back then. I didn't consider traditional riding lessons, I began on the ground, with natural horsemanship. Horse whispering, or horse listening, really, it means observing and interacting as if I'm another horse, not a domineering human. The thrill of that powerful animal willingly walking and trotting alongside me, cantering in a circle around me in an open field, taught me how to step forward and face fear.

Bareback on my new tutor, a chestnut mare named Cosun, the trails of Cortes Island became the ley lines for learning a new way of being, with myself, with animals and nature. Riding with her, through the forest and along the ocean shore was the perfect anti-dote to the responsibilities of work and a disintegrating home life.

Meditation teacher Michele Mcdonald gave me a book that would chart a new course. Her gift, *The Tao of Equus* by Linda Kohanov, ordained the marriage, in me, of spiritual life and the magic of horses. I began training in Equine Guided Learning—how the intelligence of horses and our communion with them can help humans heal, grow, and thrive. And for horses, too, the bond with a respectful loving human shifts an old paradigm of dominance and control.

At last, the long dark night that had come with loss of bear-ings and loss of purpose began to lift. To mark this new phase of life, I planned a pilgrimage to Bhutan. Not that I had the funds to go, but a cottage that had been in my family was up for sale. I wanted to arrive in Bhutan primed in the spiritual atmosphere of the country—Tibetan Buddhist meditation. So I continued daily practices with renewed dedication. The cottage didn't sell in the summer, though, so I cancelled the trip to Bhutan, disappointed yet curious about the significance of losing that opportunity.

Looking out at the herd on this sunny birthday, I remember the other day in the pasture, when I lay down on the grass with the horses grazing just across the fence. While I was deep in the earth-descent meditation, something came over me—an unmistakable inner call.

"Lie your body down on the earth of Africa."

Africa?

Honestly?

I have always wanted to go there.

Yesterday the realtor called with good news—she has a buyer for the cottage. This morning, as I wash the baking dishes, the huckleberry bush outside the kitchen window is draped with dew-glistened spider webs, strands of diamonds sparkling in the sunlight. Each tiny shimmer trembles with the motion of the spider weaver. A thought pops into my mind—you're free, and ready for a grand adventure.

Africa.

What would I do there?

Ride horses, of course.

How could I afford to stay for a few months?

Volunteer, why not.

I dry my hands, flip open the laptop and type into the internet search box: Africa + Horses + Volunteer.

Onto the screen spring compelling photos of horses and riders running on the sweeping shores of the Indian Ocean.

"The best beach riding in the world," the caption says. Mozambique, Africa.

My flight to the southern hemisphere leaves in two weeks, but I can't concentrate on my to-do list. I've just received a hugely upsetting e-mail from a friend.

"I'm awake all night," she writes, "very distressed about you going to Africa. As a small, blonde, white woman travelling alone, you'd be an immediate target. It's one of the real and unpleasant truths about being female. We are very vulnerable, physically, something most men wouldn't begin to understand. And women on their own, at any age, are at greatest risk. I'm afraid for you and truly hope you don't do it."

She goes on with horror stories of travel in South Africa related by others.

Crumpling onto the couch, I start to bawl; it has taken everything in me to have enough faith in myself to follow through on the call to go to Africa, and now—this vote of non-confidence from someone whose good judgment I value. This time, her perspective just doesn't ring true. Does she not recognize the ground I've gained since the broken times last winter? Is this her own fear, projected on to me?

After two sleepless nights, I email a reply to reassure her with details of my itinerary and the horse volunteer program—in Mozambique, not South Africa—and to say that I've delayed my departure by a week to tuck in loose ends. I even manage to thank her for caring and speaking out honestly.

There's more.

Carrying hay to the horses, I inadvertently leave a gate unlatched. From behind, loud snorting. Jagged prickles along my spine—the black stallion. Hot breath grazes my hair as he strides past me into the paddock beside the mares' field. One of the mares squeals, she's in heat and prances with her hind end pressed against the fence. The other mares are agitated, too, with the stallion's arousal. They strut and bounce, swishing their tails. The stallion rears and tosses his head, full mane flaring—he is clearly about to jump the fence. Panicked, I shout for my friend—she's already running out of the barn and screams at me.

"What are you doing? Get out of the paddock!"

Later, in the house, I receive what feels like a brutal dressing down. I listen and agree with the graveness of my mistake and the injury or worse, to horses, or me, that could have followed. My acceptance of blame and quiet apology are not enough. The tirade goes on and I feel quashed: it's her farm, her house and her horses.

In the end she says, "How can I trust you? You are not to go near the horses before you leave for Africa. I will do all the feeding."

In the days to come, I feel like I've been snorted up an elephant's trunk and pooped out the back end after these two alarming episodes with trusted friends. Despite feeling punched in the gut and beset with self-doubt, nothing in me considers backing away from going to Africa. And then I remember—when I've made a life-size decision in the past, like leaving my marriage, usually there's a pushback. Something disturbing happens, that, on the surface, says, "You've made the wrong choice." But in my experience, it's usually a test of resolve. "How committed are you to this choice?"

I choose a tarot card. The archetype of Lust, or Strength, slips out of the deck. In the picture, a golden lion carries a confident-looking, naked woman astride him: courage, passion, enthusiasm. From entheos: "possessed by a god, divinely inspired."

My son, Devon, twenty-eight and wise, listens on the phone to the dramas.

"Mum," he says, "never mind what anyone else thinks. Trust yourself. And for what it's worth, I still say go."

Over the next few years, my horse friend is humbled to the ground by that black stallion as he teaches her about respecting boundaries, about listening and kindness. She will become a specialist in animal and human relationships, in love and leadership. We've remained the truest of friends and I respect her immensely.

The night before I leave for Africa, Mary stands in the round corral wearing her Haisla blanket, ceremonial garment in the design of her First Nation ancestors. The sound of her drumbeat quickens my heart. Mary is my kindred spirit, with her herd of healing horses. I've come to their farm sanctuary in Goldstream, sacred Coast Salish territory, for the true preparation before Africa. The black gelding, Prince, stands on Mary's left and Summer, gentle paint mare, sniffs the ground on her right.

I kneel in the middle of the corral, in the twilight, kindling a small fire. As the moon rises, I mix a clump of wild herbs foraged on the farm, together with corn meal that I ground in the morning, a splash of birthday-gifted vodka and warm ash, all scooped into a red Tibetan prayer flag that represents my dedication to meditation practice. I roll it up and tie the ends with saffron-coloured thread. It looks like a fat cigar. Prince and Summer come close, curious, and I hold the bundle under their noses, to receive their breath. A blessing for the journey.

"I'm going to meet some new horses in Africa," I tell them. The bundle will announce where I come from, a kind of earthy introduction. I string it around my neck, for now.

Second thing: my beloved aunt and godmother, Oriane Jane, gave me a birthday card of Spirit Horses. Into its brown paper envelope, I slide: the tarot card of Lust-Strength, a slender braided strand of my hair twined with another, of horse tail collected from the grooming brush, along with a few other sigils I've made. Tucking the packet inside my bra, I have no idea when it might come in handy in Africa. A silvery light creeps across the blackened fire-ground, full moon shining above the mountain.

How do I know, to do these things?

I lie on the earth and I hang out with horses; I listen with my heart and not my mind. And I follow the guidance I hear—no matter how far-fetched it seems or how trepidatious I feel.

Here we go.

　　　　　　　　　　　　　*The Geography of Belonging*

# Breakfast in Africa

Mandy pours the tea. As she leans over, sunglasses slip from her cropped blonde hair onto her sunburned nose.

"Lukha, our horse groom, hasn't been to work at the stable in a few days," she says. "Witch doctor problems; he's been sent home from the hospital. Not only that, the other stable boys fell asleep and the horses escaped into the neighbour's grain crop."

Millet grain. Horses love it. Local villagers make a fermented homebrew by mixing the grain with water and spitting into the barrel to start the bacteria; it only takes a few days, and is potent stuff. That's why the loudspeaker music from the barraca behind Blue Waters Resort, home of Mozambique Horse Safari, is so loud so late into the night.

Already my shirt sticks to the plastic chair as the sun heats up the day. Mandy passes a cup of tea down the table, along with luscious-looking plates of food. The crayfish this early in the morning is delicious with lime, as are the sliced mangoes, here on the glittering shore of the Indian Ocean.

"Nick says the police caught the guy who slashed that woman tourist down the beach. They'll beat the shit out of him," Mandy says. This paradise sounds a little gritty.

The woman who was attacked is in her 30's, on holiday with her mother from Europe. It's an isolated incident and won't be publicized, so as not to discourage prospective visitors or horse volunteers. That evening, Mandy and Pat talk with the distressed mother in her bungalow. Across the room, I listen to the young woman. Her right hand rests in her lap, entirely bandaged in white gauze.

She had been at the stable communicating with the horses, having done a horse-whispering course before she came on holiday. One of the grooms had described seeing her at the stable in the morning, after our riding group had saddled up and headed for the beach. She sat cross-legged on the ground, he said, by the manure pile with her eyes closed.

It's one thing to practice tuning in to horses in a safe familiar place and quite another to try that here, in Africa, especially without anyone understanding what you're doing. When one is new to the experience it can bring about an overly open state, too vulnerable. It's much better to stand up, grounded, stay alert and aware of every nuance in the surroundings—as a horse itself does.

After leaving the stable she walked alone on an overgrown path down the hill to the beach—a path which I, and other volunteers, walk alone going to and from the stable every day. A local guy grabbed her from behind and held a knife to her throat, cash, the motive, the police said. As she raised her arms to fend him off, he slashed her right hand bloody. She screamed as loud as she could and the guy took off.

I cannot begin to imagine if that had been me. The knife was a panga, one with a long curved blade used to slash and clear bush. What comes to mind is my initial training in Equine Guided Learning; a crucial piece of healing is in the question: "When did you feel safe?"

I pose this question, gently, to the young woman beside me because compulsive retelling of the incident does not help to release the trauma. I intend to turn her attention away from the intensity of the attack and toward the moment when she realized she was okay and safe.

She cocks her head and says, "When I realized the guy had run away after I screamed, and again when I got back to the cottage from the hospital and was thankful because I am left-handed." I hold out her cup of tea, to help bring her into the present, and commend her bravery and quick thinking. She sighs, takes a sip of tea, and looks out the open veranda door.

"Oh, look," she says, "the moon is so beautiful shining on the ocean."

Since the attack on the European tourist, the stable grooms have been doing double-duty escorting me, and the other female volunteers, back and forth between the stable and Blue Water Resort where we are in residence. Most often the sweet 18-year-old volunteer from England is beside me, chattering away in her form-fitting riding tights and halter-top. She's been wearing her jeweled flip-flops out riding since the mosquito bites on her feet became so badly infected that she couldn't wear her leather boots. She's going home to London tonight.

I feel awful about the infection in her feet, and responsible. She and I walked in the shallow ocean water, purposely at my suggestion, to soothe the blisters on her heels. On the west coast of Canada, the cold salty water is good for abrasions of the skin and tissue. I had no idea the warm footbath of the Indian Ocean would proliferate bacteria. Oh my god, fermenting feet.

"What on earth will her mother say?" Mandy wonders, spreading marmalade on her toast. I think her mother will be relieved it's nothing worse. It could be a lot worse.

Mandy Retzlaff and her husband Patrick are Zimbabwean, but fled the country at the height of the violent government-decreed takeover of white-owned commercial farms in the mid-2000s. Everything was left behind in the farm invasions—except their beloved horses.

"Barricaded inside our house, scared to death with our young children, the soldiers-who-are-not-soldiers setting the crops on fire, threatening us with machetes. And we were the lucky ones. We managed to get out that night. Our horses ran for their lives and followed us, otherwise, meat on the roasting spit of the marauders."

Their saga unfolds at mealtimes over the duration of my two-month stay with them. Mandy holds forth with detailed monologues and turns direst tragedy into entertaining stories. It's an epic tale of bringing more than a hundred horses, rescued from overtaken farms, across the border into Mozambique. Eventually, creating this riding-safari business in Vilanculos, as a way for the horses to support themselves.

She has saved her collection of "Letters from Africa" over the last ten years, now a blog on Mozambique Horse Safari's website; writing her way to sanity amidst the crazy-making changes in Zimbabwe—President Robert Mugabe's corruption of power, turning democracy into dictatorship—and now the unpredictable conditions in Mozambique.

"Finish up that crayfish, it won't keep 'til lunch," Mandy says. She gets up from the table and looks at me. "We've got to get moving if we're going to ride before your visit to the orphanage this afternoon."

I am herded onto a safari truck—a Mitsubishi flatbed fitted with bench seats—along with a dozen earnest young women and men in their twenties who could be my daughters and sons. But I don't feel like their elder, barreling along the pot-holed highway from Vilanculos to Pembarra, wind whipping our hair. These young people are foreign students, volunteers, in Mozambique for two months to teach English and educate about HIV/AIDS. I'm a guest on their expedition today to an orphanage an hour's drive north. Listening to their animated banter, I'm curious how a three-hour visit to an orphanage could make any real difference, to us or to the children.

The driver, a serious young American man on a mission, is fixed in his view that Africa needs rescuing. He's seemingly untouched by the sensory deluge of landscape and the hearts of the people. I cannot find a way to connect with him in conversation and wonder

*The Geography of Belonging*

how he survives in an organization here—perhaps more easily than someone with a bleeding heart who is overwhelmed and cannot function. NGO's get a bad rap all over Africa, I'm told by the local whites—too many new Land Rovers, handouts, and rooms in high-end hotels. I try not to form any unfounded opinions.

It's early afternoon when the truck pulls into the sandy yard and the passengers jump down enthusiastically. I don't join in the face-painting or ball-playing or English tutoring. Let's see what is already here. Just sit, I tell myself, and watch what happens. So I stay under a shelter walled on two sides with corrugated tin, shaded from the searing sunlight. As the volunteers engage with the children, I wonder if I should make an effort to do something useful. No, just sit, inhale the scent of over-ripe fruit and shimmering heat on sand.

Behind me, the attractive young woman tutor leans over the Math workbook across from the teenage boy who is learning. She doesn't seem to be aware that her breasts are there for all to see in the spaghetti-strap halter dress. The boy's attention is not focused on her body, however, but on the book, so I take my own view of these things and put it aside. Yet here it comes again—what were these young volunteers thinking when they brought cheap plastic toys? I bet, in their western homes, they know about recycling. Already I've wondered where the "garbage" from here goes, knowing it goes nowhere.

A little hand rests on my thigh. The slight weight of her body against mine. A picture book slips into my lap. A ridiculous book left by some well-meaning visitor. No matter, it's not about the book. A shy arm reaches for my hair, pats my head. I slightly nod and raise my eyebrows. Now two little beauties comb my long straight hair with their fingers, finding strands to braid. Their gentle tugs on my scalp are relaxing and melt any reserve I've had.

I don't know how to make *sadza*, maize porridge, or how to say good morning in the Indigenous language yet, but I do know how to love children. Another shy hand reaches up. Face paint on my nose now, tickles on my ears.

"*Aqui*. Here," I say, offering my camera into the colourfully painted little throng. Giggles.

"Press the button harder, like this..." and off it travels from hand to hand. Child to child, reflections of each another. Truly I'd love to stay a long time in their midst. Months. But always the foreign visitors leave. How kind is that with orphans? A slender boy with long, graceful hands paints himself without a mirror, seeming to savour the feel of his fingers spreading the oily pinks and blues over his face.

The eldest girl, elegant in her tiny plaited braids piled high like a bird, covers her shoulders with her capulana, the Mozambican style of brightly coloured sarong worn by women all over Africa. She keeps her distance when I admire her hair, and turns away, laughing in delight at the younger ones playing. The littlest boy in the group cries when he can't keep up in the tag game. His face seems to crumple when the other kids tease, and a girl, who is his sister, pulls him close. Am I too old for this pair to come home with me, if they'd want to come? What an arrogant thought. Maybe I'd dedicate my life to being here? Yet I have young grandchildren at home and parents in their eighties.

What is selfish? What is humanitarian?

Where and how is the truest heart offered?

By late afternoon, the sun has fallen behind the palm trees; it's time to go. We climb back onto the safari truck, the volunteers giddy and tired. The children of the orphanage return to themselves and line up by an enormous black pot steaming over a fire, plates in hand. Pressing my back against the bench seat, I feel swollen by a brew of beauty and grief.

Who was it that talked to me of suffering? Oh, yes, that Swiss man who runs a guesthouse on the ocean bluff. Tears shimmer on the man's cheeks every day as we chat on my way from Blue

Waters to the stable, he interrupting his never-ending maintenance work.

"There is suffering, everywhere," he points, "Right over there,
and there, and there. And here," he says, putting his hand on his
heart, looking around. Has his mental state frayed in the polarities
of Africa?

How could this part of the planet have exploded—so profoundly—into my consciousness? My mind is shrapnel; there
are no valid opinions or judgments or suggestions to be had, or
made, by foreigners. I want to know and hear everything. Is the
maize grown with pesticides? Why are there South African-labeled
mangos in the market stalls, right beside mangos hand-picked here
this morning? How is human genetic heritage a result of place? I
know nothing.

Pat and Mandy's stories about their country of citizenship,
Zimbabwe, the land they fled, rouse bigger questions, too. Land
reform, the government still calls it, returning the farmland to
black Zimbabweans. Problem is, the political favourites who are
given the land have no skills to farm, especially not on a commercial scale. The agriculture-based economy of Zimbabwe falls apart.
I'm learning the history of the country, formerly colonial Rhodesia,
from the perspective of the white settlers. I had no idea.

Was the new Zimbabwe a shooting star, blazing bright then
burning out? Or in the shadow of a decade-long eclipse of the sun?
Is there a systems map for corruption? On a photographic image of
the entire world on the internet, one that shows where electricity
is concentrated—the African continent is mostly dark.


"Don't mind Pat's shouting," Mandy reassures us, excusing
Pat's military demeanor as he bellows orders and summons the
grooms.

"He does it with everyone. He comes from a long line of gen-
erals and commanders."

It doesn't bother me personally, for it is mostly aimed at the atmosphere at large, but it bothers me intensely when directed toward the stable grooms, the young black men responsible for the horses' care and feeding. Harsh, denigrating, it is characteristic, I later learn, of an old-school white Zimbabwean, former Rhodesian, "boss." Unabashed condescending superiority.

This, is my culture shock arriving in Africa.

To my immense discredit in this unfamiliar world, the Retzlaff's impatience with their staff leads me to think the grooms and housemaids are uneducated or slow to learn. When Mandy herself speaks sharply to the young women who do dishes, I smile at them to try and make up for her. In the mornings at the stable, I make the most rudimentary of greetings and ask questions about the horses and chores by gesticulating with my hands.

One day, a sudden electrifying shame catches me out. Riding on the beach, I'm just in front of a thirty-something female photojournalist from a South African travel magazine. She's talking with one of the grooms, Torai—and they're in a perfectly normal animated conversation about all kinds of things, in English, as he walks beside her horse. I feel sunburned to the core. It hasn't occurred to me to do that. My unwitting deference to Pat's authority and compliance with his social order is absolutely shocking now that I recognize it. Yes, everything is new and I'm trying to find my bearings—yet, what right do I have to be in Africa, unless with an unfixed mind? Picturing the young men who care for the horses, a pale shame punctures my identity.

Regardless of their seeming behavior, I know that the Retzlaffs provide their key staff with practical support and assume a responsibility for their basic needs, just as they had on their farm in Zimbabwe. One of the volunteers tells me that Jonathan, the head groom, has four children back in Zim, whose school fees and medical care are paid by the Retzlaffs. Mandy herself has said—when I asked her what in Pat has seen them through the devastations of the last decade—that his unfailing kindness to all living things, people and animals, is his finest quality.

How to hold the contradictions?

Jonathan Driver, the head groom, is about fifty years old and has stayed with the Retzlaffs through the odyssey of their ordeal from Zimbabwe to Mozambique. He was educated in English: in other words, on a farm in colonial Rhodesia, the precursor to Zimbabwe. It doesn't occur to me, at first, that Driver is not his true surname but was, instead, his function on the lost farm. Each morning when we arrive at the stables, he greets us, the volunteers, warmly by name, keeping an ear cocked towards Pat's plans for the day. Jonathan wears what look like cast off T-shirts and baggy shorts with cracked plastic crocs on his feet. He is patient, articulate, and kind. Perhaps he's a father figure to the young men who work for him.

I sit on a plastic crate in the shade, quietly knotting synthetic twine into hay nets. One of the grooms, Jonas, burns charcoal in a little brazier. Some rusted belt buckles cleaned in acid need to be tempered in fire, a process called bluing. Pat uses the buckles as hardware when he fashions recycled halters and stirrup leathers. Pat comes up the hill, shouting at Jonas. "No, no! Do it this way, not that way!"

At lunchtime, the groom is given a cold coke, but no food. I'm flabbergasted. Do the grooms have invisible lunch kits? Does Jonas' metabolism function without food between dawn and dusk? Am I missing some cultural imperative? Within two years I will come to know this is standard practice with "workers" in Zimbabwe. Boss or madam gives lunch: a loaf of white bread to share and a coke each.

Later, Pat leaves us, with one last command to Jonas, "Escort the madam back to the stable along the beach."

Jonas and I start down the hill and I mime cracking a whip, *che-che-che*, and ask him, "Does this bother you?"

"No," Jonas says, "It's not personal to me."

Day-to-day, dust-to-dust life in Africa belongs to the ones who live here, a deeper story than what appears to an uninformed visitor. What is that story? Six years later, a Shona friend in Zimbabwe will tell me, "It is the debris of superiority of colonialism."

Later in the afternoon I purposely seek Jonathan out and find him on the beach. We sit down on the sand.

"Please forgive my ignorance and misperceptions," I say. He is quiet.

"How do you do this?" I ask. "How do you live in these conditions and away from your family?" He sleeps in a stick hut across from the stable yard, overseeing the horses and the stables at all hours, every day and every night.

"How do you keep your composure and your dignity?"

Jonathan looks out to the ocean, then turns to me.

"Difference is difference," he says. "Who is oneself to judge another or try to change them? I make a divine plan and live each day with all my faith and all my love."

He is quiet again. After a time, I ask about his family, and he asks about mine. He talks of his devoted wife, of going home to Zimbabwe one month in the year, of phoning his four sons every Sunday who take turns going outdoors for private conversations with their father.

I'm sure I'm not listening well enough when he changes the subject and says, "I was told that you, coming from Canada, would think we are savages, like the Indigenous in Canada."

The sun on the sand reflects directly into my eyes, blinding me. My stomach heaves like I'm going to throw up. Leaning forward, head between my knees, tears sting and drop to the ground.

"Now I know, that is not true," Jonathan says.

Our shadows grow longer on the sand. Gingerly I sit back up, and ask him, "Do you know who the Dalai Lama is?" He doesn't.

"Well," I say, "he hangs out with Desmond Tutu."

I take the iPod shuffle out of my pocket and offer Jonathan the earbuds. His eyes brighten when he holds them to his ears and the music begins—His Holiness the Dalai Lama chants the Green Tara Mantra, invocation of compassion.

When the mantra fades, Jonathan hands the earbuds to me. Each of us has chores to do. We stand up and clasp hands for a moment, smiling. I turn back to Blue Waters for more net-making and Jonathan heads along the ocean's edge toward the stables.

What am I to do, or say? Not to absolve myself, but to stand for human dignity. Knowing that a face-to-face conversation with Pat and Mandy won't change decades of white supremacy, after my return to Canada I handwrite a letter. Before too long, photos of the black grooms appear on the Mozambique Horse Safari website. Coincidence, or not, I don't know.

"Here come the horses!"

Although there are just two of them, it might as well be a thundering herd for the amount of excitement in the air. Six Mozambican students from the residential teachers' college near Vilanculos are waiting in the grassy grounds of Archipelago Resort. We've planned an afternoon of Horses & Leadership, to learn body language as a communication skill by interacting with horses. This assignment from Mandy is part of my contribution for Mozambique Horse Safari's community service. I recall the students, having met them before in the Conversational English class: Antonio, Carlito, Martina, Filipe, Benute, Florencia—these names are the residue of Portuguese East Africa, the colonial predecessor of Mozambique. How sincere and open the teachers-in-training are.

Horses are a rarity in Mozambique, and not one of these young adults has ever been near one. The students are nervous; several are downright scared even though they have chosen to come. We hope the session will be good community relations as well. Too often the horses get loose and trample roadside crops, upsetting the village neighbours who work so hard on the land for their food.

*Con su permiso*, meaning "with your permission," is an activity that allows the students to meet the horses up close, to approach them with curiosity and respect. I practiced it with Barbara Rector in the United States; she's the grandmother of Equine Guided Learning. It's taken weeks of patience for this first session to materialize, but I've learned nothing from horses if not to be adaptable and to improvise with changing conditions—great training for getting along in Africa. The upside of the wait has been time to become more familiar with the two grooms who will be horse handlers: Torai and Jonas, both in their twenties, are actually from Zimbabwe, so English rather than Portuguese speaking. I had explained the purpose of the afternoon.

"Who do you think would be the best horses for this?" I asked.

"Oh, I know! Brutus and Texas," Jonas said. "They are intelligent, pay attention and are the safest." It's clear, right then, that my role is to simply describe the activities and keep the group dynamics flowing because leadership itself belongs to these two young men.

"Horses are here," the students call out again.

Brutus with his dark, flowing mane and sturdy build is led by Torai who has dressed for the occasion—jeans, sporty shirt, leather-look loafers and a ball cap. This contemporary clothing is bought at roadside market stalls for just a few *metical*, the currency of Mozambique. The garments arrive by the container-load in Africa, donations from the "first world." The other horse, Texas, light-gray and nimble, is led by the ever-cool Jonas whose appearance would be completely at home in Manhattan or Montreal, though I'm not sure about his urban savvy. The two grooms are confident in their roles as leaders with the soon-to-be professional teachers.

Samantha, another volunteer like myself, skirts the field and I casually invite her in; we'll need another facilitator to keep an eye on safety. She's a horse trainer from England who competes all over the world in long-distance endurance riding. She was formerly a high-end casino manager in London, a subversive fireball, yet in Vilanculos, in tattered riding tights and ball cap, she looks nothing like the sultry vixen in her Facebook photo. I notice Jonathan Driver leaning on a wall across the grassy field and wave him over, but he declines with a slight tilt of his head toward the ground. Is he curious himself, or reporting back to Pat? Either way, I'm pleased he is here.

By way of introducing the session, I ask the grooms, "Tell us how you became involved with horses, and about your work with them." They appear to have thought about what to say.

"The horse is your friend," Jonas begins. "You can love him and trust him and feel for him, and he feels for you."

The students are giddy with anticipation. I team up with Torai and Brutus, and ask Samantha to join Jonas and Texas, each of us with three students.

A simple approach exercise sets the foundation: while the grooms hold the horses' lead ropes for safety, the students, one at a time, are instructed to approach the horse offering the back of their hand.

"Is the horse inviting you to move closer?" I ask. "Is he sniffing your hand or touching it with his lips? Is he turning away because you are too close? Everybody, breathe!"

In just a few minutes, each person walks past his or her fear into connection with the horse. Afterward, they all let their breaths out, dance around, laughing in relief.

Their second approach goes a step further—stroking the horse's neck and shoulders. I ask the kids to notice softness, warmth, and motion under their hands—again followed by a dancing release of tension. When the horses lower their heads and blow out their noses, we do too—a herd of ten human and two equine beings.

Samantha demonstrates how to cross behind a horse safely. Standing by Texas' left flank, facing his rear, she puts her left arm high on his rump and fits her torso gently against him, then walks around to his right flank. There's no danger of a horse kicking out with this close contact. The excitement level rises as the students, one by one, accomplish what half an hour ago would have been unthinkable.

For the finale, I ask Jonas and Torai to demonstrate moving their horses forward without pulling on the lead ropes.

To the students, I say, "Keep the rope loose, look ahead, picture where you want to go, then start walking."

Martina struggles, looking backward toward her horse helplessly.

"Look ahead, walk forward!" I say.

"You go, girl!" Samantha encourages.

Martina sets her sights on a nearby tree. And Texas, bless his heart, follows her. We are jubilant for Martina. She'll retain this feeling of success in her body. It's hard for a young woman in Africa to take her place and move forward.

Torai spontaneously directs Brutus to lift his hoof and coaches the students to accomplish the same thing. The students are incredulous at their own achievement. Samantha jumps in to suggest wrapping up with a debrief from each person. Jonas says he learned something today and understands his connection with horses now.

A polaroid camera appears and we take photos of one and all—students, hugging horses and stroking their manes. The grass field at Archipelago Resort mellows to gold in the coming twilight and seems to radiate love under the deepening blue of the sky. Horses do that with humans. Evening songbirds, nightjars, begin to sweep overhead, their churring sounds ripple across the stillness.

You'll remember that before coming to Mozambique I put together a small bundle of elements from nature at Mary's farm, a respectful

*The Geography of Belonging*

greeting to the spirits in the new land I would soon tread. The red prayer-flag-wrapped bundle stayed outside in the centre of the round corral on the full moon night before my departure.

Tacking up Texas this morning I tied the medicine bundle to his saddle for exposure to the elements of open sky, expansive shore sand and glittering turquoise ocean; air, earth and water. Now the beach ride is over, and I have an hour alone at the stable, while the grooms lead horses to the grazing field for the day. Sunlight dapples the spotless yard; four just-washed saddle blankets hang from the overhead rope line, three horses, who are on rest leave for the day, softly snuffle in the dry heat. A mountain of manure steams near the back fence, composting.

I untie the medicine bundle, offer Texas a sniff, and then stroke the dark patch of his coat soaked with sweat where the saddle has lain. This is a very effective grooming tool—swiped firmly across his back and belly, it works just as well as a bristle brush. I rub down the other few horses; each one wants to sniff the still-fragrant bundle.

The pile of manure is hotter than I reckoned; digging in a foot or so, my hands turn red. When the scorching becomes unbearable, I push the offering in, sprinkle some maize meal, then fill the hole. This burning is not a flaming open-air fire—it is dark, smoldering, an earth-oven.

The ceremonial moment closes over as the grooms return from the fields. Jonas offers me a drink from the rubber hosepipe. The stable's water comes from a borehole 150 metres deep into the ground, safe to drink. Jonas wants to know more about what we did together, with horses and the student teachers.

"Let's try something," I say.

"Hold your hands out in front of you, palms facing each other, like this. Now move your hands closer together, slowly. Can you feel anything?"

"Yes," his widening eyes say. "Like butterflies in my hands."

Looking around the stable yard I ask, "Which horse do you feel the most?"

"Fleur," he says quietly.

Fleur is a petite mare, endeared to us all by her floppy ears—an untreated tick bite can progress to this outcome.

"Okay, walk toward her and notice what you feel in your hands, your whole body."

"I notice something," he whispers, slowing, then steps again toward Fleur.

"I'm sure you are already feeling the horses' energy," I say, as Jonas reaches out to stroke Fleur's forehead. "Now, pay attention to it as you're with them through the day. You know, when guest riders don't really care about the horse, and the horse is restless when they try to get on."

"Ohhh!" He gets it.

"Like music," I say, "You can't touch it with your hands, but you feel the vibration in your body from the instruments or from the stereo speakers."

A few minutes later we return to the water buckets, and he asks if I have a picture of my horse in Canada. It's in my daypack. The beautiful chestnut mare Cosun is lying down in the photo and I'm kneeling on the grass in front of her, with my forearms resting on the ground. We are nose to soft nose.

"Ohhh, you paid attention and went close, just like me with Fleur," Jonas says.

In two days time, I will leave Mozambique and the horses. Up before daybreak I walk down to the beach below Blue Waters, and slip onto the sand near the fisherwomen, with their spirited banter, who are waiting for the tide to change. The fiery sun, rising out of the ocean, draws that glittering lava trail straight toward my feet.

Today Pat has arranged a day-long ride to a fishing village; he's guiding a short-stay safari guest and has invited the volunteers—Lisa, Samantha and me—to go along. It's my favourite route, traveling on footpaths between villages and in the afternoon heading out onto the beach for the return. We'll have most of the day on horseback, with midway stop for a seafood lunch prepared by the fishermen.

Pat rides in front on Duke, his magnificent chestnut gelding, and gives the cues for changing gait. Along with hand signals, he shouts, "Walk, trot, canter" depending on the footing and the proximity of crops and people. I'm first in line behind him riding my trusted buddy, Texas. The inland atmosphere is intimate and lush, jungle. Coming over a slight rise, the footpath widens and dips into a rustling swale of shoulder-high greenery. Jonas, on foot, goes ahead, parts the tall grass and wades into a waist-deep stream. Our horses lower their heads and blow, then, one by one follow him into the serpentine waterway. A floating carpet of mauve-tinged water lilies brushes our boots and stirrups. Pat's feet, though, are out of his stirrups and trail in the clear water soaking the hem of his jeans. He's tall and wears crocs with bare feet all day, every day, no matter what the occasion.

As the sun peaks toward noon, everything about riding comes together. Rounding a bend at a canter on the packed-earth footpath, I lean over Texas' neck to avoid a low-hanging branch while simultaneously keeping him out of the millet crop bordered by a low stick fence.

At last, after all these weeks, I feel completely in synch with Pat's instructions and unpressured by the other horses and riders who follow me. The sun is deliciously hot on my back—my effortful trying evaporates. I want to ride on like this into the heart of the world.

Thwack, the fisherman's machete cracks open a coconut held in the palm of his hand. He gestures toward a thatch-roof pavilion set back from the cliff side. Wooden chairs tilt gently on the sandy floor beside a lace-covered table, the places impeccably set for our lunch. An exotic-looking feast is laid out—lobsters caught this morning, the traditional cooked green-vegetable dish called metapa, fresh tomato salad, steaming rice, and ripe mangoes. Our horses, unsaddled, graze their own lunch nearby.

As we eat, Pat casually says of my riding today, "You're doing very well. It takes years to cultivate high-level horsemanship." I'm thrilled to the back teeth, as the Australian visitors say.

Today is the unspoken culmination of Pat's informal coaching, preparing me for a wildlife safari on horseback in Zimbabwe, a new journey I will undertake in a few days. Some friends of the Retzlaff's who remained in Zim, James and Janine Varden, guide week-long expeditions with mobile tent camps in the bush, in an area of the country less tangled in politics. My dream of seeing wildlife in Africa is coming true. I recognize the incredible light-handed support Pat has given me; I can now canter confidently on the wide-open beach and feel skilled enough to soon ride into the habitat of Africa's iconic animals—in the wilderness of Hwange National Park.

After a brief rest we're back in the saddle and we make our way down the red cliffs toward the vast reach of the ocean shore. Texas is swift and sure-footed n the steep soft-sand trails, ski-dancing downhill, diagonally traversing the slope. Once the whole group is out on the flat-packed sand, each horse and rider finds his or her own pace. Several speed along the water's sparkling edge; some meander through the shaded mangrove streams that border the cliff bottom.

Out on the sweeping expanse of white sand, it happens.

Someone comes off her horse at high speed—tumbling in the air, falling headfirst.

Oh, my God. It's me.

A lightening shock, shattering force of impact, my body slams the ground. Flat out on the wet sand, I'm detached from myself, observing from a distance and immobilized by the intensity of sensation in my body.

*The Geography of Belonging*

A pair of hands holds the sides of my head, lying in a shallow tide pool. Warm water feels good. Stay with that. The contact of Lisa's hands feels good, too.

"Does your travel medical insurance have emergency evacuation coverage?" she asks. "Do you have a doctor at home we can call?"

What if my neck is broken? I should be more upset. But I can't think about the future. Only this minute. And I'm not saying I'm fine, as people in shock often do after accidents. I know very well I'm not fine. And, I know, I'm not going to any hospital around here.

"Don't move," someone says.

I don't intend to.

"Where does it hurt?"

Everywhere, for Christ's sake.

"Can you wiggle your toes?"

Yes, barely, I can wiggle my toes. Now piss off!

Trying to breathe, I can't swallow the saliva at the back of my closed throat.

Just lie here, I instruct myself. Let the body trauma, the shock, sink into the wet sand, and out of me. Instead of trying to get up, I stay put and don't move,

Just lie here, trust the earth—the comforting, warm, stable wetness of the sand beneath me. Sink deep into that healing.

After a time, I begin to feel oddly lighter, unwrapped, transparent to the earth and sky, to the ocean and sun, as if they recognize me. Slowly, I comprehend—when I landed on the ground, some ages-old tension in me, some separateness, shattered.

Lying on the beach—with, the beach—really, I didn't fall so much as Africa leaped up to meet me, to shake me awake. The motherland wants my attention. All right, I think, let's be friends. What do you want to do together?

The scent of seawater dried on the sand prickles the hairs in my nose. Time to train all my attention on my body, keeping perfectly still, letting it inform me of its state.

The conversation with myself continues.

Can I turn my head at all? No.

Can I move my leg? Slightly.

Can I shift my weight, one body section at a time, and roll onto my side? I don't know. Let's try.

It's a good half hour before I'm on my right side, head cradled in the curve of my arm. Lisa and Pat, in slow motion, help me into a sitting position. Way too painful. Slowly, shifting weight in micro movements, I move onto my hands and knees, head down to relieve my neck. This feels best so far. I start to growl, from the belly, howling out the uproar in my body.

I'm an animal, a wild animal. Oh shit, that's in a few days, the riding safari in Zimbabwe.

How the hell will I ever get on a plane the day after tomorrow?

Never mind. That's two days away. Don't think, don't go there. Then, I hear an inner voice, or is it Texas, his head bent low to the sand beside me?

"Be like a horse, don't anticipate what might happen anytime ahead of now. Stay here, in the present; it's all that matters."

"Can you stand up?" Pat asks.

"Piss off!"

We all laugh. Oh crap, that hurts, too.

Let me rest. Let this pain drop out of me and into the ground, the healing earth.

At long last, I feel no boundary between my body and the beach; now, I'm able to move. Pat and Lisa form a sling with their arms and walking sideways delicately carry me the rest of the way to Blue Waters. Seeing the swimming pool in front of the casita, my little home, I ask, "Just roll me gently into the water, please."

Lisa carefully pulls my boots off. I slide into the pool. Floating face down, like a jellyfish, feels soothing, and arcing my back raises my head just enough to get some air. I know this rhythmic flexing movement will release more trauma out of the nervous system. I peel off my clothes inch by inch, except underwear, and give myself over to the buoyant support of the water.

Sometime later, propped with pillows on my bed in the casita, I remember the young woman who had her hand slashed and my question to her: "When did you feel safe?"

I feel safe right now, in my room. Wearing the copper coloured skirt with glitter from India that my sister gave me for my birthday. Ice on my ankle. Door open to the beauty of the ocean framed by palm trees. Receiving visitors, one by one. I am intact. Yes, I feel safe.

Mandy comes in and says falling off is part of the sport.

"Everyone falls off," she assures me. "Riders at every level of experience."

She continues with dramatic stories of injury. Samantha, the English horse trainer, has a steel rod in her leg, kicked into multiple fractures by a fiery mare. The young woman who runs the stable on Benguerra Island was kicked in the head. She had to be airlifted out and flown back to England for surgery and rehabilitation, returning some months later to the Benguerra stables with a titanium plate in her skull. I wonder about her devotion to the Mozambique horses and I question my own imperative to ride. How resilient is a sixty-year old body? How much risk is worth this adventuring?

Pat comes in to vent, his way of expressing concern. He's upset by this morning's guest rider, who rode right past the scene of the accident without stopping. Pat cannot fathom her self-interest or lack of compassion, especially as the previous week she'd fallen off a horse herself on safari in Botswana and had to be airlifted out of the wilderness.

I try to unravel what happened. Three things stand out: the first is the moment I felt flattered, that tiny prick of ego, after we'd come down the steep trail onto the beach, and Pat directed the woman to follow Texas and me back to the stables. Pride cometh before the fall, indeed. I would have been a fine leader, I think, had things not escalated with the guest's eagerness to get back to her bungalow and her late afternoon plane flight, though we had plenty of time. This urgency led to the second element. She was riding Black Magic, a big forward-going exuberant mare who speeds up at the slightest provocation and loves running like the wind. She's also very sensitive to people and surely felt the woman's urge to finish the ride.

Initially Texas and I were in an easy canter along the beach. But, leagues beyond my capability, Black Magic and her rider were coming up much faster behind us, soon to overtake us like a steam engine speeding by. This is extremely discourteous between riders. A horse person knows that horses respond to pressure, and pressure from behind propels them forward. I could feel it, just before Black Magic reached us neck and neck: as if the accelerator had hit the floor, Texas broke into an overdrive gear I hadn't experienced before, tossing his head in a torrent of energy.

Thirdly, I was not skilled enough to stay in the saddle in this kind of rodeo. I did the opposite of what restores control—I leaned forward, and gripped hold of his mane to keep from falling off. This is a cue for acceleration. Fine if I'd had more stability and balance in the saddle and was not at risk of falling off at high speed. Keeping your seat, it's called.

By evening my right ankle is swollen tight and colouring with deep bruising. The left side of my neck is frozen and prevents my head from turning in any direction. The back of my throat feels kicked in. My lower back is crunched, my waist on both sides aches like crazy and I cannot stand or walk upright. I've never had injury like this before. The occasional fall off a horse or motorcycle slowed me down for a day or two, but this is different.

After Mandy's assessment that no bones are broken, we don't call a doctor or go to the local clinic. I'm sure, with arnica cream for the bruising and anti-inflammatory tablets for the pain, I will manage.

*The Geography of Belonging*

In the early evening, a tap on the doorframe and Jonathan Driver stands on the threshold step looking happy and sorrowful at the same time. His hat is in his left hand. I'm so pleased to see him.

He says, "I am happy to see you are not more severely injured, and so sorry the accident happened. I needed to come and see that you are all right."

"Thank you very much, Jonathan, for coming. May I ask you a question?"

My visitor nods.

"Tomorrow morning, I planned to go shopping, but Lisa may have to go without me. To buy new T-shirts for the grooms, a thank-you present for their kind attention and hard work on behalf of the volunteers. Do you think this is an acceptable gift?"

"Oriane," he says, "anything is a good gift, if it is given from the heart. Anything at all."

Saturday morning sees no improvement in my condition. My whole body amounts to one bundle of everything contrary to agility and ease; the bruising on my leg a psychedelic emergence I pray doesn't spread. In the tack room I find some bright green, stretchy bandage-wrap for horses injured or weak in the fetlocks and I bind the wide strip around my ankle and foot. Still, a throbbing lower back threatens to knock me under, despite potent pain-relief tablets

I'm irrationally attached to my plan for the grooms' farewell gifts. Yes, I can leave a gratuity in cash, and I will, but in travels over the years the gift of choice for my son, Devon, has been a T-shirt from wherever I've been. I feel maternal and grateful toward the young horsemen who've enriched my stay in Mozambique and the shirts seem to represent the enormity of what I've received. I want each one of the grooms to know that he will be remembered.

The taxi trip to town with Lisa is successful, and we return to find Pat engaged in an all-day cooking marathon for my farewell dinner tonight—Indian curries from scratch. He looks exhausted, not necessarily from his effort in the kitchen, but more likely from the accumulated weariness of trying to survive in the conditions of Mozambique with others dependent on him. He's faced challenges like Cyclone Favio, three years ago, that hit the coast and destroyed everything he'd established; finding the engine missing from the old Land Rover he keeps for spare parts, even though the vehicle is locked in a guarded storage compound; being pulled over by the Policia every time he does an errand in town; securing food for the horses and having to train every groom from the ground up—all this piled on the past ordeals in Zimbabwe. I can only hope today's elaborate meal preparations take his mind on a bit of a restful road trip.

Mandy and their adult daughter Kate arrive for dinner, sick with some kind of coughing infection for which they are popping antibiotics. Sam is sullen and pissed off about something, though she comes around after some food. Lisa keeps everything going in the background, I'm impressed she has not yet set her sights on going home to the U.S.

The neighbours, who've been exceedingly hospitable to the Retzlaff's horse volunteers over the months, are seated with their plates around the big, square wooden table. I've come to appreciate these exiled Zimbabweans; their stories have helped me understand the unmitigated challenges of trying to forge a new life in uncertain times, when loss is the prevailing climate. True, the world over.

Pat is flattened against the back of the couch, plate on his lap, head discreetly down, eyes closed. Seize the moment; tapping a fork on a wine glass, I stand up from the table and look around the verandah.

"I have received so much more than I have given," I say, hoping sincerity over sentimentality will see this through without tears.

"First of all, Pat's riding coaching—his patience, generosity and wisdom have given me the confidence to go on safari in Hwange next week, with more horses!

"And Mandy—who else wears her best, white, clothes and elegant sunhat horseback riding? As she says, 'Darling, you mustn't save anything for later. It could all be lost anyway.'"

The rest of the guests perk up, several are teary as they raise their glasses to the Retzlaffs. I smile at Pat and Mandy's twenty-four year old son, who took four of us volunteers to Gorongosa National Park.

"And cheers to you, Jay. I'll always remember sharing your love of the wild."

The paraffin candles in the centre of the dining table are pooling in their saucers. Smoky incense burns from the mosquito coils set on the windowsills.

As the shuttle van to the airport accelerates slowly out the Blue Waters driveway in the morning, Jonathan Driver comes running breathless from the stable; the sliding door beside my seat is open.

"God bless you, Oriane! Safe journey!"

The van stops and I step gingerly onto the ground, careful not to stress my ankle.

"Jonathan! Thank you for coming!"

Joyfully I extend my hands and hold his calloused ones in mine. I'd wondered if he already has a Swiss army knife. Doesn't matter, I reach into my pocket and offer him the shiny red knife that's been mine for twenty years. He accepts the gift.

"I used to have a knife like this," he says, opening and closing the myriad blades and tiny tools. "And have always wanted another."

"May I ask you a question, Jonathan?"

He looks at me and nods.

"Would you please tell me your real surname?"

"Mazulu. Jonathan Mazulu."

"Bless your heart too, Jonathan Mazulu."

In the overnight hotel room in Johannesburg I'm alone, feeling panicky. My lower leg has ballooned above and below the wrapped bandage. Unwinding the green elastic binding, the bruising looks like a rogue tattoo now covering my entire lower leg, foot to knee.

No one answers when I dial "O" for the office. I can't work the telephone to order food in. And I can't imagine walking anywhere, now, or in the morning through an airport and onto a plane.

Stop everything. What do I need right now? Pain medication. Okay let's do that; it's in my backpack. I can crawl. Now what? Lie on the bed; knees up, put your feet flat on the blanket, the pillow under your head. Stay here, just breathe.

What's next? Get up and go into slowly, slowly, into the hallway and rouse someone, ask for something to eat. Shuffling in my bare feet, my eighty-seven-year-old father comes to mind. He walks just like this, without a cane. By nightfall, the swelling recedes and pain comes only with wrong movements, but the kaleidoscope of bruising is a sight to behold.

Mid-air, destined for Zimbabwe; in the cocoon of the SAA airliner, I stretch out over two seats in a row to myself, content for the moment. Flying over Botswana is a thrill—I wonder what animals, invisible from the sky, roam the earthy green? The Okavango Delta took on mythic proportions when I saw a YouTube video of horses galloping through its waterways. A few weeks before leaving Canada, I sobbed my way through watching it, desolate, thinking I'd never be able to ride like that. Yet, my riding gear is in the cargo hold of this aircraft, though heading to Zimbabwe savannah woodland rather than Botswana river delta.

As the plane begins its descent, I see a mammoth curtain of smoke on the ground, miles away, a distinct linear uprising of silver-gray. A firebreak, I think, created on purpose in the dry season. But the smoke isn't rising further into the sky—it isn't smoke, it's Victoria Falls from the air.

*The Geography of Belonging*

The airport is small and quaint; at the immigration desk, it turns out I don't have the $75 US cash required for the visitor's entry permit. A Canadian $100 bill won't do, and there's no currency exchange counter.

"Madam, you must ask your countrymen in the queue to lend you the money," says the female immigration officer, "and be seen making an effort to try." Oh, really?

"Someone will lend you the money." Just who is that someone?

I can't believe I'm actually going down the queue with this story. Trying not to limp with my ankle injury, I cover my acute embarrassment by imagining myself in an audition for a movie role, until, luck of the draw, one of the passengers happens to be from my country—a Canadian Coast Guard officer on holiday with his wife. They live twenty minutes from me on Vancouver Island.

"Wait here, till we get through," he says. "Where are you staying?"

A few minutes later he returns, Canada Coast Guard to the rescue. "Your hotel pick-up is outside. Just come through with me." I follow him past the border officials; the driver lends me the cash, and I return to the immigration desk. After all that, I forget to claim my bags on the way out.

I check-in to the decorum of the Victoria Falls Hotel, having booked a discounted rate on the internet the previous week. A porter leads the way along carpeted corridors, steeped in dated elegance, and opens the door to my room. Sunlight streams through the corner windows onto a dark wood, four-poster bed underneath a romantic-looking snowy white mosquito net. Floor length chintz drapes in rose and cream complete the storybook scene. I take my time luxuriating in a deep spotless white bathtub, bubbles up to my chin. I could spend the whole twenty-four hours in the tub.

Then I remember the blight of colonialism on Africa, and wonder about enjoying its amenities in the 21st century. But I'm drawn into the mystique of this bygone era and the transition from Rhodesia to Zimbabwe. Right across the hall from my room is the suite where King George and Queen Elizabeth stayed with the princesses Elizabeth and Margaret. The windows beside my bed look onto a panorama of soaring mist from the gorge and the bridge across to Zambia, all framed in palm trees.

Settled in a towel, legs stretched out on a bronze-coloured velvet settee, I think about what to do next. Earlier, I declined the room steward's offer to unwrap the elastic bandage from my swollen ankle and massage my feet. He saw my fatigue and vulnerability.

"Why do you say no?" he said, "There is no harm in it. Why are you foreign white women so uptight?"

Oh, spare me. This is not in his job description. Or, is it? I asked him to leave.

Revived by the bath, I'm relieved to be on my own after the communal weeks in Vilanculos. I want to walk to the Zambezi River gorge by myself, unescorted. But knowing the dismal state of Zimbabwe's economy and that gratuities are essential for survival, I go with a woman guide, Patrice, who turns out to be informative and charming company.

How can one begin to describe an experience of the legendary Victoria Falls? Here goes...a pink vinyl raincoat. Yes, that's what I choose instead of a camouflage green one from a vendor at the main entrance kiosk. I'd rather have none at all, but everyone coming out of the access pathway is drenched. Those soaked tourists look incredibly happy.

Entrance to the main falls themselves must wait till morning. For now, there is just enough afternoon sun for Patrice and I to walk leisurely to the bridge over the cavernous gorge and stare.

The mist, rising since the dawn of time, settles on bare arms and face, dampens hair, fills lungs, erases the pain in my ankle. Rainbows are alive in the vaporous atmosphere, lacing the tree canopy with dazzling mist-refracted colours. Time disappears in this evanescence, until Patrice touches my shoulder to go, the ethereal spectacle dissolves in the southern Africa twilight. The sky has deepened from clear blue to richest indigo above gold across the western horizon.

On the terrace of the hotel, a waiter brings beer and an iced glass since I missed afternoon high tea in favour of the short trek to the gorge. It's that magical time bordering sunset, when all seems right with the world. Why, then, are the terrace lights flickering on and off? Intermittent power outages—the elegant Victoria Falls Hotel may be written up in "Leading Hotels of The World," but this is still Mugabe's Zimbabwe, failing infrastructure and all.

Awake with the first stream of sunlight, eyes still closed. The Falls are an omnipresent, thunderous vibration, a singular never-ending bass line held by every instrument in the cosmic orchestra. The low-belly tone is very grounding. Good tonic for living beings. When I button up the pink raincoat after breakfast the occasion turns light-hearted, as if the happiest child on earth is on her way to a very special birthday party. Patrice accompanies me to the main visitors' gate and leaves me to enter alone.

A footpath winds through the lush rainforest that grows only along the perimeter of the gorge. Almost immediately, I face head-on the massive sheet of river across a heart-lurching chasm. A continuous avalanche of water slips over the precipice directly across from my lookout point and catapults into an explosion a hundred metres below. Nowhere to fix the eye—the eternally moving water has no beginning, no midway, no end. One can't walk away because there is no moment when something is finished, no moment when there is a change in shape or speed that signals an intermission. Some primal, quivering, joyous upwelling inside me asks not to be abandoned.

Agog with the sensory extravaganza, I'm about to burst apart when two full-figured black women emerge from the green foliage strutting their way toward the edge of the precipice. Tourists from Malawi the two of them, with no raincoats, barefoot on the path in their dressy western clothes; they carry their glittery shoes in their hands by the straps. Like me, they are beyond astonished. Spontaneous shrieking, we erupt in delirious whole-body laughter.

"God's Creation! Heaven on Earth!" they shout.

In no time at all, we are singing together and dancing on the lookout pathway, our hair sopping and feet squinching. We rhumba-bump hips and rub shoulders, everywhere an effervescent, sparkling glory.

A narrow trail leads back to the hotel through the scrub brush, where sometimes stray elephants wander. Today a few vendors call out their wares. A young man in Rasta dreadlocks and a green T-shirt over his jeans quietly offers a hand-carved wooden bowl painted with zebra stripes. We agree on a price, not in negotiation but in recognition of craftsmanship. I now have a vessel to hold handfuls, armfuls, of joy. I add two tiny stone carvings, one fish for Mozambique, one zebra for Zimbabwe, each threaded on a short length of waxed twine. Patrice returns my pink raincoat to the kiosk.

During the two-hour drive in the shuttle van, south from the Falls and toward Hwange, I contemplate the river waterfall's one hundred thousand years of existence, predating the first European explorers, who arrived less than three hundred years ago. Two hundred and fifty thousand years of existence, some sources say. Even at that, the present waterfalls are the eighth in a sequence of precipices eroded by the mighty Zambezi River over the span of one and a half million years. More erosion and gorges will form over the eons to come.

# Rendezvous With the Wild

The plan set in motion by Patrick Retzlaff for the safari, on horseback, into the wilderness of Hwange National Park has delivered me to the park's main entrance to meet up with James Varden himself. Several travel publications I've read note that Zimbabwe has the most comprehensively trained guides in all of Africa, and I have heard that Varden is among the best of them.

Occupied over the last two days with compromised mobility and getting myself to this rendezvous point, I haven't felt apprehensive about riding again after the fall in Mozambique—until now.

I'm scared, my breathing ragged, as I zip on my worn half-chaps; the familiarity of strapping the riding helmet over my braided hair is not full of the happy anticipation it usually is. I'm nervous about meeting my horse and being a hindrance to the other riders. I wonder if I'll be able to keep from crying.

I decide to try out being a different person, stronger, someone not succumbing to emotional fragility, so I keep my trepidation to myself. Just concentrate on the symptoms—quivering jaw, disinterest in the other riders, closing throat, fatigue—calm myself, and betray nothing outwardly.

I reported my ankle injury, as a matter of medical fact, to James earlier this afternoon at Umbtchibi Main Camp, where the horses are stabled. Now I'll let my performance, my riding capability in this physical condition, speak for itself, whatever that turns out to be. I'm not going to apologize or diminish myself ahead of time. Instead, I pray for strength while focusing on one small task at a time.

Stand beside my horse in the tall grass. His name is Manini. Okay, put my hands on his neck, feel the smoothness of his dark hair. Lean in and smell him, familiar and comforting. Now someone has made a step with his hands to boost me onto the horse's broad back. I can feel my seat in the saddle, stability under my hips; my back aches only slightly thanks to the pain medication I found at the airport. Now my left foot slides into the stirrup, then the right. Slow deep breaths, okay, settling down. Let's sit for a minute in the warm sunlight. Then with a slight squeeze of my legs Manini steps forward, and I find a reservoir of calm inside that can see me through this ordeal, freed from the tyranny of emotion.

The orientation ride does not go well for me, it turns out, but my presence of mind survives. Moving at a walk or a trot through the open clearing is fine, though I'll need more pain relief tablets to ease my bruised body. But as soon as we all transition from trot to canter, something in me comes unglued. My feet come out of the stirrups, and I can't keep my seat. I have to grab hold of the gullet of the saddle to stay on the horse. So be it, there is no disguising my incompetence, from the injury, as I bounce around. Seeing this, James hollers a cue for everyone to slow down and stop, which brings my horse to a halt. Relief threatens to swamp me with tears—we're all in this together, and I am safe.

This communal response is standard protocol riding out on safari I learn later. But will they ground me for the trip? Will they relegate me to traveling in the supply vehicle between camps?

Something profound happens in being accepted as one is, included. And something more profound in feeling safe and looked after. My confidence returns. In the morning, with arnica salve and an elastic bandage on my ankle, I'm boosted onto Manini's back and ride out from Umtchibi Main Camp with everyone else.

Four days later it's dusk as we ride into Jambili Pan camp after our day of the "real good encounter" with the lions. I remember the conversation with Joseph, about the gift I've brought from home for the spirit of this wilderness place, a gift of thanks for my being here. The cement barbeque, or braii, is not my notion of where to burn a sacred offering. Never mind, I think. You never know what's coming next. Indeed, the cooks arriving earlier in the day by truck saw two more lions up the sandy track.

The horses are unusually fussy. Everyone pitches in to tether them further inward from the temporary electric fence, powered by a vehicle battery, that forms a boma, an enclosure for the safety of the horses and our camp. Care of the horses comes first, so our personal gear has been neatly piled under a round, thatch roof. To ward off lions in the night, the grooms build a bonfire just inside the entrance of the boma. That guardian fire surely must be the place for burning my offering.

Coming to sort out our personal gear in the thatch shelter, we find each person's bedroll tagged with a bit of corrugated cardboard tied on with black baling twine. As we go through the tags, whoops of delight erupt with the handwritten script assigning our roles in this expedition.

Who the heck is Old Lady Chiredzi? I am the oldest, but certainly not from Chiredzi. That would be Theresa, who collapses with laughter on the sandy ground after our long, lion day. Overcome with the giggles, Single Lady—my own bedroll label—eases down onto the pile of mattresses in the shelter, reveling in this release after the tense exhilaration of our day.

Theresa unties her bundle and asks me, "Are you missing the privacy of having your own tent?"

Not at all. This minute, the familiar act of closing my eyes in a horizontal position is all the respite I need. It will be true time and again, finding myself at home by lying on the ground.

Thank you, I say silently to the camp crew who plainly wrote what they see. I tuck the cardboard tag into the back of my notebook. My new identification tag feels perfect. Not divorced, not formerly partnered. Pure and simple—single. Solo. One. Whole.

After showering under the canvas bucket filled with hot water from the cooking fire, I walk over to the boma entrance where Stephen is tending the bonfire. He's taken off his leather riding chaps and put on a plaid woolen jacket over his T-shirt and jeans; his clean-shaven head reflects the firelight. He brings two camp chairs for us to sit.

I show my little offering packet to him and find myself talking too much, maybe because Stephen's voice is harder for me to understand than the other grooms. He says nothing, and I continue feeling an awkward urge to explain.

"This safari is an adventure for my sixtieth birthday, a new beginning after too much change."

He is incredulous, "You are older than me, eleven years? No, I do not think so."

After a time, he says, "My wife, she passed away, four years ago. Cerebral malaria when I am in the bush."

Could that be the source of the sadness I detect in his face at times? He gestures an invitation for me to put my offering into the fire. After untying the saffron-twined packet I hand the buckskin-coloured envelope to Stephen.

I place the Spirit Horse card and packet contents, adorned with a spray of wild sage leaves, onto the flaming wood. It flares in brilliant colours, as if the tarot card inside is coming to life—the one for Strength, Lust—the one picturing a woman and a lion, befriended.

"You could make an offering yourself, if you want," I say. "Maybe put your prayer into the envelope."

Stephen blows the paper envelope from his hand into the fire and bows his head. I can't hear the few words he says to himself. Then we sit side-by-side, his legs stretched out very near to mine.

"I have got six children," he says. "First born, she is thirty years, married. Second born, he is twenty-five years, not yet married. Last-born, he is nine years, lives with my sister now, no mother."

We sit in silence, what can I say? It doesn't feel right to pierce the soul of the moment with questions about his family. Sparks streak into the darkness from the burning logs. I sense his head incline toward me and hear him say,

"Do you feel purified?"

"Indeed, I do."

"Me also," he says to the fire.

Bloomer, the ranger, still packing his weapon, joins us. His bantering does not diminish the intensity and energy of what's happening. What is happening? It's dark. The fire is beautiful— blue flames above orange coals inside an arch of logs. Stephen's boot leans against mine, the edges of our soles touch.

Theresa has come over, standing for a moment in the light, then says I must come and hear the elephants bathing. I get up and walk away with her, regretting I had not found the grace to say, "Please excuse me," to Stephen and Bloomer, hardly hearing Theresa explain, "The guys need some down time from us," as we head into the dark silhouette of the bush toward dinner.

We're sleeping without tents at Jambili Camp, on the ground under the stars and baobab trees; horses snuffle close by, tethered on long lines overhead. Invisible soundscape expands and contracts into the distance—it seems I hear every vibration for a thousand miles. Getting out of my sleeping bag I make my way toward the loo, a bottomless bucket with toilet seat over a hole in the ground, concealed by a canvas sheet. I tread slowly, staring upward into the magnetic black sky, not looking ahead. Suddenly, a penetrating, sharp zap on my breast. I gasp. Alarm dissolves to a giggle of relief—I've walked into the ribbon of electric fence. I sit on the bucket seat a long time, savouring the night to myself.

Returning to my bedroll, I'm keenly aware of Munhondo and Manini and the rest of the horses. I'm sleeping, or rather not sleeping, in their resonant field. My body feels electric, and I know it didn't come from the fence. There is a current of energy pouring through me, and I'm streaming out in all directions, not consciously breathing but pulsing with something primordial. The night sky close as a lover—each star assigning itself to a cell in my body—charges my entire being.

In the morning, I remember that the electromagnetic field of a horse's heart is five times vaster than the human heart. What about elephants and lions, what about baobab trees, and the earth itself? What about Africa? Could following the compelling urge to lie on the ground of Africa actually be my response to an invitation originating here?

What is seeking me? What is being asked of me now?

In camp, James wears khaki shorts and goes barefoot. Never mind ticks and thorns and whatever else is on the ground. Just before riding out, he puts on leather chaps seasoned by the elements and pulls on ankle boots with no socks. Stephen too has pull-on paddock boots, the kind from Australia, and I'm pleased to match their practicality with my own well-worn boots, the same as theirs. As for Janine, she wears blue jeans every day with her lace-up paddock boots, always a kerchief around her neck, and an assortment of colourful button-front shirts with the safari logo above the left breast pocket. My favourite is the pear green one with mango-coloured T-shirt underneath; these are colours of the flap-necked chameleon and the desert hibiscus flower. On the eve of my departure she will produce a similar logo'd shirt for me in a khaki colour with a lovely feminine fit.

Early morning, after our lion encounter, we're gathered for breakfast, informally sitting on folding canvas chairs around the campfire. James describes what we'll need to take in our daypacks for a walkabout of Jambili Pan on foot. The horses are resting

*The Geography of Belonging*

today. The mug of hot tea in my hand has the fragrance of wood smoke. Everything made with hot water smells of smoke from the cooking fire: tea, oatmeal, washed socks, and the shower water poured into a canvas bucket suspended overhead. I haven't bothered to wash my hair; long and thick it won't come clean in a brief drench. Sometimes I hold it across my nose and mouth, deeply inhaling the olfactory evidence that I am really here in Africa.

An hour later James and I sit on the collapsed remains of an abandoned termite mound while the same harem of zebras that we met yesterday grazes its way nearer and nearer in the pre-sunrise twilight. James quietly tutors me in the construction of termite mounds, how the insects mix their saliva with mud to create these complex towers of earth. The interiors have corridors and ventilation shafts that allow air flow with constant temperature and humidity; they're remodeled each day to suit current weather conditions. The raised pile of earth we sit on conceals a subterranean eco-system that may have endured for hundreds of years. I tell James about biomimicry, the practice of applying principles found in nature to create solutions for the human world. He's not surprised to hear that the Eastgate Centre, a shopping mall and office complex in Harare, was built without conventional air-conditioning, using design methods inspired by original Zimbabwean stone masonry and the African termite mound.

When the sun flares above the horizon, we get up from the ground to continue our walkabout before the day's heat intensifies. We catch up with Theresa who is introducing her family to the sturdy trunk of a tall Acacia galpinii, or monkey-thorn tree. She points out the shiny whorls of marbled red and cream just above our heads. Elephants rub themselves against the tree trunk to remove ticks from their hides, sanding through the bark to the inner hardwood and making polished spirals. Her nephew has boosted his sister onto his shoulders so she can inspect this marvel at eye level. Underfoot, the dried elephant dung is adorned with a kaleidoscope of butterflies. Each elephant dropping, the size of a marshmallow-shaped soccer ball, is aflutter with butterflies: petite butter-yellow Euremas, the black velvet Yellow Pansy with spot of blue-opal, and dazzling African Monarchs. A few metres away, James joins Theresa's niece lying on the ground to photograph tiny mulit-coloured beetles that look like handmade ceramic beads; the two of them are like five-year-olds on their first nature outing.

Later, in the lush mid-afternoon stillness, I take my folding chair to the edge of the grassland, bush at my back. The zebras have come up close to this threshold, where the horses are also tied to graze. It's hot. A single giraffe lopes in the distance and stops. An old one—its colours dark, more saturated than the paler young ones. Lifting my hand to shade my eyes, I sense my arm is not a corporeal limb but a gossamer wave of extending motion, as if it can be received by something light years away. Noticing Stephen on the far side of the pan, scything grass for the horses, I feel the rhythmic swing of his torso echoed in my own body.

Much later in the day, when we clients have rested, James invites us on a second walkabout to investigate flowers, insects and the minutiae we don't see on horseback. It's too hot still, and I decline.

"Fine," says James, "the grooms will take the horses onto the pan for water and grazing soon, so you can help."

He points toward the centre of the boma where Stephen and Gobo are standing by the herd, and I make my way over to them. My tiny metallic-green iPod Shuffle is clipped to my shirt. I pass it to young Gobo, while Corrine Baily Rae croons *Livin' My Life Like It's Golden*. Gobo's face lights up, he presses the volume louder and rocks out like he's on stage. I'm enthralled, the boy can move, never mind we're in the middle of the bush. I groan at my unconscious arrogance—this is where dancing originated.

Gobo gives the iPod to Stephen who holds the earbuds to his head and listens a moment. I know which song this is, Chaka Khan— explosive, with Stevie Wonder on harmonica—*I Feel For You*.

Stephen beams a shy nod of approval and moves more modestly than his young companion, but more exquisitely, I think. After that, we three lead the herd onto the grassy pan and sit together on the ground. We are silent. Gobo gazes at the deepening sky, horses graze before us in the rose-gold light.

Stephen reaches over to a low bush and picks a sunset-coloured flower, petals furled. He offers the blossom bud to me.

"Hibiscus," he says. "Only opens at night."

Is this really happening? Has my imagination conjured its own dream?

I tuck the stem of the silky flower into my buttonhole. Feel the sweetness of another human being. Nothing more.

In the evening, Janine magically produces a camp cot for me, respite from the hard ground in consideration of my injury.

"Would you like it by the horses?" she says.

"Oh, yes, please!"

Once darkness falls, the cot is luxurious under the stars, just a few metres from Munhondo and Bhura who are tethered to the long-lines overhead, and fewer metres from the thatch roof on poles where Stephen lies in his bedroll. Heaven. I can hear the soft, fluttering snoring of his sleep, the gentle shuffling of horses' hooves on the ground.


It's now two days after the lion encounter, and we ride out as the sun begins to brighten the treetops. Our last long ride, having vacated Jambili Camp for the final leg of our safari; we'll arrive at Umtchibi Main Camp by tonight. It's mid-morning. A bit of a meltdown is happening. Mine, apparently. We've been trotting along the elephant track and James cues, "Ready for a little canter?"

I cannot, just can not summon the wherewithal today for a fast ride, and tears of fatigue and embarrassment well up. Theresa looks back at me, as she always does when a gait change is signaled.

"Are you ready?"

I shake my head, "No."

A drink of water, a few drops of Rescue Remedy, deep breathing, and an arm on my back are all freely offered.

"No worries, Oriane, we'll take care of you." James' words are the sweetest balm. Just before midday on the trail, anticipating our lunch break and rest time, he rides over to Manini and me.

"Oriane, you graze here with Bloomer and Gobo; stay in the trees for a bit. Turn your horses away from the rest of us, then they won't follow. We're going to canter across the veldt. We'll see you on the other side, up there and around the bend, where we'll stop for lunch. Take your time."

Perfect. I'm obviously not up for a fast ride through open space on the heels of that lion escapade a few days ago, and I'm glad the rest of the riders have the chance to let loose. After the others are out of sight, the three of us—Bloomer, Gobo and me—turn our horses and leisurely make our way through the high-grass plain.

Freed from the distracting pressure of the whole group of riders, it's easy to unwind in the safe company of Bloomer and Gobo. To be entrusted to their care by James is deeply touching, recalling Mozambique where the grooms didn't ride with the guests, only walked or ran alongside the horses.

Crossing the veldt is luxurious, I hear and feel everything visible and invisible, thrumming biosphere.

"It's pretty cool riding with you guys, just the three of us!" I smile to Bloomer and Gobo.

Bloomer grins, "You are the Queen; we are your escorts."

By now, with days of his bantering company, I'm pretty sure he's having me on.

"Well, maybe the Queen Mother!" I say, laughing, as a flock of snowy white cattle egrets disperse to the sky from a baobab tree.

In the distance ahead, a figure rides back toward us—Stephen, with braided whip in hand. He joins our mounted party, to assure my safety I hear later from Theresa. As his horse falls in step with mine I am happy beyond all reason.

In due course, we meet up with the others, and I join them for lunch—hefty sandwiches and coconut cake. The guys, as they're routinely called, tend to the horses before eating their meal. When I tell James the escort story he laughs.

"Too bad there wasn't someone to take a picture, that would have made a great photo for our website."

After a restful lie-down in the filtered shade, we ride contentedly through an endless afternoon of bushland and wildlife. As the day's heat recedes and the light leans toward dusk, it takes a few minutes to recognize that we're traversing our first landmark, Umtchibi Pan, marking the culmination of our full-circle journey. We head for the watering hole, where we set out a lifetime ago. Cameras appear out of saddlebags; the pictures will show us lined up, horses and riders, facing the water's edge. Our reflections on the liquid surface are surrounded by billowing clouds in the magnum opus of the African sky.

Our safari support crew is waiting, enthusiastic and welcoming, with the truck at the gate to Umtchibi Camp. Seeing Joseph, the farrier, I burst out, "I did it, Joseph!" and he meets my hand in a jubilant high five.

The all-important group photo shoot, once we're dismounted, shows Bloomer crouched, hand still on his gun, eye to eye with Manini. James hugs Janine who has an armful of greens for our dinner, and various groupings of us pose, beaming, guileless and disarmed by our days in the saddle. No one else notices, I think, that Stephen and I have wordlessly ended up beside one another in every shot.

That's it then. Stephen and his crew lead the horses to the stable compound, and their own meal, as usual. The rest of us wash up, taking turns at the cement basin, and change into clothes we'd left here for the finale dinner.

As James pours champagne by candlelight under a black and starry sky, I sit down beside Theresa and the conversation turns into a fond review of the last seven days. We've ridden with giraffes, marveled at elephant families, made friends with several herds of zebra, sighted kudu, eland and sable. And oh, yes, encountered lions. We were saddened, too, coming across the bleached bones of a white rhino, killed long ago for its illegitimately-prized horn, and the intact body of an old leopard two-days dead, its coat still shiny. We've seen a puff adder up close, flap-necked chameleons, billions of insects and myriad birds. Of the birds, the African Jacana is my favourite with its sleek white neck and bronze-coloured, iridescent feathers.

To experience the wilderness of Zimbabwe with life-long residents is a mind-bend immersion in an entirely new world—accessible to me because of joining Theresa's family trip with a big discount on the usual safari cost, thanks to the Retzlaff's friendship with the Vardens. I hope being the weakest rider didn't hinder the adventure for the rest of the group. And because of this desire to not slow others down, I'm inspired to take up more riding coaching before I come back. Before I come back?

Sunrise is a two-hour gala in the ballroom of sky. I stretch out in the bedroll while the African night slips away and the world begins to glow. Then I get up and stand facing eastward, as happens on many continents every morning, humans honouring the new day. A shimmering light on either side of my face, dew drops of gold in strands of my hair. The golden tarot card; woman and lion.

Manini and the herd wander into the back garden near me. I kneel low in the grass among them, and match my breathing with theirs, taking in every scent and every sound. A pearl of wisdom shines though, with this herd of horses that thrives in the wild. It's the shape of courage. Coeur, French for heart. Courage is what happens when I say "yes" with all my heart, and don't look back.

*The Geography of Belonging*

"The guys are here to say good-bye." Janine finds me in the garden.

Quickly, I need to come up with a little gift. My duffle bag is a tangled jumble of earth-smudged clothes yet, there, in a zip pocket, a new shoelace, leaf-green and threaded with a tiny wooden heart with a cross-etched into it. Tucking it into my shirt pocket, not knowing if it's suitable, I'm reminded of Jonathan Mazulu the head groom in Mozambique who counseled me that anything is a good gift, if it is given from your heart.

The camp crew and grooms are lined up along the pathway that leads to the thatch-roofed kitchen. I'll be departing before the others and must make my way along this path in a formal farewell and expression of thanks.

"Thank you, Joseph, for everything." For lifting me onto my horse the first day when my injury humbled me into accepting your help; for your affirmation of an earthy spirituality; for the welcome back to main camp after the time of my life.

"May I give you a hug?" I ask. Yes. Enveloping, bear-like and brief.

After shaking hands with the two cooks, adding exaggerated expressions of tummy satisfaction, I now stand before Stephen. Taking his proffered hand between my two, I fold in the little gift, smile and lean in to say quietly, "God bless your children. This is for good luck finding a very fine new wife."

After a moment I step back, letting go of his hand. I offer my thanks to the other support crew, sharing a vigorous handshake with each of them. One of the cooks ties the shoelace around Stephen's neck. I wonder if I've overstepped, but everyone is laughing so all is well.

I run to the breakfast table to hug Theresa and her family. They're driving back to her farm in Chiredzi via Bulawayo. James hoists up my duffle bag, and I head to the truck; the guys are still on the path—a whole row of beaming faces and thumbs up.

Janine opens the truck door for me, and says, "Thank you for coming to Zimbabwe."

*Rendezvous With the Wild* 57

The Land Cruiser, with James at the wheel and me in the front seat beside him, moves slowly along the dusty track away from Umtchibi Camp and the horses. We're going to meet the shuttle van that will take me to Victoria Falls airport. I ask James for more lion stories, his best.

"We just had one of the best."

He reminds me that it's actually safer for humans to encounter lions on foot than on horseback. On foot, James can make lions retreat by shouting and shooting his gun into the air. However, horses are prey animals and lions are their predators; instinct in either can take over with a change in the wind. He tells me that Bloomer, riding last in line, confirmed seeing the lioness trot behind us, and she slowed only as the distance from her cubs meant we were safely away from them. I picture Bloomer's face. His curiosity was a match for mine, and he wanted to know about the wild animals in Canada. I've seen bears, cougars, wolves, elk and orca whales and could describe them in their habitat, to his delight.

James and I drive on in silence. I look down at my new khaki safari shirt with its green logo—Varden Safaris Riding-in-Hwange—on the breast pocket, and lean back to catch the wind from the open window. I feel the contact of my body with the car seat, the hot air on my skin, the dampness of my neck—at the same time, a glow from inside me caresses the land and the trees as the truck cruises along the tar road. In return, a vast presence flows through me; I'm sure it's love, from the earth.

James shifts gears as the park headquarters appear up ahead. Looking out the side window, I see something I wouldn't have noticed one week ago—a small herd of grazing zebras, almost invisible, in the shadows of the distant brush.

At the tiny Victoria Falls airport café, the waitress shows me to a table set back from the others and brings a grilled cheese sandwich with tomato, and black milky tea to drink. The dim light is relaxing, an hour alone to catch up with myself. I can't fathom going back to where I came from, to the known and familiar. Theresa told me her niece will cry and cry back in Switzerland, and ache when she looks at her safari photographs because her heart stays in Zimbabwe. I know how she feels.

How can the spirit of Africa be assimilated once I get home? But I cannot say that I'm going home, only that I'm returning to the west coast of Canada.

There, I will lie on the earth with horses, and begin to tell my stories of Africa. This journey has not been sitting with women in huts, tending cooking fires and caring for babies in my spare time, as I thought volunteers do. Rather, it's been men and horses, earth and masculine soul, about a seascape in Mozambique and a landscape in Zimbabwe beyond what my imagination ever conjured. Everything conspired, it appears, to usher me through a crack between the visible and invisible worlds—into that dimension of human experience found with immersion in nature.

Finishing the toasted sandwich, I begin to "make a plan" for what I'll need back in Canada. First thing to do, once off the plane in Vancouver, is go to Eva, a huge-hearted Percheron mare stabled by the river near the airport. She's a beauty, a black and white paint. I'll sit on her bare back, wrap my arms around her neck, allow her scent to bring the safari horses home with me—horse medicine.

Getting up from the café table, I switch on the tiny iPod clipped to the pocket of my safari shirt, to block out the airport bustle. Earbuds in place, the music is glorious and loud. I bring my hand to my heart where the still-rosy hibiscus flower rests inside my bra, delicate on my skin. I am returned to the bush, filled with elephants, horses and the scent of a man.

One o'clock in the morning. I'm near exhaustion in the Johannesburg guesthouse. Sobbing and laughing with the enormity of the last seven days and nights. My whole body is literally vibrating, billowing, beyond any capacity to contain this genesis. The streaming energy will remain for months to come. My mind has unraveled, as well, a good thing really, more access to what's real. Already I miss Theresa, Old Lady Chiredzi, my trusted new friend in the bush. Then I notice my reflection in the mirror above the bed—Single Lady. Yes, I feel pure. No past, only presence.

Twelve hours later, thirty thousand feet up, en route from Johannesburg to London, I stand by the galley window and watch the African continent below. Raw and alive, I can feel it from here. Two white women older than me, who were born in Angola and Botswana, captivate me with stories of their lives in Africa. I want to be one of them. As we drink sparkling water, bottled from a spring in Scotland, I smile to think the interior of my body still holds the deep groundwater of Zimbabwe.

"My goodness, your hair is beautiful," the elder one says. "It's so long."

Eyeing the Varden logo on my khaki safari shirt she adds, "You're a warden. What do you do with your hair in the bush?"

"Oh, I just put it in a braid and don't wash it."

This is true about my hair, and I say no more. I turn back to the galley window, to the terrain of sage and sienna below.

Who am I now, I wonder, and what does life hold for me?

My dear cousin Myfanwy has driven the two hours from her home in Leicestershire to meet me at Heathrow. When we arrive home David, her eccentric husband, serves the most delicious chicken masala. The two of them are well-traveled and curious, so we share stories late into the evening and speculate on the fate of the African continent. David's enthusiasm for the wild on his trips to southern Africa pours out.

"Every thing is moving all the time!" he says.

"The very land pulses with life!" I gush.

I don't say, however, that my entire physical body is also pulsating right in his dining room, energy streaming outward in all directions.

*The Geography of Belonging*

Eventually, Myfanwy shows me into a guestroom. The luxury of white linens, lace bedcovers and Egyptian cotton sheets receives my travel-worn body. I lie awake in stillness, with tender ankle and tingling pleasure in my belly. Africa is unfurling inside me.

A covering of snow sugars the ground through the window-panes as I rise the next morning. By midday, I feel heavy and slow, deeply fatigued, my back aching. Maybe I have malaria. In private moments I'm overcome—exhausted and wired all at the same time. Could this acute state be a kind of grief? The loss of not being with those kindred spirits: James and Janine, Theresa and her family, Joseph, Bloomer and the Shona horseman Stephen Hambani. And, most of all, the land.

A version of Hafiz rings true:

Just sit there right now
Don't do a thing
Just rest.

For your separation from God,
Is the hardest work
In this
World.

Let me bring you trays of food
And something
That you like to
Drink.

You can use my soft words
As a cushion
For your
Head.

Though I cannot be sleeping on the ground in the wilderness, solace for that loss is at hand. I bring the big sheepskin rug from the floor into the bed, and lay it under my body, sleeping naked on its mammalian comfort. Waking in the night, I feel soaked in the outpouring of where I've been.

Early Sunday morning Myfanwy and I walk to the stone parish church. On the windowsill beside our pew, lilies and daffodils glow in the morning light. We're part way through the first hymn when it hits me with a shock. I whisper to Myfanwy.

"Oh, my God, it's Easter!"

She rolls her eyes, snorts softly and pats my arm.

Easter is my favourite of the Christian holy days, the story of resurrection. At the back of the chapel a floor-standing candelabra holds votives flickering in red glass cups. I get up from the hard wooden seat and tip-toe to the tiered wrought-iron stand. I take a long wooden skewer, light it from one of the burning candles and touch its flame to a new, unlit wick.

"How can this experience, of Africa, be offered back to the world in a beneficial way?"

On our walk back to the house, a sharp pain suddenly pierces the ball of my foot. What the heck has stabbed my sole on this Easter day? Down onto the grass verge, pull off my paddock boot to find a long acacia tree thorn from Hwange has pushed its way through the heavy-duty rubber outsole, sticking up like a needle from the insole of my boot. The African landscape is claiming me, still.

# Restless Liminality

My aunt and namesake, Oriane Jane, turns eighty in June and I call to let her know I'm back in Canada. She's my father's sister and also my godmother. Auntie Oriane says prayers to a special angel every night, though no one else in the family but me knows this; God and angels are our shared secret. I picture her soft gray curls that match a cashmere sweater she is probably wearing, her sparkly eyes and iridescent pink lipstick. She picks up the phone right away.

"Oh, sweetheart. I'm so glad to hear from you," she says. "Now tell me, did you fall in love with a beautiful African man?"

I hear myself say, plain and simple, "Yes, I did." Based on barely anything at all.

"Oh, tell me!" she giggles.

It's classic, predictable even—foreign white woman, exotic location, propriety and inhibition shed, thinks she's in love with the safari guide, the wildlife tracker, the native beach boy, the horseman. Projecting her unfulfilled fantasies into his life. I've read the book and seen the film version of *The White Masai*, and the culture clash that breaks the marriage between the white Swiss woman and the African Samburu man. I tell myself that I'm in a more mature stage of life.

Why would I turn away from this most unexpected, though conceivably unfounded, prospect—for fear of the bubble of fantasy popping, revealing a disappointing and unpalatable reality?

I can live with that.

Still, I find it confusing to account for the radical change inside me when I haven't made any plans to alter my life in practical or visible ways. I'm not moving to Africa; I don't even have a ticket to go back. How much patience does it take to "stay with" a deep internal recalibration inside oneself and not prematurely make plans to shift allegiance in the outer world of home and work and geographical place? It's tough to be in this liminal state when society conspires to propel us always toward something: some place, some event, some accomplishment, some demise, something not right now.

I go to Hollyhock for a meditation retreat and the teacher, Tami Simon, leads us out of the hall and onto the lawn by the ocean. She places a brass brazier in the centre of our circle; the black charcoal she lights turns glowing orange, roused by the morning breeze.

"We begin with a ceremony," she says, "introducing ourselves to our enlightened predecessors in this Buddhist lineage."

I know that lineage also means the Beloved in Sufi tradition, the Creator in First Nations, God, the Goddess, the Divine—and the Ancestors in African cultures.

"Our sincerity is met by an equal force of sincerity from their unseen presence," Tami tells us.

One by one the meditators place a twig of green juniper to burn in the sacred fire—for letting go or asking for help, for offering thanks, or inviting clarity or wisdom to come. When it's my turn, I feel into my pocket for the glass vial of red earth from Zimbabwe, where the elephants roll. A pinch of that atop the smoking juniper. I speak to the Ancestors.

"How can I serve unselfishly, this call of the soul, the call to Africa?"

Or is the call from Africa?

Alone on the beach after lunch, I lie down naked on the soft glittering sand beneath a clear blue sky and slip into the Earth Descent practice. I don't notice the incoming tide creeping up over sun-heated sand—until warm seawater silk-wraps my body.

One September morning I lean against a fencepost in the pasture while the horses, Cosun and Tick, eat their breakfast hay. I'm talking on my cell phone with my mother who lives in Sequim, Washington, across the strait from Victoria. Mum is eighty-five now and I'd been a bit apprehensive last Christmas—before I went to Africa the first time—about telling her I was going. I didn't want her to feel abandoned in a fragile time of life. She still identifies as a nurse and considers grass-roots travel dangerous and unhygienic. So I didn't say I was going to Africa by myself. In a quiet moment at the end of the holidays, over a cup of tea I said, "Mum, I'm going to Mozambique to volunteer with some horses."

"That sounds like hard work. Where is Mozambique exactly?"

It can sound like Martinique, an island vacation destination in the Caribbean.

"Just north of South Africa," I say. Her best friend, also a former nurse, has been to South Africa, making it a safe destination based on nothing at all.

This morning, watching Cosun's jaw as she chews, mum surprises me.

"I think you'll go back to Africa," she says. "It's your pattern to go back to places."

Being seen by one's mother can be stunning if it's a rare occurrence. I haven't felt this close with her in a long time and the poignancy of her age surfaces with my first pang of missing her when I won't have her any more.

Mum continues, "You went back to Burma, you know."

A small black-velvet bag hangs from my belt loop, it's from the Mahamuni Pagoda in Mandalay, Myanmar. The gold-embroidered bag remained in a drawer of keepsakes for ten years, until I found it after returning from Africa. Two tiny glass vials are tucked inside—one of water from the Indian Ocean, Mozambique. And one, the earth from Hwange wilderness, Zimbabwe. Also nestled inside are thumbnail-size photos—of the safari horses, the African animals, and one of Stephen Hambani—bound together with gold thread.

The medicine bag is a home, here, for Africa and it carries a potency that keeps me grounded in situations when I expect to feel uncomfortable or thrown off balance. Then again, horseback riding in the eastern drifts of the Kalahari sands with elephants and lions engenders a strength that takes root in the body, never to leave.

Mum, still on the phone, asks when I might return to Africa. I don't know, but I tell her about the email from Janine Varden, the horse safari owner:

"I'll tell you what happened to you over here—as it happened to me when I came from Australia. You've been bitten by the Africa bug—it gets into your blood and it keeps recurring."

I understand what she means. In the liminal times of early morning twilight and in full moon brilliance, the motherland finds me, even here, returning me to the continent of our human origin.

Janine describes a different region of Zimbabwe with horses. The Mavuradonha Mountains.

Website pictures of the untouched wilderness—gorges and waterfalls, rock cliffs and river valleys—glisten on my laptop screen as if finely polished. Something—beyond the purity of colours, beyond the contours of the landscape, beyond the visible—seems to emanate.

Something immaculate.

Is there anything that indicates I shouldn't be going in this direction? No, there is no contrary evidence. That night, in my field notebook, a cautious down-to-earth love letter takes form.

Dear Stephen.

Then, another fall.

Hardly breathing, I can barely look at my bandaged hand and wrist as the surgical nurse gently pulls back the layers of gauze, each layer more gruesome-looking, stained with the residue of surgery and the beginnings of healing. Oh my god, I'm going to faint—what are these metal skewers doing sticking out of my wrist and through my hand?

Last weekend I sat, too absent-mindedly, on the bare back of Tick while he quietly chewed his hay. Cosun made a move toward the hay pile and Tick lurched toward her. I slipped sideways and put my arm out to break the fall. My wrist hit the flat stone first and then my hip on top of that. I understood the expression "bent out of shape," when I managed to shift my weight and see the skewed angles of my wrist and hand.

When the nurse murmurs sympathetically, something turns loose in me, sobbing floods the sterile room. Never mind telling me about the long healing process, never mind scheduling the weekly all-day trips to the hospital hand-rehabilitation clinic, never mind instructions for the twice daily bandage changing and mobility exercises. I came to my senses a few weeks ago and determined I must go back to Africa before the end of the year. My body is getting on an airplane in eight weeks time. My body is going back to Zimbabwe, back to the wilderness, back to the bush. But now, my return to Africa hinges on this post-op examination of the traumatic injury.

I hear a voice in the room. "You won't be able to lift anything over five pounds for three months, and it'll probably be about six months before full mobility and weight-bearing are restored."

The orthopedic surgeon might as well have said I'd never ride again.

The nurse offers some Atavan, but the reality remains, I am not going back to Africa any time soon. Shiny steel rods pin the fractured bones, and me, to this geographical place for now.

Curled up in the car on the ferry back to Cortes Island, a friend at the wheel, my breathing begins to fall in with the rolling swell of the ocean. Inspecting the spanking clean white gauze that wraps my forearm from elbow to fingertips, I find that my hand and wrist are held stable inside a custom-moulded plastic splint—it's clear that I am safe and will be sound. This injury will heal. I did not pick up a land mine, nor have my wrist severed by a machete, nor find my arm in the mouth of a crocodile. I am fortunate, exceedingly fortunate.

Mid-winter, I'm house-sitting my friends' waterfront lodge. Early morning, new moon, the gradual lightening of the night sky is too promising for staying in bed. Bundled in winter weather gear I go out to the ocean's rock edge just as a sliver of sun colours the eastern horizon. A glittering path of orange light streams across the ocean surface to my perch on the rock. I've placed a framed photograph of Stephen with his dark horse Chacabikwa on the rock, and it, too, is lit up with early morning gold. At first, I think the sound is my own breathing, until a movement to the right catches my eye. Not ten metres out, a long line of Dall's porpoise, a pod of thirty, breach and swoosh right toward the spot where I stand on the rock. My chest begins to rise and fall in the same cadence as the communal swimming of the pod—my whole body fills and then deflates with the porpoises' surfacing and diving. When the trail of moving water disappears on the far side of the bay, I lie down on the rock and look up at the brightening sky. The vapour of my breath floats for a moment in the cold air.

Opening the lodge door much later and taking off my gloves to plug in the electric kettle, I hear my cell phone ring.

"Hallo. It's me. Stephen Hambani, in Zimbabwe. When are you coming?"

I can barely make out the rest of his words on the overseas line connecting Africa with North America, but his enthusiasm is clear. It's been two months since I mailed the letter to him and now, all of a sudden, I am pierced by the sound of his voice. I can smell the safari horses and the dry-earth heat.

"Yes, come," he says, "But not good time to come now. I am having new job, not in the bush, in town, training horses. It is rainy season and too hot for you. Come in May. I will make a plan."

Come springtime, my wrist and hand are not quite fully functioning. I feel vulnerable and incompetent. I can't fathom traveling by myself again, and won't put myself in an unknown situation, in an unstable country, even without the pressure of finding out who Stephen is. The two of us met in one of the most potent landscapes in the world. Now he's in the city without that wilderness mystique. Africa is no place for unnecessary uncertainty.

All year I've been tracking the recommended news sources for Zimbabwe. The reports are, at best, uninformative—it's so frustrating to look for information in their national media and to find only word circles that go nowhere—and at worst, downright alarming. Journalists and dissenters tortured, jailed or "disappeared." Intimidation of villagers in the rural areas. Fear that the economy will nose-dive once again. I wonder if all Zimbabwe suffers the aftershocks of trauma.

On a warm sun-lit morning, I sit cross-legged in the pasture while Cosun nibbles her flake of hay a few feet away. My stomach is churning; I'm deeply troubled by the book I'm reading—the absolutely hair-raising memoir of a 40-something Zimbabwean, now living abroad, that details the horror, in present-day, suffered by dissidents in the country—and I can't quell my sharp distress about the dangers, and my safety, if I return to that land of beauty and sorrow. I'm an innocuous visitor, some in-the-know would say, but still, what is the difference between faith and naiveté?

Close your eyes, I counsel myself, and focus on the sound of Cosun's chewing. This helps, as I try to relax. I sense Cosun come toward me, her hooves quiet on the short mossy grass; a soft rub of her nose on the top of my head. My heart rate settles with her warm breath in my hair. Silence, except for the crows flying from one tree to another, their wings swish-stirring the air. Cosun stands over me as she would a new foal, her horsey smell bringing me back from a fearfully imagined future.

The dark feeling inside me evaporates and my sense of "self" falls open like the petals of a blooming flower. She continues breathing into me, and I'm filled with a deep conviction to make life choices and decisions based on arriving at the end of my time on earth without regret.

When I open my eyes everything is glowing and super-lucid—the cedar trees are deepest emerald green, fat dew drops glitter on blades of grass, bed sheets on the clothesline billow perfectly in the breeze.

In the afternoon I book two months with Varden Safaris' new volunteer program—with their horses in the wilderness of Mavuradonha Mountains.

My flight to Zimbabwe leaves in two weeks. Communication with Stephen by cell phone is static-riddled, awkward, and it feels perilous not being able to understand exactly what he says to me. He doesn't text in English and though my friends assume we'd use email, he's never touched a computer. Stephen promises he's arranged accommodation for me at a guesthouse, in Borrowdale on the outskirts of Harare, where he now lives in a room beside the stables. He says we'll have five days and nights to ourselves, before I go on to Mavuradonha, though he'll be training horses in the daytime.

But the limb of faith I'm out on is about to crack. I feel in thin air, like the mythical boyfriend has vanished, vapourized. No answer when I phone him to confirm my arrival details and no response to my text messages. Anxiety clutches my chest, shadowing the self-doubt that grows, hour by hour. How could I have counted on a stranger, really, in a foreboding place, to come through?

*The Geography of Belonging*

By now I've arrived at Mary's Farm, closer to the airport, for the few days before my ticket date. I go out to the barn. Summer stands, dozing, in her stall and I lean my back against her belly. I don't know, yet, how expensive international airtime is in Zimbabwe, and that Stephen hasn't the money for this extravagance. Nor that beat-up cell phones don't charge properly.

With Summer's breathing, the rise and fall of her belly against my back, my misgivings begin to clear and then, as if she speaks to me.

"You have only to trust Stephen."

That's a tall order, but what else can I do?

I can understand there is more at play than meets the eye, it's not all up to me. Trust the deeper call of Africa. Keep moving ahead and checking off the to-do list.

Back in Mary's kitchen, I'm putting away groceries when the phone rings.

"Hie," he says, "It's me, Stephen. I need to tell you something."

Oh my God, I think, as my stomach flips, what are you going to say to me now?

"I loooove you!"

I hear myself laughing a new-born delight, and disregard the disapproval lurking in the back of my mind. Sunlight streams through the window onto the ripe mango I've just cut open and I remember something Paul Theroux wrote in the DVD liner notes for "Concert for George" (Harrison).

*If the dream is pure enough, and the dreamer unselfish, the dream will come true.*

# The Bedroom Dress

The art of buffing my fingernails to a shining finish, French polish it's called, becomes a ritual preparation for the passage to Africa. The sheen of light on my nails as I travel alone is a way to remember something deeper, more organic than the air-conditioned terminals of one airport after another, and a way to weather being confined in an airliner cabin with so many other bodies.

By the time I enter the arrivals hall of Harare International Airport, port of entry to Zimbabwe, I am one hundred percent grateful for my shiny fingernails. I need to focus on something specific because my legs are shaking and my breath is ragged. I feel faint in the heat and in the unnerving anticipation of what lies on the other side of the immigration officers and baggage claim.

A quiet voice says, "Oliane."

I turn toward someone I hardly recognize. He is more slender, taller than I remember, and is goofily dressed for the city in baggy dress pants that drape over his running shoes, frayed button-down shirt and synthetic-suede windbreaker. Stephen Hambani is here.

After my bags are stowed in my room, we walk up a grassy hill in the glow of late afternoon to stretch my legs after the long journey. I feel like a teenage girl—black t-shirt and blue jeans, long hair loose—soaking in her new boyfriend.

In the guesthouse dining room for the evening meal, just the two of us sit at the long white linen covered table. I ask him to tell me about each of the horses he is training, and he goes on at length about the five of them. I don't know this, yet, but Shona custom is to be quiet when eating. When our plates of grilled fish with roast potato wedges and glazed carrot sticks are served, Stephen bows his head, puts his palms together.

"Asking for Jesus, not church Jesus, but here," putting his hand on his heart, "to hold us in a nice way, you and me, together."

After dinner we return to my room—a once elegant, thatch-roof circular rondaavel beside a pond on the far side of the grounds, behind a tall hedge and hidden from view of the main house. The air inside has a slight musty smell, the flower-print upholstery on the loveseat is faded, but otherwise the room feels cared-for and safe. Stephen takes off his windbreaker and sits down on the side of the bed. I remain standing by the bedside table, silent, unsure. When he reaches for my wrist, I sit down beside him; my hand looks tiny and pale held in his, as he inspects the scars from the steel pins.

"Sorry, sorry," he says. "Are you strong now?"

His thumb strokes the pulse point on the inside of my left wrist.

"Yes," I say.

When I begin to ask about his family, his children, he says nothing. He suddenly lets go of my wrist, spreads one of his hands on my chest and the other between my shoulder blades, and leans me backward onto the bed.

Instinctively, I push up onto my elbows.

"How can I welcome you if we do not lie together, right now?" Stephen says, puzzled.

Oh, my God, right now? I am not ready.

I sit up and press my back against the headboard. I'd imagined getting to know one another, before an intimacy of bodies. Stephen looks bewildered and sincere.

Calm down, I tell myself. Don't panic. Take a breath. Stop trying to have things go your way, with your expectations. And most important—remember, and trust, the trail of evidence that has led to this moment.

"Okay." I say. "First, something I need to tell you."

"All right. I am listening," he says, his Shona English accent rolling the "r" and deepening the vowels.

There are two things I need to say, actually.

First of all, before coming to Africa to meet up with Stephen, I'd had a crucial conversation with my friend Torkin. She co-founded the Bead for Life project in Uganda, and her husband, Charles, an MD, is an HIV medical specialist who teaches in Africa. I knew she'd have the answers to my questions. Not only did she give me the comprehensive gospel on safe sex, she also gave me the unvarnished fundamentals about stereotypical relationships between foreign white women and African men.

"You have to understand," she had said, "that the woman is perceived as a trophy, a sugar mama, who ups her man's status."

Torkin counseled me to resist the inclination to pay for everything, even though I appear to have so much more money relative to Stephen. She counseled me to notice how, and if, he reciprocates, in his own way, within his own means, and not to overstep that balance of equity.

Stephen hears the safe-sex condition and nods.

The second thing I tell him—horseman, trainer and wilderness tracker—or rather confess, is that a woman of my age needs warming up, in the same way that a horse is warmed up for a jumping competition or before a long gallop.

"Yes, I understand the system," he says.

This talking makes space for my mind, totally unstrung by his advance, to find its way back to my body and to my heart. Okay, long exhale.

Now, I am ready.

He smiles and his face lights up with a dimple in his right cheek. Stephen is not only taller and more slender than I imagined, he is more youthful in his physicality—muscular and agile. Unclothed, he seems thirty years old, not fifty-one.

But I find he is wrong about knowing the warm-up system for an older woman, me anyway, and with his fervor, I come up against my own constriction and want to cry out, almost desperately, "I can't do this."

But I don't cry out. The present grabs hold of me and says, "What if you can, do this?"

What if you stay with body sensation, like in the somatic meditation practice, like riding horses bareback? Relax, and let your self go, go, instead of tensing up? And see what happens.

"Slowly, more slowly, let me catch up with you," I whisper.

Truth spoken, Stephen relaxes as well. He looks at my face. He shifts his weight from two hands on the bed to one. Places his palm under my sacrum—sacred bone where the soul resides—drawing me to him. With that tender cradling, something long-held in the secret interior of me, gives way. In the sheen of nighttime, I arrive in Africa. As we lie in stillness afterward, his low voice feathers my ear.

"*Maita basa, bebe.*" He is saying, "Thank you."

The next day, my first whole day in Africa, I meet Stephen for his long lunch break in the field beyond the horse paddocks with a picnic from the guesthouse cook. We sit down side-by-side on the dry grass and lean comfortably against a mounded stack of cut hay. I set our food out on the striped tea towel—avocado halves with lemon, tomato slices with fresh basil clippings, fluffy biscuits and cheddar cheese.

Bareheaded under the soft blue, high noon sky Stephen reports, "I need sunglasses today. There are no clouds, and the sun is too bright, makes my eye sore."

He knew last night in the dark bedroom, in the blankets, that the sun would be too bright today. His eye is a barometer for the weather. The entire surface of his left eye, including the pupil, is an opaque, milky bluish-white, in a starburst shape.

"You know, when I was little boy, two years old in 1962, my father is boss of many workers—manager working on a big farm. The farm owner, a white man, does not tell the workers what job to do each day, he tells my father in the evening before. So in the morning my father tells the workers which job to do. Workers are jealous of my father because he is their boss. Some workers have to do a job they don't like, maybe cleaning the shit drain, so they hate my father and go to witch doctor to make juju.

"That witch doctor, the *nanga,* makes bad medicine, it looks like a snake, against my father's first-born son—me. The snake comes in the night to the house, through the thatching, its tongue moving-moving across the place I am sleeping and spits tongue's poison in my eye.

"In a few days my mother says my eye is leaking fluid and coming bigger and out from my head. In the medicine clinic, nothing they can do and send us home. So my father goes to a different *nanga,* one for good things, pays him some money. That one sleeps and dreams about what is the problem with my eye, and what to do about it.

"His dream says the problem is what I tell you now—the juju from workers who hate my father and go to a bad *nanga* to give bad medicine to my father's family. So, the good *nanga* gives African medicine plant to my mother to rub over my face, says that my eye will not see but will be all right in my head. In a few days my eye comes small again, like the other one.

"And so, my parents leave that farm. First my mother takes me and my older sister to new place, another farm. In some days my father comes. And that new place is fine, my father is a good manager."

The term "witch doctor" conveys a dark romance about Africa from western-world childhood. I'm surprised Stephen uses it, but then, he speaks in the post-colonial English of his generation, not his own first language, Shona. So much sediment remains from decades of the European world colonizing the southern hemisphere and renaming "their" bounty—reclassifying the Indigenous world in its own image, according to its own civilized ethic, and more often than not, demonizing nature-based ways of life.

By now I have lain down with my head resting on Stephen's blue-jeaned thighs, utterly enchanted. The palm of his brawny hand, fingers spread, is a welcome weight on my belly. I can imagine how a spirited filly finds contentment in his care.

When Stephen returns to work, I stay on the flattened grass to watch him ride in the field. It's beautiful to see him jumping the horses, clearing the hurdle rails effortlessly, his body so loose and natural. Later in the afternoon, back at the stable, he cleans the riding gear and returns the last-used saddle, the numnah or saddle pad, and the bridle and equine ankle protectors to the impeccably kept feed and tack room. His 26-year-old son, Hambani, is here too, apprenticing as a groom: cleaning stalls, sweeping the yard, mixing the horses' feed, and leading them out to the field to graze. He's also learning to ride like his father.

"Good afternoon, ma'am," Hambani says and I respond with a smile.

"Hambani, I'm not a ma'am or a boss."

The young man corrects me, "Good afternoon, mum, I am saying to you."

Stephen smiles and raises his eyebrows, then hands me a curry comb when I say, "Show me how you do this, so I'll know your system for grooming the horses."

Professionals each have their own way of doing things, and beginner's mind is best in an unfamiliar situation. Stephen starts to meticulously groom the dark bay thoroughbred beside him. First, he runs a currycomb vigorously over the horse's whole body, followed by a soft bristle brush, and lastly, a hairbrush through the lustrous dark mane. He asks the horse to lift a foot, and he cleans

*The Geography of Belonging*

the hoof with a small metal pick backed with a stiff little brush. Finally, he swipes a thick cotton cloth everywhere, polishing, he tells me. The horse's coat really does shine, treasure in the late afternoon sunlight.

Stephen is a horse professional in every sense of the vocation; he knows the animals from the inside out—from correct feed to farrier work, from intuitive veterinary care to problem solving troublesome horses. At the moment, the six horses he is training, along with the dedicated teenage girl and her father, the owner, take top places in Harare dressage and jumping competitions. In Canada, Stephen would command industry respect and financial reward. In Zimbabwe, I observe, a horse groom or trainer is subservient. He's like other workers in a family's corps of household help, employees who receive minimum wage at the end of the month. It's baffling to try and find my bearings in the unfamiliar territory of an overtly segregated society. I can relate somewhat with each demographic, one human heart to another, even in the short time since my arrival, but I am not at all comfortable in the no-fly zone where the two worlds interface.

Inside the stable now, it's my turn to groom a quiet, mature Arabian mare. When I finish brushing her silken coat, she lowers her snowy-coloured head so I can reach her forelock and comb her beautiful, long mane. She gently rubs her cheek against my shoulder.

In the rondaavel after nightfall, I read a story aloud, slowly, with dramatic emphasis. It's the one I wrote about noticing Stephen in Hwange last year, interlaced with scenes from our safari adventure, the lions and the rain. Now he is my lover, tucked into bed after a cold shower, or "baff" as he calls the bathing, with the wool quilt up to his chin against the chill night. I sit astride his hips on top of the quilt in my red nightdress from India, printed papers in hand, reading the part where he rides back to join Bloomer and Gobo in escorting me across the grassland.

"Stephen, did you put a spell on me, some magic, last year on the safari in Hwange?"

"No, I did not."

"Well, what did you do?"

"When we were at the bonfire, the one I made by the gate after we saw the lions, you gave me the papers from your offering, the wrapping. I put it in the fire and asked God to make you my wife."

That sure sounds like a spell to me, a petitionary prayer, perhaps.

He listens intently to the rest of the story and is impressed with what I remember, the small details of what happened and the things we saw.

"People will like to hear this," he says earnestly, takes the papers out of my hands and drops them to the floor.

Later, resting on my side with Stephen's arm cradling my neck I feel unbounded, as if we've made love with all of creation. He asks for another story, and I tell him about visiting the orphanage in Mozambique last year, the closest I'd come to any black African way of life.

I stop and ask, "Do you understand everything I am saying to you?"

He looks straight into my eyes, pauses, and says, "I am listening to you."

I mean to hold nothing back and to find out everything I can about being with him, because I don't know whether we'll see one another after my volunteer time in the wilderness.

I remember Mandy Retzlaff saying, "You mustn't save anything for later."

So, every offering shall be poured into these few days. And then we can see where we stand.

After the storytelling, I reach for the iPod on the bedside table and delicately push the earbuds into Stephen's ears. I click play and turn up the music that's been my comfort and way of feeling him with me in Canada. He smiles, eyes closed for a few minutes.

*The Geography of Belonging*

He sets the iPod back on the table and lifts the bedcovers, inviting me to slip in beside him; the press of his thigh, and more, through the night, transparent.

In the morning when he has showered and dressed and is ready to walk to the stables for work, Stephen opens the door of the rondaavel and peeks out, looking around outside before smiling back at me, and then steps over the doorsill to begin his day. I notice this happens every morning, and he doesn't answer in a definitive way when I ask about this cautious behaviour.

At first, I think maybe he is ensuring that his nighttime presence in my room is not public knowledge, but it doesn't take long to see there are no secrets in the guesthouse employee community—from the office and household service staff to the myriad gardeners and groundskeepers who arrive very early in the morning. Then one day, Stephen talks about his two years in the military reserve during the war of liberation, the bush war that preceded Zimbabwe becoming an independent republic in 1980.

"Never look straight ahead first of all—always look to the sides, right beside you, in case someone with a gun is coming to you. And even after that war is finished, when I am in the bush for horse safaris, always keep looking all sides. Yes, that's why I'm doing that every time, even nowadays, must see if there is danger before going forward."

Alone in the rondaavel, with the door open to the green fields and brightening blue sky I recognize the liability in not having a first language in common. It's too easy to hear someone speaking an additional language, like Stephen in English, and unconsciously presume he is less intelligent or educated or articulate than he really is. I resolve to hear beyond the charming simplicity of Stephen's often-literal way of saying things in English and to learn some Shona language myself.

At lunchtime, I ask him to translate for me. Let's start with, "Hello, how are you?"

"Depends on time of the day," Stephen coaches. "Morning time, say, '*Mamuka sei.*'

Other person says, '*Tamuka, mamuka oh?*' 'I am fine, and you?' You say '*Tamuka.*' 'I am fine.'"

Because of our intimacy, I think, I hear the nuances of accent and inflection in his Shona. I'm not simply reciting words or phrases, but sensing and saying back to him the undercurrents of meaning in the pronunciation and tone of his voice.

After Stephen and Hambani have finished their work for the day, and bathed under an outdoor bucket shower, we sit together on low stools by a fire outside their brick sleeping room beside the stable. Their living arrangement is primitive, given we're in sub-urban Harare and not a rural village. Hambani puts a big, black enamel pot of water on top of the rickety iron grate that is supported by bricks above the fire. "*Sadza,*" he says with undisguised pride and shows me his specially carved hefty wooden stick with one flattened end, a paddle-spoon for stirring the maize meal he has sifted into the heating water. The mealie meal, as he calls it, looks like finely cut rolled oats, but it's actually milled corn. This is the dietary staple of Zimbabwe, with a very particular method of cooking. After the initial cup or so of mealie meal has come to a boil, the *sadza* is vigorously stirred in a folding pattern as subsequent cupfuls of mealie meal are added. The whumping sound of the wooden spoon against the potful of thick porridge is synonymous with: "Dinner is almost ready!" The side dish is called relish whether it's *nyama*, meat, or *miriwo*, vegetables. This evening the relish is finely cut chomorio, a green vegetable, like kale, stewed in a small pot with onions and tomatoes and an overly generous measure of soybean cooking oil.

Hambani bends down to my height and pours a thin stream of cool water over my hands while holding a plastic bowl underneath.

"For washing," he says.

He does the same for Stephen. Hambani hands us each an enameled metal plate heaped with steaming *sadza* and relish, then, sits down with his own on his lap. The heat of the metal plate burns my knees, so I put it on the ground and watch the two men scoop a small portion of *sadza* with the fingers of one hand and press it into the palm, dip it into the relish and then into their mouths. When my food has cooled, I do the same, not quite as deftly.

"I need to buy a cell phone, an inexpensive one with a local SIM card and some airtime. Can you take me to a shop?" I ask Stephen, at the stable on his lunch break.

"Yes, let's go," he says. "My friend has got good price."

We hop off a heat-swamped kombi, the people-packed mini-van commuter bus, in front of a thatch stall on the roadside. The cell phones displayed on a faded towel on the ground look like cheap plastic toys, and the vendor has airtime cards only in one-dollar denominations. I know it costs fifty cents per minute to call Canada. No wonder the young Hambani, and his unemployed friends who come to the stables, are always talking about their buggered phones, trading power cords and attempting to make them work by taking them apart or setting them out in the sun.

"Buggered" means something is not working and can likely be fixed, usually temporarily. "Fuck-ed" means something is totally buggered and beyond repair. This distinction will become a useful means of discerning whether we'll be stuck somewhere a long time "for fixing problem" or whether we'll simply go off in search of another course of action.

I can't imagine living like this, on the "have-not" fringe inhabited by the "wekkahs," workers, in Zimbabwean society. Light years away from the romance, the allure, of horses—and horse-man—in the wilderness.

I hadn't noticed the upscale shopping plaza across the road with a billboard for the Econet shop, one of three telecommunication companies in the country. The shop is air-conditioned and staffed by young black women and men in dark blue skirts, or trousers, and white shirts. Stephen has never been inside. Although the line-up is long and slow-moving, when I reach the service counter it's as if I'm the only customer of the day, receiving the attention of two sales agents who together outfit me with what I need, a basic phone with SIM card for calls and text messages, plus a handful of five-dollar airtime vouchers. Stephen, who has been patiently waiting beside me, is incredulous at the extravagance of my expenditure, so I give up my preference for the two-dollar taxi ride back to the guesthouse and follow him into the next muggy kombi bus that comes by.

I'm relieved to know these small, but revealing, truths about Stephen's life, now, at the beginning of my time in Zimbabwe, before going off to the horse volunteer program. Oddly, I don't feel disappointed by the disparity of our savvy in the urban world, instead, I feel grateful for finally meeting the mystery.

What outcome will these revelations lead to? I do not know.

Despite our differences in the outside world, these five days and nights in the sanctuary of the guesthouse estate have been an unreserved fulfillment.

A month from now, when I return to Harare, Stephen wants to take me to the village where his older sister lives with her extended family. I would like to go. How ethical is that, I wonder, when our future together is indeterminate? I ask him what she will think of me coming with him to the village, especially if we are not betrothed.

He says, "She will think I am clever."

I ask him what clever means to his sister.

"You care about this country, Zimbabwe. You like us, the black people," he says. "I like white people but they don't like us, they look at us down. For myself, I am not loving a white person before. I'm black people, but you give love to me. For that my sister thinks I am clever."

In the evening, Stephen and I retire to the rondaavel. After undressing, he sits up in bed, and painstakingly writes in my notebook, in English, the name and birth year of each of his six children. It's our last night together.

"For you," I say, reaching into my backpack for the parcel of reading glasses donated "for Africa" by my friends in Canada, "maybe these will help."

Stephen peers at me over the spectacles now perched low on his nose.

"*Iwe ziva kuchengeta, murume wango*," he says in his beautiful first language. "You know how to keep, how to care for, your husband."

After writing the list of facts, he talks about each child, five of them young adults—where they live and their life circumstances, and what happened with each of the three mothers, two divorces, one death.

He tells me about the customs of his culture in the time of his grandparents, 'the old people from before.' He tells me about a traditional wedding in those days and the long strand of tiny seed beads a husband gives his wife to wear around her waist in the night for their pleasure.

"I will give you some beads like that," he promises.

The shredded practicalities of life in today's Zimbabwe hit home again this morning as I prepare to leave the guesthouse in Harare for the month in bush camp without internet. Forgetful of unexpected lapses in wireless connection and unpredictable electricity cuts, especially in the city, I'm writing an email on the laptop that Ann, the guesthouse owner, has lent me, just to let my son, my sister and my elderly parents know that I have arrived safely and that I'll be out of touch for a month. There's just time for another quick message. I get a little carried away writing to a very close friend at home and am alarmed to find that my exceedingly personal message about the last five days will not send, nor close. It remains on the screen. The wireless connection is gone. In my disoriented panic, I imagine that my message will reappear when the computer is turned back on, by someone else.

When I ask Ann to close my email message herself, if it appears on the screen when the internet comes back on, and confess to her why she should do this personally rather than leave it for one of the office staff, she says, "Fine. We'll just publish your letters in The Herald, the most gossipy of the local newspapers."

"Perfect," I say, and our friendship is established.

# PART TWO

## MAVURADONHA MOUNTAINS, ZIMBABWE

# Beneath Our Feet

As soon as we're out of the truck it's clear that "here" is different—Siya Lima Farm, the Varden's gateway to the Mavuradonha Wilderness. Stretching my back after the long drive, something in the atmosphere causes me to spread out, to take up more space, but without intruding myself on anything.

Is it the smell and the heat in the air? The enthusiasm of light? The colours and formations in the land? Yes, all these qualities that visitors remark on, and something more: an invisible presence seems to welcome the human animal of me, a newcomer, into its fold.

Janine and I walk out into a pasture that slopes to a pond. We sit on the ground, apart from one another, silent in the dry grass while her horses graze and drink. The surface of the pond reflects cumulus billows overhead, a floating mauve water lily bobbles as the horses wade in and out. Four of the horses, greys, seem a lustrous pearl-white in the green foliage along the water's edge. And then I recognize Munhondo, Bhura, and Manini from the safari in Hwange; their earthy smell stirs a memory. I really have come back to Africa.

An hour or so later Janine and I walk to the house, horses trailing behind. The Siya Lima farmhouse, with adjacent stable, is an extraordinary architectural apotheosis, poignant in its faded eccentric grandeur, a remnant of Zimbabwe's lost agricultural economy. Janine leads me inside, along a narrow hallway, up a short flight of stone stairs and around a corner to my room. The Blue Room.

Interior designers would dare to match the non-faux construction, now patina'd with neglect. Beneath an arched plaster ceiling, a two-person raised oval bathtub is the centerpiece of an adjoining alcove, flooded with afternoon light through floor-to-ceiling windows. But there is no running water. Janine pulls a faded turquoise upholstered chair into the bedroom, and I sit down. She leans back on the thick, hand-printed bedcover and begins the story of how she and James came to be here.

She tells me that they began leasing the farmhouse, along with a small portion of surrounding farmland for the horses, when the owner and creator of the estate, Mike McGrath, moved to Harare. His right to grow commercial crops was rescinded by the regional authorities in 2004 during the first decade of farm invasions. The Vardens, friends with McGrath, were already leading safaris from Kopje Tops camp and saw the potential of Siya Lima to accommodate visitors, as well.

Janine has a perspective of present-day Zimbabwe that is hopeful, different from the fear and gloom of recent years: three years ago, in 2008, hyperinflation was 80 billion percent.

"Paper banknotes stuffed into a shopping bag were barely enough to purchase a loaf of bread," she says, shaking her head and laughing. "And even at that, shelves were mostly bare in the food shops, no petrol at the pumps, no wages paid, and erratic days-long electricity outages. One quarter of our population left the country!"

I'd heard these facts around the campfire on the safari in Hwange last year and was astounded then, by the take-it-in-stride ingenuity of the Zimbabweans who stayed put. Their motto, "Make a plan," actually means: "We'll make it up as we go along, and hope for the best." In tough times that means different things at different economic levels: scavenging seeds for some and pooling the most meager of edibles; bartering goods and services; foreign bank accounts and buying trips to South Africa for others, who bring back petrol, food, and other goods. Since dollarization two years ago, in 2009, when U.S. dollars became the standard currency of day-to-day commerce, there seems to be a move toward recovery. I've been in several supermarkets filled with food and household necessities, though, of course, only for those who have the money to pay. But that's the surface picture. The country is still on tenterhooks, and I'm cautioned not to question anyone about politics or the economy. They could wind up in trouble.

Janine casually asks, "How's Stephen?"

"It's hard to say," I reply, "I have no frame of reference."

"Did he say why he left us?"

I don't know why he left Varden Safaris, but I can tell her what Stephen did say to me.

"Janine is one hundred percent."

I imagine that he misses their working companionship with the horses and the camaraderie of the other grooms in camp now that he is working independently in town.

Janine says, "Stephen didn't seem to fit in when we all returned to the stables here at Siya Lima after the Hwange Horseback Safari concession closed. He had a lot of freedom in the Hwange bush, managing the horses there, warranted by his knowledge and strong sense of responsibility."

I refrain from adding that Stephen told me his autonomy was diminished at Siya Lima, by others, peers in leadership positions. "Can have only one cock in the chicken yard," he'd reflected.

"Is he happy?" Janine wants to know. I can only say that he had a community and companionship and a place he belonged, working with Varden Safaris, and now he seems not to.

When Janine leaves me to rest, I notice that the two wall sconces above the bed are matching halves of a woven basket, plastered onto the turquoise wall. I stand on the bed to look inside one of them. Yes, there's a light socket, but no bulb, and a mound of dead bugs; no electricity at the farm anyway. The loose end of a furled mosquito net is twisted neatly into the other sconce.

The elegant decrepitude of the farmhouse is captivating, partly because it is not accompanied by a smell of dampness, mould and decay, as it would be where I live in the temperate west coast rainforest of Canada. Throughout the African rainy season, everything dries out in the midday heat. The handmade ceramic floor tiles are warm on my feet; no chill, either air-born or underfoot.

When the light of dawn blooms the next morning, layers of peeling pastel wall seem to glow. Alice, the housekeeper, brings tea in a thermos to my bedside, and a plastic bucket of hot water for washing. The towel smells of woodsmoke. Before breakfast I set off on a hike with Marvin Mutangara, the volunteer coordinator; he's in his mid-thirties, well-educated and well-traveled. Two other safari staff who seem similarly aged, come with us. They're from the local community and have worked in the Mavuradonha safari camp all their adult lives. Marvin guides the way across the unsown crop fields and up the steep incline of an enormous, treed rock mound, a *kopje*. From the plateau on top, we can see the extent of the former 3000-hectare farm and the clusters of new settlers' huts on the far side of a small, man-made lake.

Marvin sits on the flat granite surface with his blue-jeaned legs stretched out, and gives a well-prepared orientation talk about the F.E.E.T eco-tourism project. He is big on acronyms and mottos; F.E.E.T. stands for Field Eco-Equestrian Traveler. I'm the first, and so far, only, volunteer. "Our" mission is to explore the unique archeology of this wilderness wonderland.

That's it? I think. No grunt work involved?

Aloud, I muster, "Privilege to be with you in this mission. Thank you."

Marvin explains, "The presence of more foreign visitors will help save Mavuradonha from the threat of mining, and preserve it as a wilderness-education safari destination."

After asking for my hopes, expectations and potential contributions, he asks Pension Nyamare, bush-kitchen guru, and Douglas Chinhamo, wilderness guide and lead horseman, to introduce themselves, which they briefly do, then he prepares to move on.

Wait a minute.

"Marvin, you and I had long hours of travel, driving here from Harare, to become acquainted. And me, enthusiastic about what lies in store. Now we surely must ask Pension and Douglas more about themselves and their choice to be involved in the project."

I want to know if they're here simply for work, or if they have some deeper investment in what we'll be doing together. After all, this is their home territory. I ask for their thoughts.

Pension lifts his long rangy arms towards the mountains and says, "I like to cook in the bush for visitors, to show them eh-ver-y-thing we can make on the fire; even bread, cake, butternut soup." His pride makes me smile.

Douglas, on the other hand, doesn't say anything about himself: he tells me with conviction that my main contribution will be to tell others, after I leave, about the beauty of Zimbabwe and the goodness of her people who are trying to sustain themselves on the land.

"Please bring more visitors like your self," he says, "Who understand the value of protecting the wilderness."

Marvin, too, affirms that tourist dollars speak loudly to the priorities of the regional government. As I survey the landscape beyond our perch on the kopje, Siya Lima is a confounding place, it seems to me. Different eras of Zimbabwe's history demand attention: the original perfection of nature, and first peoples; then the superimposed—and later deposed—post-colonial European imprint. After McGrath left the farm, Shona veterans of the war for independence claimed ownership of buildings further afield on the grounds and on most other properties in the region, then left them to decompose. The veterans' designation as *wovits* comes from the southern African pronunciation of "war vets." At present, small family compounds with garden plots are scattered over the land; they were settled by displaced farmworkers who formed a community in their own right—the present-day Siya Lima and neighbouring Penrose. Now, nature has her way with the stonework arches, the red-tiled roofs, the untended commercial agriculture fields and pastures, the unused machinery.

The Vardens occupy the diminished Siya Lima homestead in the active sense of the verb. The tenancy they maintain with domestic animals and resident caretakers is the slim thread that keeps the farm from sliding into the hands of encroaching re-settlers, off-spring of the original *wovits*. The Varden's few staff for the horses, the household, and the camp, are locals and liaisons with the community. The horses stay at the farm when they are not out on safari, rather than in the corral at the bush camp further north, in the Mavuradonha Wilderness—the stable at the farm is fortress-like, much safer from lions. Sometimes safari clients en route to the camp stay in the farmhouse, though power lines from the road were cut and the windmill blew over last year. With no electricity and no functioning pump for running water, it's more work than bush camp for Pension the cook and Alice, the housekeeper.

A late breakfast is already set out on the patio in the protected courtyard, overhung with deep pink blooms of bougainvillea vines that infiltrate crevices in the walls. The beautiful, ornamental creeper is an "exotic" species in Africa, not native, imported evidence of European settlement. Twelve wicker armchairs fringe a long plank table, each chair lined with worn, floral cushion padding. But before James, Janine, Marvin and I sit down to eat, we take a brief side trip. The phone booth at Siya Lima farm is a small fenced area, once a rose garden. A huge, metal-webbed satellite dish sprouts from an overgrown flowerbed, juxtaposed with the monumental rock crag of the sacred mountain, Nyambare, in the distance. We leave our cell phones here in the sun, hoping they catch intermittent signal and download a text message or record a missed incoming phone number in the call log. No one in Zimbabwe has voicemail on a cell phone; listening to it uses up expensive airtime minutes that cost the recipient. Back at the breakfast table, Janine describes their plan of restoring utility services to the house and once again making the farm a destination in itself. I think it would be a perfect artists' or writers' retreat.

It's been two weeks since I left Canada, after months of preparation both practical and prayerful, in anticipation of entering the Mavuradonha Wilderness. And now, outside Siya Lima stable, the moment I've waited for. Horses saddled and ready, I'm putting on the full-length fringed suede chaps, my friend Mary's gift, that have held the promise of riding in Africa again.

Out of the blue, sunlight fades from Nyambare mountainside across the way, subduing the landscape and my mood. Something is missing, some brilliance. Oh, I'd imagined wearing the chaps with Stephen and riding in the bush with him. He is not here. I feel his absence acutely with these familiar horses, the ones we rode in Hwange. I miss the rapport we shared and his attentive support in the bush. I fumble with the long side-zipper on my chaps, determined not to cry. When I stand upright, with the weight of the suede settled on my hips, the bleak feeling just evaporates. The horses nicker, ready to go, the sun returns brightening the day.

Marvin, Douglas, Pension and I are going to Kopje Tops bush camp today with kit and gear for the month. Douglas is ready on the spunky gelding Gizmet and trails Skanky by her lead rope. Skanky is a spirited young paint mare, white and sorrel, given the job of packhorse today, as part of her training in the trustworthy composure needed on the trail with riders aboard. Pension, tall and lanky, is on foot beside Skanky; his kitchen supplies are stowed in her saddlebags.

Marvin is on steady Basera and trails a beautifully conformed young palomino mare, who is just starting her training in the bush. Her name is Jecha, the Shona word for sand. From the wood benchseat that doubles as mounting block I swing into the saddle on Moonlight, fifteen-hand grey mare, who initially checks me out with a tentative buck or two when I ask her to move ahead: Does this woman know what she's doing?

The red dirt roadway beyond the farm has been recently bulldozed wide and flat for the gigantic yellow dump trucks that transport mineral-laden earth to the mine-processing plant visible on the horizon a few kilometres away. Marvin points to a low mountain some distance behind the farm.

"The Chinese are strip-mining just over that hill," he says. "That's the urgency for getting Mavuradonha better protected, by securing status as a national heritage site."

When dust clouds foretell the looming approach of the frightfully driven trucks, we pull neckerchiefs over our noses and mouths and head immediately into the roadside vegetation, facing the horses away from the road to spare them the brunt of the dust. It's a short, thirty-minute ride to the trailhead, but the way feels treacherous, not only because of the road hazard but also because of the far-reaching implications for once-intact environments all over Africa.

After crossing a stone bridge over shallow running water, Douglas guides Gizmet off to the right, into the tall bushy border, and the rest of us follow in single file. A path of flattened grass opens up and once off the road, the unsettling realities of the mining vanish. The pathway, animal and human-made, traverses gradually rising slopes of miombo-treed woodland; this is the single entranceway to the wilderness region and to the Mavuradonha Mountains much further north. Our moving line of five horses and four humans slows as the path underfoot narrows and a head-high stand of grass obscures both the ground and the distant view. Each stalk of amber-coloured grass is rose-tinged at the tip, a blush that brushes our temples as the horses glide us through.

I expect a few hours of riding before we'll reach the Raphia Palms Botanical Reserve. Janine told me the reserve has a distinguished reputation in the world of plant biology: an unblemished eco-system alongside the Tingwa River. The immense fronds of the Raphia Farinfera palm tree are by far the biggest leaves in the plant kingdom—up to eighteen metres tall.

Douglas eventually slows his horse at the crest of a low rise, allowing the rest of us to fall in beside him. The grass just skimming our thighs, he points to a posse of zebras running helter-skelter up the far hillside. In just a few seconds the shiny stripes disappear, camouflaged by a canopy of trees. Then I see it—a clearing about the size of a soccer field.

Coming so unexpectedly upon the beauty of the botanical reserve sweeps me away. I feel small. As if the shiny peel of a giant Ambrosia apple, with its scarlet, yellow, russet and green, is spread over the landscape—a mantle of deep and glowing variegated colour. In the distance the huge skyward fronds of the Raphia Palm trees at the river's edge appear molten, reflecting a silvery rather than a golden light. Moonlight lowers her head and blows out through her nose, she follows Douglas and Gizmet's meandering lead toward the river. The silky brocade of tall grass in the meadow surrounding us ripples gently, handprints of wind. The low river burbles and sparkles over rocks. The illusion of liquid light on the palm fronds melts away as we pass underneath them. A world of unfiltered perception opens to me, one that I imagine painters and fine art photographers inhabit.

The horses carry us, further, into a surrounding grove of mujanje trees where we wind through their foliage, sunlit, at eye level. Each hand-size leaf is a vessel of mercurial water, until one comes very close, and then the reflected sunlight fades and disappears. With changes in light through the coming days I will find that every ride into the botanical reserve unveils new facets of the flora. I resolve to study mirages and the miracle of photosynthesis.

The Kopje Tops main lodge burned down six months ago, so there is no formality in camp now, simply an acceptance of making do, which Zimbabweans of all stripes are used to. One of the thatch-roof, stone-wall, guest chalets now houses the food storage and prep with cooking fire outside and another, the dining pavilion.

Marvin's guiding motto is to have me, his volunteer, be "happy, safe, well-fed, and well-informed." I appreciate his intelligence and his thoughtful perspective in many domains, and ask if he has considered being a community leader in the future. Yes, he has spoken with his parents, who, hesitant initially, concerned for his safety, came 'round to give their blessing.

"They have entrusted me to the care and protection of *vadzimu*," he says.

I understand *vadzimu* to be akin to "the lineage" in Buddhism, to the primordial force of creation, the unseen presence, and to "the Ancestors" in African Shona culture and other Indigenous cosmologies. Marvin suggests that I must have prepared very well with the *vadzimu* myself before returning to Africa, given what is showing itself to me now.

Good morning in Shona, *mangwanani*, means, "tomorrow is here." I wonder upon waking, seeing Gizmet and Jecha in the paddock beyond my window, what is the wisdom to be learned with this herd in Mavuradonha? Going to meet Douglas and his camp groom, Clemens, to tend the horses before breakfast, it's delightful to be able to say "*Mangwanani!*"

Marvin is staying in camp today, so I saddle Moonlight to ride out with Douglas and Clemens. I discover a welcome simplicity in being with the two of them: we don't talk since it is an effort to converse in English and takes attention away from observing the surroundings. Our silence lets the mind down gently and my usually overt curiosity disappears. I just listen: the familiar rustle of grass on our horses' legs; the conversation of the trees with the wind, of the cloud shadows with the cliffs they scan, and the bees dusting the voluptuous creamy-coloured protea blossoms.

I notice that Moonlight is responding to my thoughts: about which side of a tree to pass, whether to ride beside Clemens or in front of him, to slow down and pick up speed; she feels my intention the instant it's formed, before I've purposely moved my body or spoken to her or even made a conscious choice. This. This is natural horsemanship.

After a while Douglas begins to tell me, in his understated way, about the inner bark of the sweet thorn tree, which is good for thirst; I ask to try some and find that sucking a strip of fibre brings the tree to life in an unexpected way. This is no longer the Latin-named Acacia karroo species, defined by specific physical characteristics; this living organism is a friend, the source of rehydration at intervals in one's journey across the land. As we ride through the bush, conversing becomes easier. I am able to hear more accurately Douglas' accented and dated English, while he casually teaches me Shona expressions. It becomes clear that he continuously discerns what will benefit his community in a sustainable way into the 21st century. It is not an easy mission to put into practice.

After we leave our horses tethered in the scrub brush with Clemens, Douglas leads me high up a granite-strewn hill—toward a vertical surface of rock that's set back under a massive overhang. A huge flat-topped boulder, as if a platform, lies in front. As we get nearer, the atmosphere changes from the sentient woodlands to an uncanny sense of spaciousness, as if all persona and preconceptions have fallen away. Then, without any fanfare, we are standing on the boulder—face to face with hand-drawn images of the iconic animals of Africa.

"Rock art," Douglas tells me, paintings ten millennia old, the language of his ancestors, leaving messages for other hunters about where they have found certain animals for food and hides. "We can come back to these shrines," he continues, "and I will tell more about the spiritual and supernatural significance of the pictures." The zebras are vivid, animated. The elephant is immense and the human figures are tiny behind its legs.

Something minuscule moves, a living spider creeps across the long, curved horn of a sable antelope painted on the cliff. Something inside me moves, too. I feel a bit light-headed and have to lie down on the boulder. When Douglas tells me the granite rock underneath us is more than a billion years old, I just let go.

When I wake up, I can feel a distinct heartbeat, but more than my own: the boulder, the hill, the earth are pulsing in time with me, or I with them. I am them. Breathing is the same: a boundless invisible presence breathes through me; with each inhale I am filled with the whole universe, when I exhale my breath disperses to the incalculable reaches of the cosmos. *Vadzimu*, indeed.

When we return to Kopje Tops camp, Nesbert Mafusire, the camp manager and second-in-command safari guide when James is away, is waiting for his weekend clients. I'm beginning to get the feel of camp life and notice that Nesbert has a rifle case slung from his shoulder.

I ask Douglas why Nesbert carries a weapon. "Ah, because he is a certified hunter as well as a guide."

There is no hunting in Mavuradonha.

"That's not what I mean," I say quietly, "we were out there without a gun and perfectly safe. Is it for emergency encounters with wildlife? Or just for show for the clients?"

In a low voice, Douglas says, "I prefer just in the early morning before we go out, to make a prayer to my Ancestors and ask the spirit of this place to keep us harmonious with the animals, to guide and protect us. No danger will come to us then. I do not need a gun."

The horses begin to shift weight slightly, sensing the distant Land Rover approaching camp, carrying the weekend clients in time for lunch.

Low clouds shroud the surrounding hilltops in the pre-dawn, such a contrast with the grandeur of last evening's sunset that relinquished itself to the dark cosmos and the diamond sharpness of stars that echoed sparks from the camp fire. Going out to the paddock to be with the horses, even before Douglas emerges from the tack shed where he sleeps, I begin to sing quietly, resting my hands first on Moonlight, then Skanky, the words of a mantra, a musical prayer, gratitude.

It's time to pay my respects to this land, to say hello to the Ancestors long gone and to the spirit that animates the biosphere today. When the horses are saddled, Marvin, Douglas, Clemens and I cross the Tingwa River toward the tumbledown Carew House, hidden a short distance from camp. The house was the original two-storey thatch and mortar family home of the first safari outfit in Mavuradonha. Marvin describes the restoration he has undertaken with some of the craftsmen who were its builders in the 1980s. As we proceed upward into the hills behind the house, I confess to Marvin a desire to have Stephen come to camp as my riding coach, offering to pay the extra expense, thinking it quite out of the question. He doesn't reply.

After a diagonal ascent this way and that, Marvin, Douglas and I leave the horses in Clemens' care and climb the rest of the way up a steep *kopje*. Unbelievably there is dried elephant dung on the very small flat space at the top. Marvin accords with my purpose, perhaps indulging me, by stretching himself out on his back near the edge. Douglas follows. I do the same, with my knees bent and soles of my feet flat on the granite, then, I say a few words about the earth descent practice. Though I feel silly saying what might be perfectly obvious to the two men.

When Marvin reminds me that the rock supporting us, the sentient terrain of Africa, is some of the oldest on the planet, any perception of separateness evaporates with his testimony. In just a few minutes a pulsing current surges through my back—the earth in conversation with one human body.

Afterward, we sit in silence with soft-focus eyes on the valley below. Douglas by gesture invites me to begin the informal ceremony, to present the offerings I've brought from Canada. Mindful of the tufts of dry grass in the rock crevices, I light a slender beeswax candle and secure it on the rock; I uncork a tiny clear glass vial of seawater from my Pacific Ocean home and another of earth from the base of an old-growth cedar tree.

I unwind a shiny saffron-coloured ribbon from green Tibetan prayer flag fabric that holds the wee femur of a fawn, one of the barebones of a baby deer we found in the forest of Mary's Farm. To the visible, and invisible, my prayer:

"Thank you for opening the way, for accepting my presence.

"How can I serve this wilderness, the preservation of Mavuradonha, and all that is sacred here?"

"Douglas, Marvin?" I ask, "Shall we send a prayer from our own hearts to whoever out there in the world has a contribution for Mavuradonha, and ask them to come?"

"Yes," they agree, and we bow our heads for a few minutes, then look, out, beyond the distant mountains.

After this Marvin is ready to move on, to a different spot at a higher elevation to receive signal from his cell phone service provider. We continue on foot up a slick grassy hill. At the pinnacle, my cell phone doesn't have reception but Marvin's does; he has a different brand of SIM card, and surprisingly he calls Stephen right there on the hilltop.

He looks at me, "Stephen can come next week, to be your riding coach. When you arrive back at camp from the overnight trek to Bat Caves, he will be here."

As we slide down the hillside toward the horses, a small lemon-looking bird zooms above us, an African Golden Oriole. When I'm back in the saddle on Moonlight, Douglas hands me a finger-length bright yellow feather. Everything is perfect; Stephen is coming.

Down the mountainside we slide; at camp we find Pension making a remarkable lunch over the fire—roast chicken, olive oil baked squash, sautéed greens with peanut sauce (the traditional dish is called *muborah,* made with pumpkin leaves) and bush tea from foliage he has collected.

"Get your weapon, Nesbert!" shouts James, handgun holstered at his waist, as he disappears down the path to get his rifle from the locked storeroom.

Four of us have been assembling gear in front of the stable this early morning, preparing to undertake a multi-day trek on foot along the perimeter of Mavuradonha, around to the Mzurabani Tribal Lands on the eastern side of the wilderness. Actually, three will tackle the formidable full route; I will stay "out rough" one night and return to camp late tomorrow with Nesbert Mafusire who will come to collect me. Then I'll resume exploring the territory of Mavuradonha on horseback with Douglas, and Stephen.

Barely twenty minutes ago, Janine had set off in the land cruiser heading back to Siya Lima farm. She has just returned in haste, skidding to a stop in the field, breathless and angry.

"The Chinese are opposite the Raphia Palms," she bursts out. "Let's go!"

The purpose of the trans-wilderness trek, surveying current conditions, has just escalated to anti-poaching and illegal-prospecting patrol. Leaning into the truck window, Marvin tells Janine that prospectors have a right to be in the area, but first must have officially informed, and received permission from, the local tribal council. Janine knows this and is hotly intent on determining the legitimacy of these apparently trespassing prospectors. Douglas remarked to me a few days ago that his brother-in-law is one of the Shona locals on the prospecting crew and pleased to have a job to supplement his meager farming income, however temporary. Douglas is an ethical man and knows this dilemma is classic worldwide: preserve the environment or feed your family. He is set on educating his community about "sustainability," living in a reciprocal relationship with the land, as the great-grandparents did in the time "before." He often talks to me about the short term and longer term needs of his people and I wonder how he navigates where to place, or how to split, his allegiance as a respected young leader in his community?

"Got your ID, Nesbert?" James is back. "We may have to arrest the motherfuckers and take them to the police station in Guruve."

Nesbert Mafusire's quiet nature belies his former career as a special services police officer with the authority to arrest and detain; he was posted around the country for twenty-one years, 1978 to 2000, until the political climate changed for the worse. Today, a .458 Mauser rifle is slung over his shoulder, he knows that two firearms will be more intimidating than James' pistol alone. The two men leap into the back of the truck along with Marvin and the newly-arrived game scout from Mzurabani, who must, by regulations, accompany our wilderness trek.

"Better you stay here," James warns me as the truck heads out at speed.

Having no idea if they'll be back in an hour or a few days, I walk to the dining tent where Alice and Pension are industriously clearing up breakfast, to study the big plastic-covered topographical survey map that leans against a canvas sidewall, looking for revelation in the natural contours of rivers, mountains, gorges and vleis.

The map was compiled manually, from air photographs dated 1960, more than fifty years ago and covers 1000 sq. km. The original typeface labeling the country "Rhodesia" is overwritten by hand in thick black marker, "Zimbabwe." The Mavuradonha Wilderness protected area boundary, 600 sq.km, is outlined in black marker on the plastic oversheet.

In the early 1980's, just after Independence, the white, now-Zimbabwean, farmers whose properties bordered the uninhabited Mavuradonha Mountains region went to the Mzurabani Rural District Council, the regional government, seeking to preserve and protect the land as a wilderness area. They foresaw an intact habitat for wildlife, in part for sustainable game hunting which requires a natural ecosystem. Mavs would need protection from animal poachers, from habitat destruction by potential mineral exploitation, from homesteading wovit settlers and even border-dwellers' firewood and timber harvest.

The bid was successful, and in 1988 the Mavuradonha Wilderness was gazetted by an act of parliament into a concession with the same protection and provision for tourism as National Parks. A few years later the Carew family secured the right to run photographic safaris (as opposed to hunting safaris) in the wilderness, which became among the best in Africa, I've heard. Eight years ago, the Vardens took over from Carews, in 2002, unknowingly just as the land reform program began spiraling the country into the ground.

Orienting myself in the bottom left corner of the map, the "You are here" spot, the Tingwa River winds diagonally upward, along Raphia Palm Botanical Reserve, traverses the map and meets the Musengenzi River in the east. The Musengenzi flows northward through the Mavuradonha Mountains and eventually into the Zambezi River, which continues eastward through Mozambique to the Indian Ocean.

Sitting down on the sisal floor mat in front of the map, I realize it was just yesterday that four of us, James, Marvin, the game scout and I walked the first leg of our trek, from Siya Lima Farm over the northern hills into the wilderness and on to Kopje Tops camp. My thoughts return now, to the shocking first sight of the alluvial strip mining just beyond Siya Lima—a hair's breadth away from the southern boundary of Mavurdonha. At first exhilarated with the physical exertion of hiking and by the holy spirit of place, our feet and our hearts fall heavy as we walk over the stripped land, and bear witness to ruination. I picture James leading us over the chromium mine site, the deep red earth gashed, bulldozed raw, yet glittering, as if strewn with diamonds and dew in morning sunshine. Trees uprooted, scraped into the Tingwa River bed, a convenient burning ditch, cutting off water flow to village communities and natural habitats downstream.

The conversation between the three men jars my ignorance. I hear their shared opinion that Chinese mining is taking over the continent, that geological Africa is still seen as a boundless treasury of natural resources, as it was a few centuries ago by infiltrating non-natives. And here in Zimbabwe, as everywhere that exploitation on the planet occurs, the lure of immediate cash to a few locals for hard work gives no clue, initially, of the destitution that follows when ways of life integral with the land fall by the wayside just like the heaps of slag left by foreign resource extraction operations.

Where mining is officially authorized, more often than not the staggering amount of incoming revenue doesn't get past the personal pockets of the government and corporate heads, with no benefit to a community, nor to infrastructure in the country unless it serves the exportation purposes of the mining company.

"A vigilant presence," James says, "is the best counteracting force to unsanctioned foreign loot and leave operations."

I walk off to the side, eyes to the ground, a clutch of anger and sorrow bites fiercely. "Made in China, Raped in Africa," the title of a Facebook page that monitors this mining activity with widespread opinion, across demographic differences, that the Chinese will colonize all of Africa for natural resource extraction; and not for the purpose of making a home or society here, as the Europeans did so long ago for better and for worse, but to plunder the earth's treasury and leave a desecration of land, wildlife and human culture on a scale so monumental that the continent, and indeed the planet, will never recover what has been lost.

Dark thunderclouds threaten the nearest range of peaks as we continue northwest over the next hillside; is it my imagination conjuring the howls of grieving animals that echo into the far-off mountains? After that, grim silence, save for the occasional scrabble of loose rock under our boots.

After a time, to lighten our mood, I demonstrate Monty Python "silly walks," and the guys gamely follow the goofy gaits from the British television series "Monty Python's Flying Circus." Everyone makes up his own steps; a crazy trail of spoor on the gritty game track along the rocky ridge.

The sound of the land cruiser returning to camp brings me back to the prospect of resuming our trek; I leave the map and walk back to the field. The sun cranes overhead, hot. James relays that the prospectors took off in their truck speeding back to the walled Chinese mine processing compound about five kilometres south. Nesbert went on to the authorities in Guruve and filed a report; within the month he will hear that the chromium seekers were charged with trespassing in the protected area and have been heavily fined—dissuaded from further incursion, one dares hope.

Despite the intense pre-noon heat, the four of us hoist our backpacks and one by one enter a footpath into dense shoulder high grass on the far side of the field. With that, a wondrous uprising quiver of colour, a corridor of butterflies ushers us into the bush. James, behind me, elaborates: Gaudy Commodore are the deep purple ones, they unfurl from cocoons in the dry season for a fleeting two-week appearance. There is a bigger paler Commodore, orange, longer lasting. The fiery Acraea. The citrus Swallowtail. Closing my eyes and listening for Marvin's dry grass footfalls ahead of me, my face, ears, neck, and bare shoulders are feathered with an effusion of butterfly kisses.

"The damselfly closes its wings when landed." James, ever the guide, continues, "Dragonfly wings stay open when landed." The red Scarlet Dragonfly, the Navy Dropped Wing and the blue Julia Skimmer. These winged air jewels, too, weave their flirty gossamer flightpaths into the head-high thatching grass all around us.

By mid-afternoon we've forded streams, climbed up and over bare rock *kopjes*, and fallen silent along time-worn animal trails. The narrow track abruptly shifts to an expanse of smooth stone, and the sound of rushing water. Elephant Gorge—the boulder banks of the Mavare River. Mavare, Shona name for the Raphia Palm tree and for one of Janine's favourite safari horses. A wedding-tiered frothy white waterfall tumbles into a deep pool; James pulls his shirt off and abandons himself, laughing, under the cooling downpour.

Excusing myself from the men I wander upstream; a moment alone in the bush is hard to come by as a novitiate in the wild. Usually, the best opportunity is going off to pee behind some tall grass or thorny shrubs, or even an anthill. I take my boots off. The gorge's rock surface is blessedly hot on my bare feet so I pull off shirt, shorts and underwear, lie belly down. The heat of the stone receives my tired and utterly grateful body. Then, the lure of jade cool water. I wade in to float on my back, arms wide, a five-pointed star. My long hair streams a halo on the surface, like the energy emanations in the rock paintings above.

This evening in a clearing of higher ground above the Tingwa River the campfire is ablaze. The day's moderately strenuous trek behind us, we're enveloped by the simplicity of the bush after dark. Crickets chorus, a lone baboon's haa-call, the silky hush of the water stream below. Otherwise, penetrating quiet. Marvin returns from his river bath with a well-worn gray and white striped Kube cloth sarong wrapped from waist to shin, and an earth red blanket draped around his shoulders. He stands pensive, silhouetted by firelight, facing the massive rock wall across the river. James is barefoot in the dark, puttering with cooking pot and provisions, unsheathed knife in hand. The game scout zips up a one-piece camouflage coverall over his daytime uniform, saying it's for the chilly night.

"Bush pyjamas," I joke to him. It seems that returning to the wilderness is the restorative elixir that sustains each of these men in their conservation quest.

James announces, almost offhandedly over the pot of steaming pasta, "This. This is why we do what we do. It's for this we take action against those who destroy it."

He goes on to tell us about safari clients on riverbanks in the evening who confess an ineptitude for happiness, and find their internal compass re-calibrated by time in raw unexpurgated nature. One client, now friend, returned to America and initiated a philanthropic foundation out of the compassion which seized her, deeply infiltrated her, by sleeping on the earth and waking disarmed, in this natural state.

Some wilderness outfitters declare in their promotions "Our Safaris Change Lives." Not quite the truth for James, who offers integrity not promises.

"Yes, it can happen," he says, "but not as a marketing ploy."

In the soft-focus of firelight, a more apt tagline occurs to me: "Our African Safaris Bring You to Life. Wild Life." That's what is happening to me, from the inside out.

Marvin appears to have an additional mission: re-educating Zimbabwean native African communities about the value of their Indigenous culture, its dependence on the land, and that without culture or land they, as peoples, will not exist.

"If there are no lions left, for example," he says, "then that particular ancestral animal totem is lost in the tribal culture as well; the mythic and spiritual underpinning of that family's life on earth vanishes."

I understand that. Vanishes.

I ask Marvin, "Have you read *The Wayfinders: Why Ancient Wisdom Matters in the Modern World*?"

The author, ethno-botanist Wade Davis, a National Geographic Explorer-in-Residence, among myriad other accomplishments, is

Canadian. His accounts of the interdependence of humans, geographical place, the spirit of those places, and all forms of life on earth come from his first-hand experience all over the world; his too-true stories pierce any illusion that human practical, cultural and spiritual life on earth can exist in the void of habitat loss.

I promise to bring Marvin a copy of the book next time I come to Zimbabwe. Toward midnight our sleeping bags form a loose triangle around the last red embers of fire, and I lie awake. The dark-night sky, arcing from here to kingdom come, has taken up the earth's daytime mineral sheen—the billion-diamond stream of the Milky Way that seems as close as my breath.

But the next morning's pre-dawn finds me wakened with alarm, my hair wet with tears, gripped by a dream. The dark red soil of the strip mine has become an earth surgery gone awry—a visible viral advance across the African landmass; spreading like a fungal blight infects a forest, as the pine beetle decimated the boreal pine tree forests of western Canada in the late 2000's.

Lie still and feel the ground underneath my body, find my breath. Listen for the river—that sound of ribbons in the wind. Stay in my sleeping bag and relax down into the dark nurturing womb of earth, the earth descent meditation, deeper down than all the pain of the surface world. Find the stability that enables wise action. In time, I am collected enough for a wash in the river and to join the others for a cup of boiled powdered-milky tea and breakfast of Jungle Oats, a Zimbabwean favourite.

By the time our gear is stowed in backpacks, Nesbert has arrived on foot to escort me back to camp with his own instructive route in mind, different than yesterday's, with our own pace and preferences. I remember seeing him the other day ironing his freshly hand-laundered shirts and trousers with a heavyweight iron filled with glowing hot coals from the fire. Not an antique, this household appliance is available for sale today in hardware stores. Now I know how he maintains his look of distinguished leadership in the bush; the secret is in this ironing, and those ever-polished boots.

As we walk, I dare ask about traditions and customs of his Ndebele culture—about family life, inheritance, education and opportunity in current day Zimbabwe. But mostly I'm curious about the difference, or changes, between the generations of his grandparents, his parents, himself and his children. And how that timeline is overlaid by the historical and current affairs of this country.

The sun rides the mountains in the west by the time Nesbert leads me back into camp; a golden glow saturates the eastern hills. The day is waning and still I'm anticipating the sound of hooves in the distance, or the faint snort of a horse that would announce Stephen's arrival with Douglas. But it's become clear since being in Zimbabwe that a plan is only what starts a chain of events, and has nothing to do with how or when the outcome is achieved. Strolling down the red rock track in the direction they would be coming, I stop beside the gurgling stream of water to pick some tiny flowers, pink and blue ones, and to set down the disappointment in Stephen's non-arrival. Back in my room, flowers arranged in an eggcup of water, I stretch out on the bed, pink silk prayer shawl over my legs, and snuggle against the lumpy pillow at my back. The unexpected solitude before dinner allows the last few weeks to settle inside me. Twilight comes and the sienna plaster walls glow, the roof thatching forms a vaulted golden-grass ceiling.

I keep the window shutters open at all times and never unroll the bamboo blind above the wide doorway that would block the view. Outside, the ratching sound of Clemens splitting wood for the hot water boiler. The eight-foot-high brick chimney tower that encases a metal drum is about five feet from the outside wall of my room; a water pipeline runs overhead from the drum to the rock-walled indoor bathroom. How much more efficient, I think, if the towers were attached to the outer wall of the chalet to lend some warmth to the evening chill inside at this time of year. Oh, of course, in the summer heat season, it would be an unbearable addition.

Awake in the night, half-moon waning. The ornamental iron bedframe silhouetted in the open doorway is wetted in pearl light, a scrolled heart in the centre—a heart exactly as embroidered in gold on my black velvet medicine bag, the same design etched in the water glasses in camp, exactly as embossed on my small Italian leather-bound journal, a going-away gift from Devon.

Will this heart sanctuary in the wilderness become the re-meeting ground of Stephen and me? No, not any time soon, for his upcoming contract as my riding coach must be strictly professional. Marvin informed me of Janine's condition: because Stephen was formerly an employee and head of the horse grooms, apparently it wouldn't do to have him sporting with a foreign client, setting a precedent of expectation for other staff. Still I can dream, for he is, after all, half of what brought me back to Africa, paired with Mavuradonha itself and these horses. My thoughts go from musing about extending my visitor visa to wondering how to go about becoming a resident of Zimbabwe.

In the morning Pension and I go on foot to the Carew House to check the progress of the young guys clearing away the brush surrounding the house. We come back with the front of my shirt forming a basket to hold green lemons that Pension picked to make lemonade for our lunch.

A glance through the trees—horses in the paddock!

How did they arrive so quietly, and in the last few minutes, so that I didn't hear them?

Lemons still in my shirtfront, I skip across the shrub bush to the stables. Stephen presents me with a red mesh bag of *nanjes,* easy-to-peel oranges.

Over lunch in the dining tent, he and I talk about plans for our horse time together. Then we set off for an open, though overgrown, former polocrosse field beyond the Carew House. It's a more private location for our cantering practice than the area in front of the paddocks. I haven't ridden Munhondo before, but Stephen and Douglas figure his bulk and stability will counteract my apprehension that comes with speed. As I follow Stephen's instructions, he beside me on Water Spot, I notice it's the possibility of uneven ground, dips or holes, a stumble and a fall, that causes my anxiety to flare.

"Look ahead to where you are going," Stephen says, "Don't look to the ground. Munhondo knows himself where his feet to go."

That helps: trust your horse, and your coach.

Stephen is cross when I tell him he may not come to my room in the night, but I'm not about to breach my integrity, or Janine's trust in me, and contravene camp protocol between guest and guide. That also means no fooling around out in the bush, returning to camp rumpled and duplicitous.

As for this afternoon, my cup runneth over, being out in the bush with him—in the fantasy that has occupied me since leaving Africa thirteen months ago. Our horses are at rest, standing perfectly still side-by-side, head to tail, so that Stephen and I face one another in our saddles, our right knees and lower legs touching.

Through the thickness of my suede chaps, I feel an electric charge in that slight physical pressure. A current of energy rises, slowly, upward into my thigh, and beyond, to the sweet spot where my body is held by the saddle. Just breathe, let it be.

Stephen nods with a trace of smile. A glossy starling flushes up from the tall grass, wings thrumming as it zings across the blue-white sky. This, is enough. More, than enough.

After a time, I lift the velcro'd flap on the pocket of my saddle pad and pull out one of the oranges Stephen brought. Keeping a raised eyebrow on him I peel the orange and hand him half.

"*Maita basa,* mama," he says with a wink.

Munhondo lifts his tail and I stand up in the stirrups to release pressure on his back as plops of manure drop to the ground; a passel of lemon-coloured butterflies convenes, flittering around the grass-fragrant dung.

Pension walked to Siya Lima while we were gone this afternoon and has returned carrying a slaughtered goat across his shoulders like a shawl, in honour of Stephen's arrival. To feed their co-workers, and friends, for the days he's in camp with us. Friend, *shamwari*, is one of Stephen's favourite words. Wari, means God, literally "existing everywhere all the time."

Dinner, to my relief, is at the kitchen fire tonight, rather than in the dining tent. Informality returns with no other guests in camp. I love listening to Nesbert and Stephen tell stories, mostly in English for my benefit, and sometimes in Shona which is so helpful for sensing the undertones of the conversation.

By now, I've ridden five of the horses. Moonlight mostly, a real sweetheart, but at the moment she has an abscess on her belly and is grumpy. This morning she is out with the other horses grazing, tethered on an overhead longline. Stephen runs his hand underneath her and squeezes the abscess releasing a globby spurt of bloody pus. Moonlight lowers her head and snorts, with relief, I'm sure.

Water Spot is a good follower, of both my direction and the lead horse when we ride, so after Moonlight he feels safest to me on a challenging trail. I found riding Munhondo too effortful for my level of strength and endurance. I have not yet ridden Gizmet or Kody. Gizmet needs a stronger leader to head off his tendency toward spontaneous expressions of independence. Kody responds best to an adventuresome cowboy kind of rider like Marvin. Basera is easy to ride, he feels comfortable at all gaits, yet with not quite the sparkle that Skanky and I have together.

Indeed, I feel most at home riding the beautiful paint Skanky, her chestnut and white coat gleam in this morning's light. Douglas reminds me that her initial training was with a specialist in natural horsemanship, the way I learned to ride. She's attentive, responsive and today something syncs up between us while Stephen coaches us in changing gaits gracefully. Trotting in the field in front of the paddocks, I feel fresh and alive on her back. Then we, four horses and three riders, head out of camp to practice the finesse of bush riding. Skanky and I are in the middle. Douglas leads on Gizmet with Jecha in tow while Stephen follows me on Water Spot. After a while, Douglas hands Jecha's lead rope to me; now it's my turn to help train her as a safari horse in unfamiliar and strenuous territory. Jecha, adolescent palomino mare that she is, tickles my heart; her mane and tail are the same colour as my own fair hair.

When Douglas turns back, returning to the stables with the now-tired Jecha, Stephen and I curve off the trail with Skanky and me in front. I am learning bundu-bashing, bush-whacking—heading into the pathless underbrush of the woodland terrain. Stephen, with his innate sense of orientation, guides me from behind, his verbal directions take us further and further into the territory of wild. Arc left between those msasa trees, wade into the river stream and allow your horse to make her own way up the bank, lean forward and pass on the uphill side of that boulder. As we ride deeper into the bush I begin to feel Stephen's inner compass as my own. Africa opens herself to me.

Later in the afternoon, heading back to camp, the horses are on a loose rein; Skanky and Water Spot know the way home. The cloud cover is low, giving a sense of intimacy with the distant hills. We pass through a grove of flowering protea trees and I slow Skanky to admire the huge creamy coloured soft-spikey blossoms. Stephen leans out of his saddle and touches one of them, comes round beside me and gently drops a tiny jewel into my hand—a shiny green protea beetle lies underside up in my palm, furry orange underbelly tinged with pollen.

On the last morning of Stephen's coaching time in camp, I walk into the grass field to join the horses, stretching out on my back on the ground, propped up by my elbows so I can see the beauties who graze close by. Three of them, the black and white paint Gringo, Basera, and Fundi are also lying down, or rather have their legs folded under them on the ground, their heads up. I can feel the slight flare of nostrils as they breathe, my own body-boundary dissolving, at one with the herd.

Someone comes up behind us from the stables. I know the sound of Stephen's footsteps, and he squats down beside me. I sit upright and reach into my shirt pocket.

"*Maita basa, tatenda, shamwari*," I say. "Thank you, very much, precious friend."

I fold a small paper packet tied with a strand of raffia into his hand, the customary thank you conveyed by a cash gratuity. Ah, the same action, coming forward from the past, of folding the small wooden heart into his hand in Hwange last year.

Stephen nods, "Yes, myself, I thank you, too."

He says something in Shona and asks in English, "Do you know what I am saying to you?"

His shapely clean-shaven head inclines gently upward toward my face, caress of air that quivers.

Yes, I know the Shona words. "I love you."

On our way to Harare in the land cruiser, Janine is at the wheel. I'm in the front seat beside her, Marvin and Pension are in the back seat. We're going to town to restock supplies and three of us, Marvin, Pension and I will return tomorrow. Stephen is in the truck bed with camp gear, keeping an eye on the horsebox in tow. Skanky and Fundi are coming to the Varden's property in town. Watching Stephen's reflection in the truck's sideview mirror, the impulse to doubt arises—of course I'd be under the spell of an exotic horseman professing his love and desire for marriage. I'm sixty-one and a half years old and enthralled with Africa. All I know is the gratitude I feel, doubt be damned.

Marvin, alpha-host, as he calls himself, has an agenda for our overnight re-supply trip. He says it's my chance to try out the back-packers' hostel he intends to book for future volunteers when they arrive in Harare. I could have predicted my distress, arriving just out of the bush to a city hostel, alone amongst new strangers I don't care to meet, The tall unkempt Englishman who looks quite gaunt and sick, the slight young woman from Ireland talking too loudly at the bar, regurgitating a litany of her stints teaching English abroad.

A 40-ish unmarried man from Finland ticks off his travel bucket list, as he streaks through as many continents and countries as he can on his holidays from work, taking great pride in the frugality of his journeys. Showing me the overflowing cache of fresh produce he purchased for one dollar at a street stall, he accepts the worn dollar bill I offer for one of his huge avocadoes in the hostel kitchen. An odd entrepreneurship for a foreign visitor in this country, I think.

I regret not having returned to the Borrowdale guesthouse for the night, instead of the hostel, to share a meal with Stephen and Hambani, and to lie with my horseman from twilight through sunrise. My compliance with Marvin, in light of the intimacy Stephen and I have already shared, rattles my conscience. I recall the soothing sound of Stephen's voice guiding my pronunciation of Shona phrases. Was he really offering to give me a manicure? Listening carefully and observing his gestures showed that yes, he would like to file my nails, but in a very particular fashion, one that leaves certain fingernails longer for running along his cheek in front of the ear and gently down his throat.

"Is this Shona tradition," I asked, "or just for you only?"

He smiled, "For myself only."

Another time, his hand smoothed the fine light hair on my unshaven leg and he was mystified, Africans do not have such body hair. "Soft, feels like feathers, good to my hands."

I phone Stephen from the hostel to tell him I miss him, and that my allegiance to Marvin's plan was misplaced. He offers to come, a long complicated bus ride, but it's already late with a very early morning start back to Mavuradonha. It's enough to hear his voice. With that, I understand there will be more challenges in my stretch toward integrity. Though I'm alone in the barren single room, sleep comes easily now that contact with Stephen is restored.

In the grocery store first thing this morning, searching for biscuits, I notice a change in my mood, as if prospects for the day have just grown brighter. Two young women stocking shelves on either side of the aisle are singing, each softly in her own sweet melody, and I feel threaded with tendrils of happiness. Uplifted, I carry on to the craft and flea market stalls on the deck of the shopping centre's old parking garage. Looking in vain for some cashew nuts, I am distracted by Agnes, who propels me into her display of handcrafts and describes in detail the carved wooden bowls, the miniature animals made of shiny glass beads and wire sculptures of musicians embellished with bottle caps. The sun visors made from soft drink cans will be perfect for my goddaughters. Back at the hostel, I sit on a bench outside with my gear waiting for Marvin, a friendly black cat curls himself around my hip. Later, as we're driving, I remark to Marvin about the young women singing in the grocery store.

"Because things are so much better than a few years ago," he says. "During the economic crisis that peaked in 2008, there were no jobs, no food on the shop shelves. Last year, 2010, Zim sales for the international Spar grocery chain rose 50%."

# Questions of Identity

Dani's loose blonde curls jiggle as she talks. Nico, her fiancé, pulls his canvas-back chair close to hers, so their shoulders touch. Marvin sits opposite his two friends, at the long wooden table that fills one side of the khaki canvas tent that serves as camp dining room. I'm on the bench beside him. The rest of the space is furnished with an antique buffet sideboard, overstuffed armchairs and sofa topped with wildlife design dust covers. Marvin still has on his faded green camouflage jacket from our day in the bush, though his brimmed hat with one side snapped jauntily up is parked on the table. The four of us are having the obligatory gin and tonics before dinner, except that Marvin's, as camp host, and mine are straight up tonic. Dani is Marvin's best friend, she is also in her thirties and also Zimbabwean by birth and current passport. Nico is from Kenya. The young couple are fourth generation white African. Her forebears were from England, his from Italy.

"Nico and I are trying to start a life together in Zimbabwe," Dani explains.

I listen intently as she describes the bureaucratic process, in case her experience will be useful to me in the future. The topic shifts and the three friends become engrossed in a conversation about being black African, white African, Zimbabwean, Kenyan. Regardless of nationality or family origin, they each believe they belong to this continent.

Africa as an entity, and being African or not African, is spoken of daily by everyone I meet in Zimbabwe—those here by birth or ancestry, by migration and as visitors on a short or long-stay. Personal and social identities seem entirely interwoven with place in the landscape of Africa. I try and imagine that being true in Canada. In my own experience as 6<sup>th</sup> generation white Canadian in 2011, national or continental identity isn't the subject of reflection, nor usual in everyday conversation. But then, I haven't spent much time with First Nations communities or immigrant families.

The country of my birth occupies almost half the continent of North America—and is bigger than all of Africa south of the equator. Canada's population of thirty-five million is mostly compressed along the bottom edge, the southern border shared with the United States. No generalities can be made in the diversity of geography, weather, peoples, economies, or livelihoods.

What is Canadian, I wonder? A curious question, one that I haven't given much thought to before coming to Africa. On the surface, I don't feel representative of anything definitively "Canadian." I don't watch hockey, hardly ever drink beer, I've never eaten anything at Tim Horton's fast food chain, I didn't vote for the current Prime Minister, and some days I don't even listen to the CBC national radio.

Out of the blue, Dani leans across the table and says to me, "What did you leave behind at home in Canada?"

Awkwardly, no words come; it's hard to respond to questions about my life in Canada in the course of mealtime chatter, to talk about a life there with any conviction, for I have been solely focused on coming back to Africa. The fact is: I don't actually have a home in Canada. At this point I feel like a stray, tentatively making myself at home wherever I happen to be.

The flame of the pillar candle on the table flutters as Pension, the camp cook, sets down a bowl of homemade butternut soup in front of each of us. "The starter course," he says with pride. I cup my hands around the bowl's warmth and bow my head in thanks for just a moment, trying to settle my thoughts. It would be useful to come up with a story to bring out on these occasions of enquiries about my life, so as to avoid my own discomfort and that of others' in having asked a perfectly normal question that I can't answer.

"That's a tough question, Dani," I say, thinking out loud. "Whatever I've left behind seems exactly that, left behind, a phase of life completed. Yes, my family is there, my thirty-year-old son, my elderly parents and closest friends, but I feel them very much with me, not left behind. Mostly, what I've done in the past in Canada holds no interest right now, and I have no idea what the future will bring.

"I think, for my parents at least, there is a vicarious and nervous delight with my being in Africa, daring to step into the unfamiliar. They love receiving my emails with tales of romantic-sounding bush camp contrasting with the gritty realities of day-to-day in Zimbabwe."

Dani's question wasn't polite or superficial it turns out; before long the discussion returns to deeper questions of self-definition, of values, of nationality, of our origins, really.

I look at Marvin beside me—he has asked before about the Indigenous people where I come from, and I tell him now, "The name Canada may have come from an Iroquois First Nation word *kanata*, translating as settlement or village."

"Oh," he responds with surprise, "That sounds like our Shona word, *kumusha*, the rural home in the village. All of us have *kumusha* where our grandparents live, if they are alive, where we go on the holidays back to a simple life."

Marvin asks me, "Why do you know about Indigenous in Canada?"

"Marvin, I don't really, but it's my responsibility to know the human history of the land that is my family's home. To be aware of the people who were there in the beginning, before my great-great-grandparents emigrated from Ireland and England and Scotland. You know what? It wasn't until I took an Anthropology course in university that I had any idea about the cultural genocide of the First Nations people in what is now Canada. Their uprooting from the very land where their ancestors lived from time immemorial. Discarded by the colonists, segregated, and immured on native reserves that still exist today."

When Pension leans in to replace our soup bowls with plates of fragrant chicken stew and rice my tablemate sighs and rubs his chin. I leave unspoken the memory of feeling envious as a kid in suburban Vancouver riding in the family car through the then-Indian reserves located right on the waterfront, reminiscent of my coastal inlet birthplace. I didn't know back then, the reserves' social troubles that put a very dark shadow on the clusters of First Nations people. Through my child-eyes they seemed to have a place together, an identity, a community, however artificially delineated on a map. I didn't have that; my family didn't have that.

"You know what, Marvin? I can still see the packed university lecture hall, forty years ago, and the young man wearing a jean jacket with his shiny black hair in long braids. He stood at the lectern, shaking, and shouted, 'Your white ancestors did this to our people! You are still responsible.' It blew my mind, to have been so ignorant. And I was angry at the magnitude of this omission in my education."

"You mean like what happened to Native Americans in the United States?" Marvin asks.

"Yes, the same. I've heard stories of the reserve near where I live; that mothers and grandmothers sent their young ones into the forest to hide when news came that the police were on their way to seize the reserve children and rustle them off to a church-run boarding school––and strip them of their native identity. I heard, too, that parents who didn't hand over their children were arrested. Some of those children, now adults, are younger than me. This happened in the 1970s and even '80s, not some long-ago past.

"There is no getting around the real story of Canada's First Peoples after Europeans arrived. It's a shame that seems impossible to reconcile. Yes, the government is seen to be trying, with the Truth and Reconciliation Commission established a few years ago. We'll see where that goes, and whether the findings are followed by action. What I find more hopeful is the contemporary Indigenous writers, and visual and performing artists who are creating a regeneration of the lost cultures.

"In a small way, too, I take heart, knowing that my Irish grandfather intentionally formed an abiding friendship with the community of First Nation knitters who supplied his Vancouver Island store with their handspun wool Cowichan sweaters. I remember mine, child size, and how cozy and dry it was in the cold rain of winter."

The candle light flutters again as Pension comes in with our dessert plates, earnestly naming the ingredients in his pineapple upside down cake.

I remember something else. Modern history shows that Ireland was the first land and people to be colonized by the English.

"My grandfather wrote a letter once, to the Canadian government, in support of the Ugandan Asian refugees who fled Idi Amin in the early 1970's and were welcomed into Canada. I have the thank you note he received from the Minister of External Affairs."

Does this gesture of my grandfather's–– extending the welcome he had received fifty years earlier to those who followed––absolve anything of the desecration that preceded him?

Marvin says, "At least you don't turn away from the truths of history."

He offers this perspective about Rhodesia, before Zimbabwe: the colonial land barons saw the traditional customs keeping morale and productivity up in the native labour force, so turned a blind eye as long as they were kept within the workers 'compounds' on their white-owned farms. The compounds had schools and medical clinics, as well. But now, there remains an expectation by former farm workers that their families should be taken care of, by someone. But who, nowadays?

I see what he means. In Harare, Stephen calls the primitive staff quarters at the Borrowable guesthouse, "the compound." And I heard the night security guard only half-jokingly ask me, the white woman, "Where's my birthday tuck box?" Tuck, sweets.

"Dani," I ask, "Who were the British who came to Rhodesia?"

"A history teacher once told me," Dani says quietly, "that Ian Smith, early Prime Minister of Southern Rhodesia, recruited the 'best and the brightest' from post WWII England to come out to the new colony—pilots and intelligence officers, agriculture scientists, engineers, geologists—and the ones who couldn't make the grade went back to England, so a select gene pool was intended to reproduce and populate the country."

A moth has landed in the liquid candle wax and flutters in vain to extricate its papery wings. In the morning it will be embedded in the hardened waxy surface.

How were the Europeans who made their way to North America different from those who settled in southern Africa, I wonder? I wish my great-grandparents were still alive to tell me their stories, to explain their values and listen to mine. In a faded sepia photograph, my well-dressed great-grandfather stands with his cronies, leaning on the butts of their long-handled axes beside the massive stump of a fallen Douglas fir tree. On the back of the photo, in elegant old-style script my great-grandmother wrote: Prince Rupert. British Columbia. Canada. 1918. Their daughter, my grandmother, is the young woman with the picnic basket sitting daintily on the ground.

All of this "civilizing" superimposed on both continents over the span of barely a few centuries is a nano-fragment in the timeline of human existence, and seems ironic when genetic science considers the human species to have originated in Africa. I look around the table and voice my thought.

"Marvin, do you know about the GenoGraphic Project of the National Geographic Society?"

He doesn't.

"The purpose is to map the human migration patterns out of Africa beginning 60,000 years ago that eventually populated all the habitable regions of earth 15 - 20,000 years ago.

"Anyone," I continue, "can send away for a kit that samples their DNA with a cheek swab. The swab is sent back to the project lab and the results show––get this––where in Africa one's ancestors originated, and their global migration paths over tens of millennia. A map of one's lineage, one's branches on the human family tree!"

I haven't done the "Geno 2.0 Next Generation" test, yet, but just knowing about it gives me a bit of comforting reassurance in the face of my mysterious affinity for this part of the world, southern Africa, when I certainly don't look native to this land. Like a bougainvillea bush, I am an exotic, a foreign transplant on the continent of our human origins.

With a cheery "Good night!" Dani and Nico push their chairs back from the table and leave the dining tent for their room. I feel my way in the dark along the sand path to the kitchen tent, guided toward the light of the cooking fire, to fetch my headlamp from Pension. Earlier he couldn't see the strips of appetizer potato skins he was frying in olive oil over the fire. The sun had set and his helper, Alice, had taken herself and her flashlight to another location. So, I made myself useful and shone my headlamp over the big cast-iron pot.

Later, cozy by candlelight under the quilt and blankets in my thatch room, I feel exhausted, confounded by the quandaries of the legacy of colonialism. One striking difference between Africa and North America, I realize, is that the whites in Africa have always remained in the minority in relation to the black, Indigenous, population. What does that say?

Pressing my hands over my eyes, gradually the whurring birdcall of a nocturnal nightjar slides in from the dark. Is it this confoundedness that makes me Canadian? And on top of that, a west coast, aka unconventional, woman, to boot? My god, there's a stereotype.

A tap at the open doorway and Alice shyly brings in a thermos of hot water for morning tea and a fleece-covered hot water bottle. How thoughtful and sweet of her, though probably standard practice in camp. I surely hadn't expected that Zimbabwe would be downright cold at night in June and the flannelette pyjamas, thick socks and fleece hat on the list of "things to bring" would be among the most useful. Soothed by the residue of Alice's presence, I fall asleep between the sheets of dual worlds: past and present, Indigenous and imported. North America and southern Africa.

The next morning, Pension, picking up from last evening, asks, "Please, can give you me recipes from Canada to prepare in my bush kitchen?"

Jeepers, does Canada have a distinctive national dish served coast to coast? Not that I know of, but there are regional specialties. How about vacuum-packed smoked salmon from the northwest coast Pacific Ocean and maple syrup from Quebec? I brought some of each, left as gifts at the guesthouse in Harare. I'm sure Pension would be pleased to smoke a twenty-pound fresh-caught salmon over his fire, a traditional First Nations meal, but we're a long way from any fish in a cold northern ocean. Or maybe some bannock, traditional bread dough wrapped around a green stick and baked over red-hot coals, like school kids make on an educational camping trip. Seems a bit gratuitous.

What Canadian accompaniment would do justice to the avocadoes Pension has brought from his own garden, picked at different stages of ripeness, stored buried in a bucket of maize meal to be served at the time of perfection for each? Perhaps I could suggest Canadian wheat for the homemade bread he has baked in a cast iron pot in the fire, then carefully sliced and brushed with olive oil to toast over the coals.

Of course, regarding all questions about present-day Canada, I'm able to be more informative about the western edge where I live—Vancouver Island: the mystic beauty of the coastal temperate rainforest, wetsuit surfing in the cold ocean rollers of Long Beach, the wineries and artisan cheese makers, "the slow food" and "eat locally" advocates, and the shellfish—oysters, clams, mussels, best collected at low tide and steamed open in a beach wood fire.

"Can you imagine," I say with a twinkle to Dani over breakfast, "Salty seawater inside the shell steams the oyster open. Woodsmoke infuses the succulent delicacy and you wait just until it won't burn your tongue, pick up the half shell with your sleeve over your hand and let the oyster slide into your mouth." She loves the image, and wants to come to B.C.

But something feels sticky; for the first time ever, I can't say the name of my home province in western Canada out loud. British Columbia.

I decide, when pressed later by Pension's request for recipes, that what I can do is offer an alternative perspective on menu planning for guests like me. The regular European, Australian or North American safari client may prefer familiar food from home; Pension's roast chicken dinner, cheesy cauliflower, his crispy fish (frozen) and chips cooked over the fire are superb. But the square slices of mass-produced white breakfast toast and imported supermarket iceberg lettuce, the white rice and boiled carrots are simply too disappointing. What about guests who'd be enthusiastic about food of local origin, the myriad of vegetables, grains and fruits uncommon to visitors from the Northern Hemisphere? Yet most of the food grown in Zimbabwe nowadays is not native to this land. Tomatoes, maize and squash were brought from the Americas, by European settlers. This is not the food the African grandparents, the old ones, planted and harvested. I hope one day to taste the native grains, perhaps in a rural village: rapoko, sorghum, millet. And the tree fruits: jujube, marula plum, monkey orange.

On Waterspot's gleaming white back, I'm unsettled in a stark leather saddle that feels like a wooden plank under my backside. Not wanting to aggravate the tender tissue around my sitting bones, I make a joke so that Marvin comes over with a foam saddle pad covered in faded camouflage fabric. That feels even better than the piece of woolly sheepskin I sometimes tuck into the crotch of my riding pants for just such saddlery occasions.

Nico is bent over, closing the zippers on borrowed leather half-chaps that cover his white jeans below the knee; I wonder if his soft Italian suede jacket will tear when he brushes past a thorn bush. Dani wears her own fringed, full-chaps over black riding tights, plus oversize sunglasses, no hat or helmet for her. When we finally leave the paddocks and cross the open field into the bush our guide, Douglas Chinhamo, takes the lead position on Gizmet; just to complete the picture, I note he is wearing his practical one-piece cotton twill coveralls. Nico is second in line behind him on the ever-steady Basera, then Dani on the sweet-tempered Moonlight. Waterspot and I follow with Shepherd, the other groom, beside us on Apache.

Marvin is aboard Kody, a former polocrosse pony who matches Marvin's energy and enthusiasm. As they cavort around the field, rider bouncing in the saddle, it appears that Marvin's daring and vigour make up for any shortfall in proficiency.

We're on our way to the landmark Spilling Tables waterfall. Nico is a filmmaker and has requested an impressive wilderness setting in which to videotape interviews with Marvin and Douglas——about the preservation of Mavuradonha Wilderness and sustainable ways of life in adjoining communities. A small daypack holds minimal camera gear snug against his suede back.

Marvin and his two friends banter back and forth as they ride; I'm not listening to them, but to the rhythm of Waterspot's footfalls, klick-klock, klick-klack, klick-klock, on the shale-strewn ground. Shepherd and Douglas are silent as they scan the landscape and I watch how their bodies move in synch with their horses. I instinctively relax my own posture to reflect theirs––hips low in the saddle, legs loose, reins loose. Gradually, my friendship with the bush feels more intimate.

A while later, Marvin, riding behind me through a thicket of eye-level flowering protea trees, says for my benefit, "This species of trees, Mubonda, are some of the oldest on earth, 300 million years, are still reproducing and growing."

He remarks on one magnificent swelling bud, just about to bloom, and I imagine myself curled inside it, as if held in cupped hands, while the creamy petals unfold for the hovering bees.

After a time, we spread out to cross an open hillside that leads to the mountains, and I wonder aloud how to distinguish the different species of African antelopes. So romantic sounding: impala, kudu, eland, bushbuck. Not all of them live here in Mavuradonha, but under Douglas' tutelage I begin to learn their identification as he describes differences in colour and markings, size and shape of horns, vocalization, food preferences, and movement.

"Over there, Oriane," Douglas says, "Look, up the hill under that acacia tree. Sable, female"

The sable antelope is the most dramatic, the national symbol for Zimbabwe. I see her standing broadside on the slope not far away. The splendid grazer is on the large end of the antelope size continuum, darkest chestnut in colour, thick-throated with a short stand-up mane. Her ring-notched horns rise straight up from the top of her head, much longer than my arm, and curve backward to a fine point. As Douglas and I slow down to let our horses graze a moment, she lifts her head and turns toward us, revealing white facial patterns that line up with her horns and draw down to a wide chinstrap beneath her mouth.

"What is this antelope called in Shona, Douglas?"

"*Mharapara*. Say it like this––marah-para."

The lone doe stands still as we skirt around her at a distance and make our way up the hill toward an opening in the mountains.

We tether our horses in a small gorge by tying their lead ropes to tree branches. Shepherd, the groom, parks himself on a shaded boulder where he can oversee the cloistered herd. He cups a hand to his ear and points toward the sound of falling water.

I turn around to face the falls. The pool of water beyond our boulder foothold is dark, deep, sparked with sunlight on the surface. The river stream slides into it from above, rippling silver drapery over smooth tiered rock that looks like a swath of fallen dominoes.

Instinctively my hands find a button on my shirt, intending to drop my clothes and boots on the stone by my feet, to slip into the aquatic caress and glide the few metres across the pool–– but we're on a mission. Douglas beckons toward a steep ascent on our right, reaches for a thick vine and pulls himself up onto the incline of the cliff bank.

After a sweat-wringing climb alongside the cascades, Dani and I take our boots off on the plateau at the top of the waterfall, wade into the warm streambed and survey what lies below.

Mavuradonha is her most enchanting from this perspective. Spread before us are the gently mounding grassland and hillsides we traversed, the colour of honey, of lions, and of native grain fields at sunrise. In the mid-distance treed *kopjes*, those distinguished uprisings of rock, match our elevation and leave low-lying grass valleys and passes in between. Beyond, toward the northwestern horizon, lie the gradiated silhouettes of the true Mavurdonha Mountains. The eyes, and the mind, can rest in this muted richness that layers into the distance.

Nico sets up his video camera, prompts Marvin and Douglas in turn and begins filming their respective messages. Their optimism about the future in the region is impressive, considering the massive setbacks in Zimbabwe over the last decade.

Then Nico changes course, "What about you, Oriane? Do you have a personal story from the front lines in Canada?"

Immediately I see the mustard yellow paint of earth-moving machinery, and feel the tremor of idling engines ready to shift into gear. I recall my trepidation, and my certainty, the strength of my friends' hands in mine as we stood in a solid line across the dirt road facing the industrial loggers. I was wearing a heavy grey melton wool coat with the hood up over my hair in the cold early morning mist. Our kids were young and watched intently from the safety of the forested bank, their coloured raincoats restless like a crop of wild flowers in the wind. The independent school we started on Cortes Island, the year Devon began grade one, was founded on the principles of earth stewardship.

"In the end, the blockade was successful," I say to Nico and to Marvin who has leaned close to listen. "Cortes Island was classified 'socially inoperable' as a logging site by the off-island timber corporation."

I pause to wiggle my feet in the streaming water and to inhale the dry earthy fragrance of Africa that brings me back to the present. I take a few steps back from Nico and begin to tell him about a long-standing campaign dedicated to preserving a massive stretch of wild mountains, rivers and ocean inlets still threatened by clear-cut logging on Canada's west coast.

"The Great Bear Rainforest is named for the white-coloured "spirit bears" that live solely in this habitat, nowhere else on earth. The outlook grows optimistic due to unflagging dedication, spanning almost two decades, in a collaboration of environmental advocacy groups working with First Nations communities, forestry timber-logging interests, and the provincial government." To myself, I wonder if this sort of collaboration is in the works for the Mavuradonha Wilderness.

As geography would have it, my remote coastal birthplace of Ocean Falls, once a thriving logging and mill town only accessible by boat or seaplane, lies within the Great Bear. And just recently, the gut-surprise of looking on an internet map and finding the southern boundary of that coastal wilderness barely twelve nautical miles north of Cortes Island––my home for most of twenty-five years, where my son was raised in the forested beauty.

Curious, how we are drawn back to place. For me in particular, leaving the wilderness around Ocean Falls for school-age years and young adulthood in the city of Vancouver––then, called like the salmon back north to the wild west coast temperate rain forest; to jade green water, crystal clear down to the pebbles where tiny crabs scurry about on the ocean floor.

Curious, too, the call to Mavuradonha––whose Shona name means "Place of Falling Water."

One of the older horse handlers, Ngwenya, has shown me how to make plied rope with strips of inner bark from the Maputi tree. A necklace of sorts takes shape in my hands: from a circle of slender two-plied twine, hangs a six inch porcupine quill, similarly sized guinea fowl feathers, various leaves, red stones and dried flowers. All found on the ground and organically constellated in this way. Ever cautious about misappropriation, I ask Douglas if I may offer it as an emblem of my respect for nature, the spirit of this place and the privilege of being here. In the afternoon he carefully tucks the necklace into the pocket of Gizmet's saddle blanket and we ride to his homestead in Chingorongodzi community.

On a gentle sloping hillside, in a grouping of thatch-roofed huts, his wife is bending over a plastic basin of unshelled sunflower seeds. She is expecting me and leads the three of us into the nearest hut, her kitchen. Douglas explains to her the significance of the necklace, asking her to show it to her friends as evidence of the value of the land and animals in the eyes of visitors, and of their respect for the community's traditional way of life.

*The Geography of Belonging*

"Oriane did not decide to make the talisman," Douglas says, in Shona, "It asked her to create it, to further our mission of guardianship."

His point is for village women to tell their husbands to take care that no trees are cut down for firewood, or animals poached out of the protected wilderness area. And then he leaves us, two women, alone in the room.

Sheila Chinhamo is quiet and offers me a ripe banana on a flower-patterned enamel plate. We sit down on a worn reed mat beside the smoking fire and remain in silence. A colourful display of many more metal plates and bowls is arranged vertically according to size on built-in ledges that line the walls. Douglas had already informed me that the curved walls, shelves and perimeter bench-seat inside a Shona circular kitchen are formed from tyre rubber melted and mixed with earth. The whole interior of the kitchen is polished to a glossy silver-black finish. The bigger cooking pots and plastic five-gallon food storage buckets are neatly arranged on a set of curved steps, like half a wedding cake protruding from the wall. To me the tiered assembly looks like an altar, and indeed the kitchen is the sacred domain of the wife.

Douglas also told me that the women of Chingorongodzi are competitive about who has the finest *kicheni*, each taking enormous pride in her own design and construction. Mrs. Sheila Chinhamo does not respond to my compliments about hers, so I simply peel and eat the banana bit by bit, marveling to myself at her resplendent traditional craftsmanship, craftswomanship, until Douglas returns to announce our leaving.

As we pass by a flat rock on our way to collect the horses, Douglas points out some small clay figures.

"Here are some toys my son has made."

Their younger boy, Divine, is five years old. I crouch low to the ground and see they are tiny oxen, a herd of them. One is tethered with a length of thread to a bush beside the rock.

"He doesn't want it to run away whilst he is not there to tend it."

A few weeks later, when I return to their homestead, the earth necklace is fastened to the soot-darkened kitchen wall above the storage steps.

Early July brings new visitors to camp. A team of three people from National Museums and Monuments of Zimbabwe (NMMZ), a department of the government, has driven in on the bone-rattling vehicle supply track from Siya Lima. Marvin introduces me to Chipunza Kundishora, the chief archeologist and chief curator for NMMZ, and his two colleagues. I learn firsthand from Chipunza that Zimbabwe has the highest concentration of rock paintings on the planet and that the Mavuradonha region has barely been explored. In fact, Chipunza hasn't been to Mavuradonha before and is enthusiastic about initiating fieldwork in the rarity of an intact cultural landscape.

None of the three visitors has ever been on a horse and only one has come prepared. He arrives at the mounting block wearing, not camouflage-coloured bush gear, but a very bright rainbow-coloured jumpsuit over his jeans and t-shirt. He is a big man and looks like he just walked in from a Carnaby Street flea market, circa London 1969. I wonder if he is afraid of coming across any wild animals so has dressed to ensure he is exceedingly visible, hoping to ward off any approaching wildlife. Douglas assigns him to trusty Munhondo, the sturdiest and most steady-going of the horses in camp.

Meanwhile, Chipunza slouches comfortably in the saddle on Basera, while their younger colleague seems relaxed on the easy-going Gringo. Marvin leads the parade on Apache; Douglas walks on foot for rider security and I trail along on foot as well, to listen and to take photographs of the researchers on horses.

"Cultural Landscape" is a new and intriguing term to me, an official designation given by NMMZ. The term defines a marriage of natural history and archaeology with the anthropology of sacred sites, migratory routes and tribal traditions. The wilderness at our very backs has not been formally documented, so this first foray of Chipunza's begins the long process of securing National Heritage status for Mavuradonha, the precursor to a nomination proposal for UNESCO World Heritage Status. Both of these will ensure resources to protect this wilderness treasure.

After an hour or so of riding, the horses are left with Douglas at the bottom of a steep, treed, and boulder-strewn kopje. The rest of us, led by Marvin, begin a strenuous uphill hike. About half way to the top, I stop to catch my breath and survey the valley below.

Someone says, "Come around this way and have a look!"

I clamber around a boulder following the archeologists. Marvin isn't looking at the distant view, he is pointing at the spectacle right in front of us—a whole rock face covered with ochre and brown handprints, behind which are faintly visible images of indigenous life ten thousand years ago. Human handprints, here, in a place of origin. We are standing before a portal, Chipunza explains, a rock surface where spirit mediums communicated with the unseen world. As a place of spiritual power, it drew humans in succeeding millennia to place their own handprints, "plugging in" so to speak. Makes sense to me; on the horseback safari in Hwange last year, I felt for myself the natural energy of the physical earth that infuses the body and brain with time in the wilderness.

Over the next few days, mostly on foot, the team documents rock paintings of zebra and kudu, trance dancing and elephant hunting. Chipunza describes how the images are layered over time by peoples of different eras, creating complex meaning in a particular site. Once heritage status is formalized for Mavuradonha, the mission can shift to uncovering new knowledge in anthropology, archaeology, botany, ornithology; and as yet undiscovered treasures of this wilderness preserve. As well, when protection is ensured, animal restoration can begin in earnest.

Relaxing around the campfire after dinner on the final day of his visit, Chipunza is seated in a folding canvas chair beside me. Leaning over he says, "How long will you be in Zimbabwe? Can you come back in October before our annual conference? We could use you in this project."

Late into the evening, I watch the firelight reflected on the low trees and listen to Marvin, Chipunza, and the other two men outdo each other with boisterous stories of near fatal snake bites and encounters with other-worldly presences in dark caves.

We've seen a few pythons sunning themselves on the rocks beside the Tingwa River since Marvin, Douglas and I set out from bush camp earlier this morning, heading toward Siya Lima Farm. We traverse this route quite often, bringing horses, supplies and gear back and forth between the farm and the camp. The last time, when I asked Douglas the Shona name of the open grassland we were passing through in the Raphia Palm botanical reserve, he had said it didn't have one. I'd wondered aloud what it would be called if he were drawing a map.

"I will think about that," he'd said.

"Do you think there were identifying names in the old times?" I'd asked, "Could they be found by asking the grandparents?"

"Yes, I'm sure," he'd replied, pronouncing it "shoo-ah."

For today, we ride across the slope of thick, shoulder-high grass slightly uphill from the river stream. The three of us stay in our usual order: Douglas is in front; I'm in the middle; Marvin is behind me. As we approach the botanical reserve, the lush gold seed grass is taller than we are on horseback and mesmerizing in the noontime sun. Douglas turns around to address me, "I have the name for this place. We can call it 'Reedbuck Flay' in English, for the small reedbuck antelope who hide in the grass and, when we ride close by, leap up and run away, startling the horses. So mind where your horse is stepping."

"Oh, flay is open space without a watering hole?" I query, "and pan is open space with a watering hole, like in Hwange?"

"Yes, that's it." Douglas affirms and it dawns on me the spelling is v-l-e-i, not f-l-a-y, and that in the rainy season the ground becomes a marshy pond.

Douglas has gotten about ten metres ahead. Only a wave-like motion of shifting grass reveals his whereabouts with Moonlight, his horse for today. She's named for the pale gray colour that makes her visible after dark. I'm riding the gelding Basera, rather than Moonlight who was originally assigned to me, because his gait is longer than hers, which means fewer hoof beats to the kilometer, so a much smoother ride when trotting and cantering. The heat and stillness of the air, together with the rocking of my horse's steady gait, bring on a mellow daydreaming, a definite liability in the bush.

A loud crash, startles me out of reverie. Moonlight's hind end and rear legs burst up toward the sky.

She bucks and thrashes in a one-horse rodeo. Then, we see only a commotion of tall grass, a whirlwind moving uphill in circles. It's all I can do to hold Basera steady and ease him backward out of range, around toward Marvin, who has stopped on the spot with Munhondo, the steadfast buckskin. Together, hyper-alert, we wait out the storm, not knowing its origin, ready to respond to whatever catastrophe comes.

Douglas is still in the saddle and hollering when he and Moonlight abruptly emerge out of the bush onto the narrow track in front of me. I instinctively move Basera to one side as Douglas heads straight to Marvin behind me, swings his right leg forward over Moonlight's neck, hands over the reins and jumps to the ground.

Moonlight's left hind fetlock streams brilliant crimson blood, glossy on her dappled gray hair. A puncture wound on either side of her lower leg. Marvin is unfazed. Douglas grins as he walks slowly and deliberately toward the spot where Moonlight first lit out from the trail. He announces that he's looking for the python she stepped on; he'd seen at the time that the snake had a bulge in the middle, showing it had recently eaten a small animal and was too slow getting out of Moonlight's way, striking out at her leg instead. Fortunately, python venom is not poisonous and Moonlight will be fine.

I feel for her, though, of all the horses she is the one most infested with ticks that need to be vigorously brushed out after a day in the bush, something about the pigment of her skin. Some evenings I just pick the squishy little bodies off with my fingers and stomp them under my boots. I wonder if it might be time for Moonlight to retire. A while ago she lost her closest companion, an older horse, to a lion in the night—an alarming tragedy for all. Now she may suddenly shy away or brace when approaching a dark shadow. The other day, she would not pass by a black, rusted car door serving as a garden gate beside the pathway. Douglas was harsh with her, I thought, compelling her to go forward. That is not the way I learned to be with horses; in this instance, I would have chosen a more gradual approach-and-retreat strategy in the face of perceived threat. Debriefing the day, I query Douglas about the gate situation.

"She needs to know I am the leader, and to do what I tell her. When there is real danger, she must trust me even when her instincts say no."

The Vardens' Mavuradonha horses are sure-footed, sensitive and trained for the bush, some high-spirited and some more down to earth; their expertise is honed in partnership with the humans who are responsible for their care and schooling. Each has encountered the wild animals of Africa, and I'm learning there is nothing to do but entrust myself to the horses' intelligence and to the wilderness savvy of my Zimbabwean guides.

*The Geography of Belonging*

Following the protocol of bush riding today has ensured my own safety and peace of mind. As always, we set out in our formation of three riders with the guide-tracker, Douglas, out in front and clearing the way. If something unforeseen happens from that direction, the rear guide stays with me, as Marvin did, holding the fort and my confidence. Should an incident come up behind us, the rear guide would address it, while the lead guide would either stay by my side or direct the way out of range. And thirdly, should something ever happen to me alone, everyone would stop and one guide would attend to the horses while the other would attend to me.

The trust built up over days of riding, and this knowledge, dissolves any apprehension about the wilderness—allowing curiosity, and awe, to lead the way.

Early the next morning, before the light of day is fully fledged, Douglas and I groom the horses as they chow down breakfast grain, each nose deep in the canvas feedbag suspended by a strap behind the ears.

"Did you hear the hyena last night?" he asks me, brushing Munhondo vigorously as I pull ticks off Basera.

I didn't hear the hyena, pleased to have this fact affirm that I'd actually gotten some sleep.

"It was just over there beyond the paddock making noise, at nine o'clock and again at three o'clock in the morning."

Setting out from camp after breakfast, Douglas is in front riding Gizmet when he turns around in his saddle and says, "Look down, here are the tracks of the hyena. Can you see them?"

He waits for Marvin and me to catch up with him. We slow our horses to inspect the ground.

Douglas says, "I was making a ceremony last night for asking my spirit medium, the one for this area—his totem is hyena—to show me that we are still safe and protected from the wild animals because you, Oriane, are my responsibility."

I ask if he minds telling me how he makes his ceremony.

"First, I take off my shoes and my hat as a sign of respect, and I find a place to sit on the ground by a Mahobohobo plum tree. If not a Mahobohobo tree, then any one is all right. Sitting down under the tree, I am clapping my hands and talking to the spirit medium about what I want to know. So I ask him last night, are we still safe until the last day of the visitor, you."

I marvel at the simplicity and matter-of-factness of the ceremony Douglas describes, and the utter lack of preciousness, as if it's just a housekeeping task.

"When I finished and put back my shoes and my hat," he continues, "the hyena came by right away to show me we are still protected. I could hear it making a circle around the camp at nine o'clock," he says, pointing to the hillside, "and the second time, he was coming back at three a.m. to show me he is still looking out for us."

I turn around in the saddle with a 'can-you-believe-this?!' look on my face, to get a read on Marvin who is right behind me. He raises his eyebrows and nods his head; he is as incredulous as I am that Douglas would tell me this story, as if he is talking about the weather. In the dusty red earth beneath the horses, I can see the hyena tracks, two sets of them, round four-toed prints, right beside the fresher cloven-hoof prints of one lone giraffe. I whisper good morning to the unseen hyena.

While wildlife encounters have been a highlight in the past of riding or trekking in Mavuradonha, sightings are not guaranteed nowadays, though the possibility alone brings a thrill to the bush trails. Prospects vary from season to season. We've come across the small resident herd of zebra, a traversing elephant or two, some archetypal African snakes, plus baboons, hyena spoor, stories of recent lion activity, and always monkeys entertaining us in the trees. Optimism grows knowing that once this wilderness habitat is protected, new animal populations will be reintroduced that reflect the resident species populace of days gone by. In the meantime, I wondered how to satisfy my urge to encounter more African wildlife in Zimbabwe?

Before the safari in Hwange last year with Theresa and her family, the Vardens rescued an orphaned baby elephant whose mother was killed by poachers outside Mavuradonha. The little one stayed for a few weeks at Siya Lima farm. She slept in a stall in the stables at night with the horses for company and a groom, Clemens, beside her for comfort. Clemens bottle fed her using two-litre plastic coke bottles and walked with her in a woodland paddock during the day. Though James and Janine and the farm crew fell in love with Kimba, they knew she needed other elephants. The Vardens trailered her in a horsebox to Theresa's family ranch in the southern Lowveld to live with three rescued adult elephants. And now James has made arrangements to drop me off there in a few weeks on his way to guide horseback safaris for the Malilangue Wildlife Preserve, in the same region. But first I'll return to Harare and Stephen.

Standing in the back of the truck as it gently accelerates away from the stables and gripping the roll bar to keep my balance, I wave an exaggerated final good-bye to Pension, Alice, and Douglas and the other horse grooms who are leaning against the paddock rail. Have I really been the solo client in camp most of the time, post-mid-life foreign white woman at that, riding with Shona horsemen, drinking bush tea by the fire, sitting in sacred places on the land? Yes, it's real, the sense of inclusion in the mission of ethical custodianship. Neo-tribal, Marvin calls it. He's busy inside the vehicle plugging his cell phone charger into the cigarette lighter receptacle.

He has said the welcome mat is out for anyone with a sincere desire to ensure that Mavuradonha remains a self-sustaining cultural landscape. Our being here affirms its value and brings revenue to the cause, he declares. It's true this is one place where

I feel my presence contributes to its integrity, rather than detracts from it, and does not commodify the natural order of things.

A chorus of whinnies, as Moonlight, Basera and Jecha lift their heads from grazing and keep their ears perked toward the truck till we're round the first bend and I can't see them. Standing tall in the great expanse, I keep on waving—*Tatenda, tatenda*. Thank you, thank you. *Toonana*. See you again—to the hillside, the river stream, the zebra spoor, the Raphia palms, the sky, and the shimmering in everything.

# Invitation to *Kumusha*

Within a few days of arriving back in Harare and being ardently welcomed by Stephen once more, the two of us board an exhaust-spewing bus for the several hour ride northwest to the town of Chinhoyi and the home of his younger sister, Taffy, and her family.

"Nice to meet you, Auntie." A teenage girl in a green school uniform holds out her hand as we step down from the bus. Priscilla, Stephen's niece, leads us through the town centre, along an algea-blooming ditch, across some ragged maize plots, and into a residential area delineated by sandy paths. The house her family occupies is still under construction—cement cinder blocks and red brick, an impressive three bedrooms and separate sitting room with a television tuned all day to news or sports or canned-laughter sitcoms.

Taffy and her daughters show me how to stir the *sadza*, when I join them around a fire in the dirt driveway-cum-outdoor-kitchen. We laugh at my ineptness, and I learn more about the gender-specific role of each family member in a household; my only reference so far is Stephen and Hambani's setup at the stables—not a home—no mothers, or wives or sisters.

When the evening story-telling winds down and the television screen inside the house shows static, Priscilla takes my hand and leads me to the back of the house. She opens the door to the bedroom she shares with her sisters.

The orange glow of candlelight warms the white-washed walls. Sunrise-coloured frilly curtains overlay heavier window drapes. Two thin mattresses pushed together in the middle of the clean cement floor have been made up as one bed, with peach-colour lacey edge synthetic sheets and a plush floral blanket. I have to say, it looks like a bridal chamber.

"You and my uncle will sleep here," Priscilla says.

My belly flutters and then softens; I feel like warm bread just out of the oven, pulled apart and spread with soft butter. The sweetness of a few minutes to myself, to lie on the bed alone and let tears wash the weary day. By the time Stephen slips in beside me, there is not a care in this world that comes between us, held in the sanctuary made for us by his family.

The next afternoon we continue our journey to the village of Stephen's older sister, Diana. He pronounces her name "Dee-yanah." In the stash of people packed in the bed of the little pick-up truck traveling the few hours from Chinhoyi to the village turnoff, an old grandmother asks Stephen, in Shona: who is this white woman who-must-not-be-from-Zimbabwe-if-she-is-riding-with-us? Where does she come from and why is she not in a car of her own, and what is her business with Stephen? He tells the all-attentive passengers that I'm his fiancée from Canada, coming to meet his family in the village.

"Ooooh," they say and look at me expectantly. I nod and smile and lean into Stephen. All of a sudden, the whole truckload erupts, clapping and cheering and nodding their approval. A banana and penny sweets are pressed into my skirt lap, the grandmother takes off her scarf and holds it out to be passed along to me. I wrap it around my neck, then take off my kerchief to be handed along to her. Stephen trades stories with the old man tucked in beside us.

Hours later, after dark and beyond tiredness, the two of us walk the four remaining kilometres in the clear light of a full moon—on a pathway through an endless waist-high landscape of fluffy white cotton, ready for harvest, Stephen says. My flip-flops launch little bursts of sand with each step; I can feel every grain sliding down my bare legs underneath my ankle-length skirt. At long last, we've arrived.

On the ground by the cooking fire, I make dinner for my Shona family. Having been addressed as *maiguru* upon our arrival, and in

*The Geography of Belonging*

every subsequent introduction, I realize there is no point in protesting the title that conveys my status in the family as "my brother's wife." Alone in the smoke-filled kitchen—a modest cubicle of plank walls, corrugated asbestos roof, and packed earth floor—this is the first time during my stay there is no other person near me. I can see the rest of the family with Stephen, gathered around the other fire outside in the black, starlit night. Diana roasts newly harvested groundnuts, peanuts, in a pan over the flames. It's my place tonight, as *ambuya*, respected older woman, to cook this last evening meal of our stay in *kumusha*, the term for one's home village, the place of belonging.

What a relief to be together with Stephen, held in the warm setting of everyday life in *kumusha*. Back in Harare at the guest-house and stables Stephen is a "worker," I am a client, and never the twain should meet. Of course, this is true in reputable hotels everywhere, but in this country, even after work hours his role is subservient in white company: he addresses the horse owners as "madam," the deferential term for white women, though I notice his demeanor remains self-possessed. The contrast between that city subservience and the reception he receives here in the village is stunning. In *kumusha* he holds the place of respected eldest man in the family, one regarded for his wisdom by the community.

Steam from the big pot of white rice boiling beside me eases off, so I mix powder for sauce into cold water in a separate, smaller pot. Had I known about making dinner, I would have brought some proper ingredients from the market in Chinhoyi—leafy green vegetables, onions and maybe some beans. But this will suffice, along with the eggs now boiling, presented to me as a gift this afternoon by Stephen's youngest son, 11-year-old Teneyi, who has lived here since his mother died. I'm surprised that Stephen is not warmer with Teneyi. My system of thinking figures a boy living without his father needs paternal affection and recognition when they meet. Stephen has other views, and once again, my perspective is suspended and rearranged listening to his story about fathering.

"My second-born son, Hambani, is too soft now," he says, "because I was not strong to him when he was young. Teneyi needs to respect and fear me so he knows when he does wrong things someone will be angry. In the village with my sister, everyone is soft to him. But did you see when we arrived in *kumusha* how he kneeled and nodded his head to show respect to me? The same for you."

My modest dinner offering is ready; an enamel basin holds the rice, bordered with the sliced eggs and topped with chopped ground-nuts for a smoky roasted crunch. Stephen and I share an enamel bowl, Teneyi and his cousins circle around another bowl and the rest of the adults eat directly from the serving dish. Stephen presses the rice into a ball with his fingers and brings it to his mouth.

"Is good," he says to me with a wink.

Talk turns to events a fortnight ago and even though the con-versation is in Shona, by paying attention to people's names I can follow the story. On our walk to the village that night, we had detoured to the homestead of Stephen's nephew, Fedias, Diana's son, and found two huge rectangular burlap bales of just-picked cotton in the yard and no one around. In the morning Fedias came bicycling urgently into Diana's home site. The pregnancy of his young wife had not been going well. The parents-to-be had set out on foot to the nearest clinic, but were sent home with instructions to go into town the next day to the hospital. The medic should have sent them to town directly, to avoid the extra eight kilometers of walking for the seven-month pregnant wife. She gave birth in the night at home. At daybreak, with the premature babe wrapped in blankets and carried by a neighbour, Fedias accompanied his wife on the footpath back to the road again and sent her in a bouncing truck bed to the hospital in town, a dusty two-hour potholed endurance ride.

He ran back home, collected his bicycle and sped on to us, to tell his mother the news himself, for there is no cell phone recep-tion here in the village. Keeping his mother informed had taken precedence over going with his wife and newborn son to town. This family birth became the story of my first morning in *kumusha*.

In the afternoon of that first day, I was about to bypass all reason and purposely drink a glass of cloudy brown water. Or rather I was waiting as instructed until the dirt settled to the bottom.

"Yes, please, this is for you. A little bit of soil in the water." Jonny, Stephen's cousin, rubbed his fingers above the glass. The water had come not from a deep borehole, but from a surface well a short walking distance away.

"When you drink this, the earth will recognize you—and you will not get sick from eating or drinking anything in *kumusha*," Jonny counseled.

I could almost hear my mother, a registered nurse, and her alarmed caution: Have you lost your mind? I did not think so. Sounded like a homeopathic prophylactic to me, a micro dose of immunization. Sipping from the rim of the glass over the next hour, I pondered the consequences.

Every day brings revelations about a way of life utterly unknown to me. One bright morning, Stephen and I sit side by side on a low stool in conversation with the resident regional tribal chief, who is bundled in a padded canvas jacket against the June chilliness. Stephen is conveying to me in limited English what we are talking about. I learn that the village of Chiwiti is a relatively new community, spread over several hundred hectares; the inhabitants have lived together on this communal land for much less than a generation. When white-owned commercial farms—agribusiness that housed their workers—were overtaken in the early days of land reform, an assortment of displaced black working families found their way here for a seemingly logical reason: this land had not been a commercial farm and was therefore, they believed, not at risk of being repossessed by a white farmer when "things turned around" in Zimbabwe. The broad swath of low-hilled valley had been a wildlife refuge, home to African plains game species. That is, until it was designated a resettlement area by the regional powers and what animals remained were relocated to other game parks. The community residents have their own plots of land, but few families have money to invest in seeds, fertilizers, or hosepipes for water. Besides, this is a semi-arid climate zone so food crops are destined to be sparse, sown in unsuitable ground without irrigation or adequate rainfall—the barest version of subsistence farming. Fedias and his buddies are an enterprising exception because they are contracted by a cotton merchant who finances their cotton-growing business; the land is more hospitable to cotton cultivation than food production. Beyond the meager growing season, foreign aid subsidizes the community by trucking in sacks of maize meal and imported rice. Still, one can sense a humble pride of place emerging after more than a century of subjugation, first by the European colonialists and then by the dictates of erratic government.

Stephen talks earnestly with the chief, telling the older man about plans for his little plot of property—the clay bricks now lying in the sun waiting to be tempered in fire, the trees he will leave for shade beside the yet-to-be-built-house, the crops his adult son will plant, and Stephen's own ideas for irrigation and the community grinding mill he will set up for revenue. A big vision for a man in his fifties who realizes that the physical duress of horse training and jumping will not be his livelihood forever. I have absolutely no idea if his dream will come to fruition, no means at all to discern what is realistic or attainable.

Diana has been carrying pots of steaming water from the cooking fire to a small round mud-walled enclosure the height of a person, with no roof, open to the sunlight and purest blue sky. I'd already noticed flat, pillow-sized stones over the dirt floor, and a big oval galvanized metal laundry tub. The chief has gone. Diana drapes a faded blanket over a pole across the doorway. Stephen invites me inside.

"Baff," he says, opening the blanket curtain, following me in and letting the blanket close behind him.

Steam rises from the oval washtub. A brand-new hand-sized bar of pink soap rests on a smooth stone, a trace of floral fragrance. A hand towel hangs over a bare, curved branch wedged into the wall and soon the folds of our clothes drape over the branch as well. My long hair is piled on top of my head, secured by a slender stick angled over and under it. The morning air is still a bit chilly; my pale skin, dimpled with goose bumps, looks so silly next to Stephen's dark satin body, muscled as a young athlete. We start to giggle. Stepping into the washtub, hot water on my feet and ankles electrifies the chill out of me. I stand taller in the tub, pinprick glints of mica sparkle on the earth-mud wall.

Stephen vigorously rubs the wet bar of soap between his hands—frothy pink bubbles overflow his fingers. He gently and firmly lays a calloused man-sized palm across the nape of my neck. The fingertips of his other hand smooth the hollow of my underarm, slide down to circle my wrist. He cups the back of my hand, while the cushion of his thumb imprints a soapy spiral in my opened palm. I wait.

Stephen, delicately and methodically, polishes every curved millimeter of my body.

Just stand here, I say to myself, quiescent, instinctual as a sable antelope doe. Keep breathing, and see if I can stay with the deepening pleasure in his attentive mapping of my geography.

What lies beyond, what I already know?

Beneath his fluid hands, in the interior of myself, everything I have been, until now, begins to dissolve into coherence—as the caterpillar liquefies golden, inside the chrysalis before re-forming. When he is finished, I am covered with shimmering soap bubbles. Stephen motions me to sit down in the washtub; he cups his hands to pour streams of water over my shoulders, rinsing off the suds.

He holds the bar of soap out to me. "Now you do for me."

We exchange places, he, standing in the tub. The wet bar of soap is too big to hold in one hand without slipping, even pressing it against his skin, so I also lather the pink bar in my two hands. I remember the instructions for the first time I groomed Prince, black beauty of a horse.

"Slow down. Put your heart in your hands and begin to touch your horse, all over. Use all your senses. How does he smell? What does his coat feel like? What do his muscles feel like under your hands? What about his belly, his neck? Can you touch the inside of his ears, or does he turn away? When does he respond to your touch, and when is he still?

"Notice the presence, the pulse, within his physicality. Feel his lower leg, his upper leg, and the arc of his flank. Does he tense or relax when you stroke him?"

I find these things out.

The washtub is too small for Stephen to sit down and rinse off, so he steps onto the flattest stone, bends over to pick up the tub, then pours the water over his head, goofy and grinning. The kids in the yard just outside our enclosure are shouting and laughing in their play.

This liaison is such a mystery—compelling, with an unforeseeable future, but then, that is true of beginnings. One thing is certain: I'm letting go of any familiar reckoning about suitable men. Stephen's appearance and his treatment by the urban white world do not convey the kindness, patience and strength of this man I am getting to know. We sleep in the only bed, single-sized, usually occupied by Diana with several little granddaughters in the mud-walled *imba*. They are now sleeping with their neighbour, a stone's throw away, whose husband is off working in another part of the country. I ask Stephen for the Shona word because "hut" just seems too cliché and impersonal.

*Imba*: an abiding-place; an abode; a place or means of lodgment; a fixed shelter. Plural, *dzimba*. There appears to be room for everyone who needs a place in the *dzimba* of *kumusha*.

# Animal Nation

Mungwezi's body is silhouetted on either side by a broad band of brilliant red sunset. In the gathering darkness, I move closer and her sagging belly becomes a massive shadow at my shoulder. Before my hand touches her skin, the soft, sparse bristle of her body hair startles me and I pull back. I am glad in this first meeting that Theresa has brought enough fruit to hold Mungwezi's attention, rather than letting her trunk stretch around to enquire of this newcomer.

"Tomorrow I'll introduce you properly to the three girls," Theresa says, referring to the elephants. "And don't run into the blind buffalo in the garden on your way to bed." I'd been forewarned that he is pretty hard to detect in the dark, easily mistaken for part of the mountain range in the distance.

It's been over a year since I met Theresa on the horseback safari in Hwange Wilderness. I've arrived at her farm, Wasara, in the lowveld of Zimbabwe. At least, it was a farm—a six-thousand-hectare cattle ranch, actually, of low rolling grassland punctuated with rock upcroppings, stands of ancient trees, wetlands and dams. Over the last decade though, with the relentlessly encroaching government-decreed land invasions, the farm is now a small parcel of four hundred hectares and part of the Chiredzi River Land Conservancy, theoretically a place of refuge for wildlife and habitat. But the flood of new settlers continues unchecked and has decimated the original Wasara ranch land, surrounding the homestead, setting fire to the grassland in attempts to clear it for crops, cutting down hardwood trees for cooking firewood and poaching the wild animals practically into non-existence in the people's desperation for food.

For the first time I hear in detail from Theresa's husband and see for myself how these newcomers, squatters really, have been re-located from elsewhere. They are disoriented: left to grow crops on the least fertile and arable land in all of Zimbabwe, land that is different from the places they came from, and unresponsive to the farming methods they have practiced historically. Crop yield is sparse and food production negligible. Calling them settlers is ironic under these circumstances. Apparently, NGO's pour food aid into the area, helpless to advocate that people be located geographically in places that can sustain them. Tumultuous times continue here in the lowveld.

Listening to Theresa breaks my heart. The formerly productive ranch supported several hundred workers and their families who made their home on the property.

"They are the invisible casualties of the farm invasions in Zimbabwe," she says. "Ninety percent of them dead from political violence, HIV/aids, tuberculosis, malaria, malnutrition, and the aftermath of homelessness."

Seven white horses, in a herd of ten. Beautiful, entrancing in the sunlight. All ten of them born on the ranch, descendants of the original herd. Twenty years ago, a rancher in the area let his herd of forty horses go wild on the land. Theresa wrangled ten mares to her place, then bought an Arab stallion for breeding.

"So many foals have been born," she says, "and many lost, too, to lions."

Theresa tells me how she trained the young horses herself, before hearing of "natural horsemanship." She went by her own instincts, with love, and by observing animals in the wild.

"Our family and our visitors rode all over the ranch," she reminisces. "It was lovely! And a practical way to get around."

A few years ago, she sold the stallion—with so uncertain a future, she could not, in good conscience, continue breeding.

These days, with so little land, Theresa seldom rides and simply takes pleasure in the company of her four-hooved friends.

I've come out to see the horses by myself, seeking some familiar place to put my hands. A wise-eyed older mare approaches through the bush. As a good houseguest I've tried to maintain an inner equilibrium since arriving in the lowveld, but being alone with the horses loosens a deep reservoir of darkness.

A trail of my tear drops glitter on Nicker's satiny white nose. She blows and spatters my shirt with a spray of dusty snot. Blowing my own nose on my front shirttail adds a damp brown streak and the tears keep coming as my forehead finds a resting spot against her neck. I'm up against the ingrained compulsion to make sense of things, my own radar that seeks patterns and frequencies and revelation. Up till now, I've prided myself on being able to live adeptly with chaos and uncertainty, but my own life experience pales in this light. Sorrow comes up from the ground and presses itself to my chest.

Nicker curves her head round and nuzzles my back. Oh, how I miss Stephen and ache for the strong comforting ground he holds for me.

The beauty of the horses contrasts so painfully with the disaster evident in the surrounding landscape and in every conversation. There is no escape to another, more palatable, reality. Two weeks ago, eight remaining giraffes kept safely enclosed by an electric fence from wandering into poachers' snares were sprung from the acres-big paddock and have not been seen since. Wasara, and everything a conservancy stands for, is under siege. Not that there is imminent danger to me in particular at the moment, but if the shreds remaining of this farm are overtaken, no one will be looking out for the region's one last herd of wild elephants.

Close to fifty in number, the wild ones return regularly to visit their relatives over the Wasara wire fence. They are safer, accounted for and less vulnerable, the thinking goes, in proximity to the farm. Nevertheless, a few days before my arrival two of the wild elephants were shot and killed, taken by the settlers for food, tusks likely hustled into the ivory trafficking market. In a tragic irony, these very elephants are the descendants of a herd that was relocated to Chiredzi Conservancy in 1991/92 during a lethal drought in Gonarezhou National Park to the Southeast.

The rest of the afternoon finds me up a tree nearby the horses. Just resting, hearing the contentment of their grazing, inhaling the smell of tinder-crisp bush, the dry air in my nasal passages hotter on the in-breath than the out-breath. My skin seems to evaporate, my body becomes unbound and thoughts disperse into the sky.

At dinnertime we're joined by a neighbor, a former farmer who has somehow made peace with losing the land he'd worked productively for decades. He and his wife have re-created a simple way of living on a small plot of land; he remarks that they have no security, never did really, the same now as the majority of blacks who live day-to-day, season by season. The man's daughter was recently married and his wedding gift was a pair of polished wooden candlesticks that he crafted himself.

"I gave her beauty and illumination," he says.

"Thank you, Bob," he adds, referring to Mugabe, "for taking away my farm, my land, my security. Enormous uprooting change; now we are not complacent about anything, for which I am grateful."

His resilience reminds me of a particular community of well-off Americans who lost everything in a highly publicized financial wrongdoing, after misplacing their trust. As a community this American group became re-energized by their dissolved retirement plans, rather than passive or blaming. They welcomed living more simply and set to work creating new business ventures based on the values of ecological sustainability and service to others. Resourceful, able to change course again and again—the Zimbabwean mantra "make a plan" means not making a plan but improvising on the spot in changing conditions.

The housemaids still living at the farm have been with the Warth family for years. They do the dishes, the laundry and the cleaning, and set the table for our meals—the magic fairies, Theresa calls them. Each wears a headscarf of fabric that matches her apron. Most are lucky to be alive, testament to Theresa's refusal to leave the farm and her commitment to the health and well-being of "the people." Some have HIV yet remain healthy due to Theresa's provision of antiviral medication plus vitamin supplements from Switzerland and a nourishing organic diet from the garden.

A young friend of the family who was born and raised in Zimbabwe has come for a few days and is very good company. Heather went to university in the U.S. and carried on to swim for Zim in the 2010 Beijing summer Olympics. For now, she has returned to her homeland and is researching lion population in Gonarezhou National Park; she has come to Wasara for some respite in the relative comfort of Theresa's home. Although she is about to become engaged to an American diplomat and live in Buenos Aires after their marriage, she is passionate about Zimbabwe and dreams endlessly of contributing what she can to a restorative future.

As Heather talks earnestly about their plans, the Olympian and the diplomat, I'm struck by her stage of life, all full of promise and potential. She's a breath of fresh air along with Theresa's son Stephen, who is home on holiday with some mates from veterinarian studies in Australia. He is betting his education on a turnaround in Zimbabwe's fortune. Later in the evening, Heather taps on the door frame of my room, comes in, and seeing me in tears, sits on the edge of the bed. My dissolved state touches her and we begin to talk long into the night about this illogical world.

Animals not living in the wild are dependent on humans to feed them, and they thrive on consistency. Mungwezi and her companion Chitora, named after two rivers in the lowveld, were found orphaned and injured so make their home here at Wasara. Last year the Vardens brought the littlest one, orphaned Kimba, down from Mavuradonha, after she outgrew the horse stall in which the grooms slept too, for company. These are the three girls.

Theresa wears a photographer's canvas vest at feeding time, stuffing each pocket with fruit grown on the farm expressly for the elephants. That big garden plot, fertilized with the elephants' manure, continuously produces a lush harvest from the seeds of squash and other vegetables in the elephants' diet. The plot is bordered with bright green sugar cane stalks and enclosed by fruit-bearing palm trees. This morning Theresa's vest and cloth shopping bag are bursting with bananas, sweet potatoes, *narjes*, or oranges, and *pau-pau*, papaya, and she hands me three yellow-orange pumpkins to carry. Six-foot lengths of sugar cane and a big sack of maize meal will be waiting by the paddock.

Crunch-pop, the sound of a green *pau-pau* that Mungwezi picks up with her trunk, punctures open on the end of her tusk and tucks into her mouth. Theresa stands in front of her beloved elie, who is orderly and responsive when directed to her food, one movement at a time: "pick up", "trunk up", "tusk", "eat". Her tusks are about a foot long, filed short for safety while keeping their functionality. Heather partners with Kimba and I with Chitora to learn this mealtime ritual. After the elephants' breakfast Theresa plays with each one, in the same way we do groundwork with horses to sustain love and partnership. Then the girls line up beside one another, Theresa in front of them with her head bowed, hands behind her back. All is quiet. This happens every day.

"Are you praying?" I enquire of her one morning.

"Yes, I am praying deliver us from evil," she replies. Not surprisingly, I've been silently saying a *metta*, loving-kindness, prayer, each day; it comes naturally with Theresa and the girls.

After a few days Theresa invites me to ride Chitora, the biggest of the three elephants, from their nighttime paddock far out to the daytime grazing grounds. The mounting block is a sturdy stepladder anchored into the hard-packed dirt. The idea of climbing onto Chitora's neck is exciting, but once I am actually sitting high up on her I can see how much further down the ground is than from a horse. I'm pretty unnerved at first, and she senses my bit of apprehension. Chitora's huge ears blanket my legs on either side of her head, and I grip the top edges to keep my balance. As she steps forward, I do my best to relax and flow with her massive, languid gait across the landscape, somewhere between heaven and earth.

Thank goodness Beebo, her handler, is walking beside us as we approach the wide gate. I hear thunder rumbling in the distance and wonder if it will disquiet Chitora. A few seconds later, I can feel its vibration underneath me. Beebo looks up and nods; it is not thunder, it's Chitora sounding her way across the field, sensing a truck coming our way. Standing still at the gate until the vehicle passes, she sounds again, her low frequency rumbling penetrating my body.

I feel stirred and energized in an oddly familiar way. And then I remember lying in the circular sanctuary of Hollyhock Retreat Centre back in Canada while two Australian musician friends played their didgeridoos over the energy meridians of my body. Now, I'm in Africa, with the same vibratory sensation running through me.

We pass the afternoon keeping track of the girls in the bush so they don't break through the electric fences, which they can cleverly do by putting a log or big stick against the fence to lower it to the ground so they don't get shocked by the live wire as they walk over. We're following Mungwezi, who is on the move, when Theresa cocks her head.

"Is that music coming toward us or is that a lion?" she wonders out loud. We stop moving and intensify our listening. It's the neighbours sashaying through the bush, one of them carrying a battery-operated boom box on his shoulder, bass notes thumping, a lion indeed. We can see the faded colours of the women's zambias, sarongs, through the trees as they pass by. The afternoon stretches on. By now I'm comfortable sitting on the ground while the elephants move past, near enough to touch a foot, their skin like thick quilted leather. As the days go by, I feel more and more at home with them.

Theresa has given me an ostrich egg, huge with a thick, cream-coloured, dimpled shell surface. She offers a packing box, but I think wrapping it inside my riding helmet will be perfect. The Warths used to raise ostriches for meat and feathers—so many "used to's," even though the old days are not that long ago.

She has also lent me a book to read, *The Fate of the Elephant*. The author, Douglas H. Chadwick, describes his return to Hwange National Park in 1990. I'm tickled to be reading familiar place names from our safari there last year. All of sudden I sit up in bed and hold the book closer to the light. Chadwick writes:

"Camped upon a small knoll a little fire sizzled and smoked, helping to mark out our space against the rustling night. The field of stars was limitless and, in the dry air, pulsed with a strong clear light. I felt as if I were receiving some sort of current directly from it. My whole being tingled and then began to trill. The more the night deepened the more awake I became."

My eyes blur with tears of recognition, and I keep reading:

"… I could not imagine my own life without the deep currents of nature flowing close by…The old feeling returned, of being among not just animals but animal tribes and nations."

I close the book and wonder—how can I, as Chadwick writes, be among animal nations, with the deep currents of nature flowing close by? As I turn off the bedside lamp, two moths circle the inside of the lampshade: then, in the dark, through the open window, the barest crescent of waxing moon.

I am alone in Africa, which seldom happens. Heather has brought me for the night to Chipanga camp, a lion research outpost beside the Rundi River in Gonarezhou National Park. In years gone by, Gonarezhou was one of the most popular and accessible game viewing parks in Zimbabwe, about a six-hour drive southeast of Harare. Its trans-frontier boundary is shared with Kruger National Park in South Africa and with Limpopo National Park in Mozambique to the east. I've heard that Gonarezhou has few visitors nowadays and is a fantastic place to see wildlife on its own terms.

Heather has thoughtfully dropped me off and gone to find her colleague, leaving me in solitude in a canvas chair on the bank above a side stream of the river. Something about sitting quietly above the opaque green and still water is soothing. Sounds of the wild are layered in an outward spiral—the insect at my ear louder than birdsong, elephant calls audible in the far distance and a pervasive untraceable thrumming. This jungle is reminiscent of the atmosphere in a small tributary of the Rio Negro in Ecuador. That was another evening alone, while others were gone in the dugout log canoe. I was washing my hair and, again, enveloped in quietude and heightened sensitivity to the unseen presence.

Heather returns and we lie awake on our cots in the canvas tent. The night seems never-ending as if I am time travelling with every auditory occurrence. In the darkness each sound is a summons: hippopotamuses rutting below the riverbank, the low "hoo hoo hoo" of distant baboons, the thrash of something unknown in the bush. My body and brain are quivering receptors for the wild so close at hand.

Shortly after daybreak, Theresa arrives with her son Stephen and his mates, five of us take turns perched high on a safari bench seat in the back of the pick-up truck, Theresa at the wheel. Following the serpentine river as if the truck is an animal itself, we slow, stop and move forward in synch with the traversing herds of zebra, kudu, wildebeest, impala and the magnificent spiral-horned nyala.

We have no agenda and no destination to superimpose on the day. I can feel my breathing take up a new rhythm.

Slightly upstream the Rundi River curves through crevices, channels, and over the flowing rock formations of Chipinda Pools. The deep moving water is appealing in the mid-day heat, and I am about to pull my shirt off to slip in when a chorus of "No!" stops me short. My Canadian-bred instinct has yet again obscured the reality of Africa: beneath the benign surface of the river one must always assume the presence of crocodiles.

During our picnic lunch Theresa whistles softly and nods toward a nearby branch, a tiny jewel-like bird, turquoise, a blue waxbill. Then Stephen points overhead to the bathtub-sized communal nests of the buffalo weaver bird, built in the silvery outstretched limbs of a baobab tree. I hear about wildlife mating rituals and about dimorphic animals, ones that have a visible physical difference between the female and male of a species. After a snooze in the shade of a mopane tree, we set off on foot to explore the encyclopedia of animal spoor in the dry sand of the mile-wide Rundi riverbed. Animal tracks of all sizes and shapes: the hoof prints of the plains game herds we saw this morning and smaller more subtle tracks including those of the civet and mongoose, furry little African carnivores with long tails that resemble badgers and otters to us in the Northern hemisphere.

Late afternoon beneath the dramatic immensity of the deep red Chilojo Cliffs, I walk barefoot in the riverbed. The sand is hot, and I step into an imprint that dwarfs my own foot—the rounded pad of an elephant. I can see her in the distance as she wades in the narrow ribbon of water that sparkles at the foot of the monumental cliff face. Gonarezhou means "Place of the Elephant" in Shona, and we have seen them moving across the landscape all day long, most stunningly when an enormous bull mock-charges our vehicle—ears flapping, trunk up, a bellowing that sounds like an escalating trumpet solo, feet stirring up a dust storm. He stops abruptly, as does my heart, turns and retreats into the trees.

By day's end, the stationary and the moving merge; I perceive no distinction between large rocks and elephants, clumps of wheat-coloured grass and kudu, gnarled tree trunks and wildebeest, low-hanging branches and zebra. Gonarezhou—one integral wilderness landscape, animal nation pulsing with life. And it's not over yet. As darkness falls we're northward bound back to Chiredzi and the truck lights catch a reflection. We draw a deep breath in unison and stop. Lions by the roadside, seven of them at rest, unperturbed in the more traveled section of the Mililangwe road, quite used to vehicles. Nevertheless, their perfection is undiminished as none of us, neither human prudently remaining inside the truck nor animal on the ground, move away.

Stephen has his reading glasses on and nothing else. He looks intently at my underarm, his cell phone flashlight in one hand and my tiny sewing scissors in the other. He claims to be an expert in the field of tick removal. Snipping the minuscule multi-legged flat insect from its edges into the centre will kill it, he tells me, the barbed legs will let go and soon drop out of my skin. No scratching, or pulling as I'd been doing with alarm when I discovered the tick, because then, he says, "Bad to you and getting a sore." The charm of Stephen's intentness turns my concern into giggles, which he doesn't tolerate until the minor first aid is complete.

This is our last night together and we're in a new room on the guesthouse grounds in Harare. My usual rondaavel was already occupied when I arrived back from Theresa's farm in Chiredzi yesterday. This new room is different, brighter and cozier than the thatch-roofed rondaavel and set in a row of four along a veranda adjacent to the main house. For these final two nights we have the luxury of a queen-size bed, fluffy pink duvet and soft-underfoot cream-coloured carpeting. And best of all, we have a spotless white-tiled bathroom with an old-fashioned deep bathtub. This time of year, early-July, is chilly in Harare; the comfort of lying still and relaxing in the steaming bubble bath with Stephen after the tick episode, dissolves the tension built in to my leaving Zimbabwe tomorrow.

The two of us had a stressful day riding the crowded kombis across town to Avondale flea market for some specific souvenirs I wanted for my family in Canada, and then downtown to find some hardware he needed that I offered to buy. It was a poor choice of how to spend the precious day together and I got cranky, out loud in the middle of a crowded, jostling crosswalk intersection.

Stephen had said, "Look, over there, those people are different. Coming from somewhere else. Refugees."

At first, I couldn't see any "different" people and then, I did, as Stephen continued to point out the procession of tall, raggedly dressed Africans walking, compressed together, on the other side of the street. "Somalis," Stephen said. His gawking annoyed me.

This hadn't happened before, frustration and impatience on my part. When we stepped up onto the sidewalk curb, I pulled him into a shop doorway.

"I'm sorry, I didn't mean to speak unkindly to you."

"No problem to me," he'd said.

Sighing with regret and city-induced overwhelm, I responded, "Please forgive me. Let's just go home." Home? The pink bedroom, for now.

This evening, after the tick removal and the bubble-bath, I am entirely ready for sleep and nothing else, so I promise Stephen we can get up early-early to have some morning time together before my taxi to the airport.

It's still dark when I light a candle in the morning, though sounds from the guesthouse kitchen courtyard through the bathroom window indicate breakfast preparations are underway. Stephen looks up at me, his face lit by the candle's undulating flame. I know. Is there time for a bath? Yes.

*The Geography of Belonging*

"Wait," Stephen says as he gets up to rummage in his jacket pocket.

"Something for you."

He stands behind me. His breath, penetrating my neck and shoulders. His broad hands slide forward, onto my belly, like the touch of wool on silk. Then, his hands slip slowly backward, over the contour of my hips toward the small of my back. After a slight pressure I feel the calloused palms return to my belly, and rest there. I lower my head to receive his breath on my neck.

As I look down, Stephen whispers, "Eh,eh," and spirals the two ends of a tiny metal fastener together—a double strand of tiny glass seed beads encircles my hips, gleaming pearl white and onyx black, spaced every so often with translucent emerald green.

"Now you are my wife."

VANCOUVER, CANADA

# All My Relations

Many long hours later, travel-weary, I don't want to arrive in Vancouver, I want to arrive back in Africa—to sit by the fire with Stephen and a plate full of Hambani's *sadza* for dinner. But beyond an evening's meal outside his transient workers' quarters, Stephen does not have a home into which we may go together. No containment, no place of private refuge. Yes, he has a plot of land and bricks drying in the village for potential *dzimba*, for some time in the future, when he's done working with horses. Can I imagine myself joining him in that?

"Hey, Mum, welcome home!"

Devon stands solidly on the shiny granite floor of Vancouver International Airport, arms open, allowing me to lean in while I soak his shirtfront with tears. He feels absolutely like home. He's come back to the west coast from Montreal, feeling he just didn't belong in that eastern landscape, no ocean, no real mountains. He is a deeply rooted cedar tree, a pacific west coast species in the eco-system where he and I are fourth and fifth generation.

How would life be different, I wonder, how would it feel to have an *imba* of my own again in Canada, a sovereign place from which to come and go? A place in which to receive Stephen.

A month later, I make the declaration that I'm going back to Africa soon. I say this to myself, and to my friends and family but still my mind abhors the irrationality of it and pins me down with doubt and dismissal. One day I think that millions of people go to Africa for every kind of reason. Another day I think how ridiculous that I'd traipse again to that turbulent continent, allowing my heart to be drawn by a place, and a man in particular. Today I'm trying to unravel the dispute.

I might have missed the insidious claim that shame makes on my heart, had my lover been more conventional. Not that my life has been particularly conventional, but a financially well-off soulful entrepreneur would have been enough to keep the veneer on this primal wound. But to let love, sit in the front seat is just not done. Where did that come from, I wonder?

In my first marriage, to my son Devon's father, there was certainly attraction, probably to his success as a jazz musician, his Frank Zappa good looks, Bohemian life style and fatherly attention to me. It was actually the foundation of an abiding friendship that took fifteen years of marriage to mature.

Even then it was not okay to love a man. In my maternal family of women, my mother and those before her, I cannot recall a single conversation about feelings of the heart, or evidence even of fondness for a husband. In my grandmother, who was one of the first women to graduate from Queens University, her married love seemed secretive, a betrayal of womanhood.

One evening, deep in meditation, all these historical trappings evaporate and nothing obscures the singular truth of my heart that wants to be whole and surrender into, not resist, this love affair. Yes, I've been wary all along of projecting some courageous powerful emerging aspect of myself onto Stephen, rather than claiming it inside myself. I'm wrestling with the inner work of the soul and the shadow—I don't want to unconsciously, and irresponsibly, act it out and leave human casualties in the process. My deepest prayer is to be impeccable in my relations with Stephen; but can I know what that is across cultures?

The ocean tide is low in this last hour before sunset, exposing the glitter of pebbles covering Smelt Bay beach on Cortes Island. The mountains of Vancouver Island, westward across the strait, are dusted with snow. Picking up a slender piece of driftwood, I draw a cross in the sand, a dot in the center of each quadrant.

*The Geography of Belonging*

Then, curves join the dots together to form lines and a labyrinth takes shape on the beach. The space between the curving lines is just wide enough as a walking path. Off come my gumboots, bare feet on the cold wet sand.

I'll just walk following the pattern, and see if any further clarity about my conundrum of Africa occurs when I reach the middle. I doubt it. The arcing path comes close to the centre of the labyrinth—oh, nearly there—and then spirals to the outer edge. The sky turns a deeper pink as I take the final step calmly into the center of the labyrinth, and wait, naked feet on winter wet sand.

"Just go!" I hear, clear as a bell.

When I return to the house, an email from my dear aunt awaits. Remember, she is my father's sister:

> Hi Dearie,
>
> Just a few lines as I have a sore finger, so it's hard to type. Your conclusion is no longer a maze and not a riddle—just pure and honest and in no way a sin. So just go for it—with an open heart and allow love to enter. Share and receive; accept and give. Use Horse Medicine and above all, enjoy this lovely space in your life.
>
> Love you,
> Auntie Oriane

A few days later, back at Mary's farm in Goldstream, her dog Quila and I walk down the trail to the ocean inlet, he, sniffing his way through the slushy remains of last week's snowfall. The black velvet medicine bag is in my pocket. I pat the outside of my jeans and contemplate the most valued artifact—the tiny rib bone of a baby deer, wrapped in the green fabric of a Tibetan prayer flag, tied with gold thread. Early mornings before returning to Africa last year, to meet up with Stephen, I would sit in the barn with the horses, polishing the bone to pearly white with a nail buffer.

And now the tiny treasure has been to Africa and back. Rib bone, protector of the heart and of the tender untried love that wanted to bloom. A warm flush comes up from the ground into my legs, and I understand: I am made from that rib, and the draw to Stephen is the longing to return to the source, the origins of humankind. Africa. I can feel myself nestled alongside Stephen's heart—inner *kumusha*, place of belonging—with he who was born and whose genes reside in the land where the human journey began. This flash of insight rings true in my cellular memory, but the Adam and Eve twist seems heretical for a woman who came of age in the 1960s and '70s.

*Horses come in the night. Into my dreams in the dark hours.*

*In a vast sun-filled field, I lie down in the middle of the grassland and begin to stretch my arms and legs, spiraling my torso, twirling my hands and feet.*

*All at once, I sense, something, coming, through the trees on the far side of the vlei. A dark form materializes.*

*An immense, gleaming, black horse thunder-gallops toward me. I press into the ground, terrorized, in the split-second of being trampled, to death.*

*But the trustworthy beauty leaps over me. Underbelly arcing above, as if I am a river.*

*He does this again and again, thundering and leaping, thundering and leaping, until my fright dissolves in the sound of his hooves, the sheen of his body, the pureness of his power.*

In the morning, Prince, black beauty of the farm, leans over his stall gate as I walk into the aisle of the barn. His horse medicine has come to the rescue of many troubled souls who've come to the farm for healing. His ears perk forward with my giggle of appreciation, remembering his wise counsel for my hands in the bath with Stephen. He nickers noisily and lowers his brawny head, breathing into my belly. I understand, then, that all my work, all my soul-searching and my mentoring with horses for others, is for naught if I don't stand on the ground of conviction, accept the horses' guidance unequivocally and walk their wisdom in this world of shadow and light, of doubt and devotion.

My forehead drops to the steering wheel and I can't stop sobbing. I feel trapped in the shadowy hold of the ship, engine noise echoes a racket inside the pale green cavernous steel hull of the vehicle ferry. I'm on my way to visit my parents before my flight to Zimbabwe next week. The car beside me is empty, its passengers upstairs in the lounge. All the cars are empty

"Mary, it's me. Help." I sob into my cell phone.

"What's happening?"

"I feel as terrible as I've ever felt, for no reason I know."

"Okay. Find your breath, feel your hands on the steering wheel. Push your body against the seat of the car."

"I'll try, keep talking."

"Now imagine Prince is there with you. He is with you, his energy. I'm standing with him right now, here in the barn."

With the sound of Mary's familiar voice, I'm on Prince and lying chest down against his warm broad back. The inside of my legs feel into his curving belly, my arms are wrapped around his full neck. His thick cushy mane is comforting against my face. And then his smell, that earthy scent of horse, begins to disperse the piercing melancholia that had overtaken me. How could I know that feeling is a reverberation from the near future?

Up till now, before Zimbabwe, I haven't given much thought to my father's professional life before he retired decades ago. He'd worked for a company with major logging and pulp and paper-making operations on British Columbia's west coast. He'd made his way up from a job in the mill at Ocean Falls, a remote company town accessible only by boat or seaplane, to Director of Industrial Relations in a top floor office in Vancouver.

In late 1967, dad was transferred from Vancouver to the U.S. headquarters in San Francisco to head up the company's Affirmative Action program. Before then, racial employment discrimination had been legal in the States and a new federal law decreed that all the company's pulp and paper mills around the country had to be integrated, moving black mill workers up into management positions. I had started university and stayed behind.

Within six months Martin Luther King Jr. and Robert Kennedy were both murdered and U.S. race relations were in turmoil. I vaguely recall something about dad having been recruited because the company couldn't find an American in its ranks who wasn't prejudiced.

"Is that true, Dad?"

"Yes," he says, smiling at the big dish of chocolate ice cream I've put in front of him.

"I was scared sometimes," he continues, "but not prejudiced. I'd never been face to face with a big black angry union boss. I knew right away I couldn't do it on my own. So, you know, I hired Milt to work with me. He wasn't scared of anybody."

I remember Milt, his wife, and their kids from visits to my parents. Before joining my father, he'd been deeply involved with social justice in his African-American community in Oakland. I ask Dad to tell me a story from those days. He thinks a minute.

"Well, one time I had to spend a whole Saturday working with your mother in the garden, convincing her to let your sister go to the senior prom with a black boy. You know I don't like yardwork, I'd rather play golf. Anyway, your mum was concerned about what other people would think about your sister. I couldn't very well stand for one thing at work and something different at home."

He goes on, "We began to have the top brass from the company to the house for dinner with Milt and Shirley. That broke a big racial barrier right there. Milt and I still stay in touch."

"Why did you retire early?" I ask.

Dad stopped working at age 55 in the peak time of his earning power; he and mum left San Francisco and lived out a fulfilling retirement of friendship, travel and community service before settling in Sequim, Washington state, just a few years ago.

"Well, by then Teresa, the first grandchild, was born and I figured your Devon and another one for your sister would be coming along. We didn't want to miss that."

He licks his spoon, puts it down in the dish of ice cream, looks at me and sighs.

"The company president whom I respected died suddenly, stress, heart attack. I couldn't stomach the vice presidents, who put profit and production ahead of people. I had no allies left in my responsibility to the employees at every level. Worst of all, and your mother agreed, was their callous attitude about logging in the old growth forests with no regard for the future. They had never been skiing up the mountains behind Ocean Falls where you were born."

"Have we talked about the Great Bear Rainforest?" I ask my father.

He shakes his head.

"Along the coast of British Columbia, our home, six and half million hectares of temperate rainforest are in the process of receiving covenants and protection in perpetuity—that's twice the size of Vancouver Island. And you know what? The environmental campaigners who've dedicated themselves to this mission went through leadership and negotiation training at Hollyhock. I know some of them."

"Boy, too bad that wasn't around in my time."

"Ocean Falls and all those mountains lie within the Great Bear."

All of a sudden Dad looks like a little boy, "Really?"

Then finds his composure, "Tell your friends, good work," he says and slurps the last spoonful of his melted ice cream.

"What's that noise?" I ask mum. She doesn't hear it. I go outside to see what the steady banging is behind the house. Dad is on the ground; he has fallen, it's happened before, and is tapping out S.O.S. in Morse code on the gutter drainpipe with a small rock.

"Took you a while," he says.

Later, at the medical clinic, Dad's primary care physician is not overly concerned after checking him out. "Yes, he's got a few more miles on him. Don't worry about him, you can go to Africa."

One more thing before I leave for Zimbabwe: a special ceremony on Cortes Island—the dedication of coastal rock bluffs and surrounding woodland as a Forest Conservation Park. A place of wild refuge, beloved by islanders, Devon's father and I were married there in a long ago time of life.

While government dignitaries and the island community gather on the beach, I hike inland from the shore, past the rust-orange bark of arbutus trees that hang over the cliffs and into the deep quiet of mature evergreens. The faint fragrance of cedar blends with Douglas fir; long beards of pale lichen drip from bare lower branches. Underfoot, thick moss covers generations of decomposed plant debris. In a small clearing, I kneel down on the velvet green and feel into the medicine bag at my hip for the glass vial that holds the soil from Mavuradonha. Ever so carefully, I lift the forest carpet, just enough to pour the richly coloured earth from Africa into this land. The essence of Mavs, held here, in a protected place, for safekeeping. I lie down on my back on the mossy bed—the ground is springy and cool under my weight—and listen to the trees.

A day later, back at Mary's Farm, I'm packing clothes and gear for the coming months in Zimbabwe. Folded in tissue paper, between the suede riding chaps, is a dress, an ivory shade of softest silk that fits my hips and flows around my legs. A wedding dress, just in case.

# At Home in Harare

Stephen walks ahead of me, along a wide footpath bordered by the lush vegetation of gardens that have overgrown their fences in the back of residential properties along the main Crowhill Road, further on from the guesthouse where I'm once more in residence. Enormous sun-streaked green leaves brush the bare skin on my upper arm. Children and chickens run across the path. We're immersed in a suburban jungle; a secondary neighbourhood, behind the scenes, the domain of the household workers and their families. Garden plots are tucked everywhere—pumpkins and squash, tomatoes, leafy greens, onions, potatoes, and of course, maize.

Stephen talks enthusiastically about the prospect of buying a car, more specifically about me buying a car, and is leading the way to one he has found for sale. I do agree, the thought of mobility and independence is appealing.

Angled out from a fence, overhung with giant-leaved ivy, the front end of an older Volkswagen beetle is just visible, cream-coloured. Stephen is beaming and sweeps his arm outward as if to introduce a star performer. What am I supposed to say? I step closer and see tires flattened from years of going nowhere, moss covering the dashboard, something green and hairy upholstering the seats, a young sapling growing through the floorboard.

"I have a friend," Stephen says, "a mechanic who can make it run, no problem."

I don't think so.

Otherwise it's a happy return, to walk with him in the neighbourhood this afternoon and recognize characters from last year—the colourfully-clothed women at the roadside fruit stand, the man with the bicycle repair shop under a tree who calls, "Hallo, madam!" And the young woman selling cell phone airtime cards who remembers my name.

My laptop sits open on a round table covered with a floral chintz cloth, under the verandah awning outside my room; the same bedroom in which I received the waist beads from Stephen last year. Beside me rests the most beautiful and fragrant arrangement of peach-coloured roses with jasmine vines trailing from the vase. Today is Sunday, around noon, and since early morning rapturous voices resound from the hillside across the road—spirited halleluiah singing from the Shona Christian church. Still, the thrumming of bees in the nearby flowering hedge is audible and the guesthouse property remains a sanctuary of tranquility and beauty, rare in urban Harare. I rest my hand on my heart, feeling as blessed as can be.

The guesthouse owner, Ann, who has become my friend, is one of Zimbabwe's top landscape designers and employs a crew of gardeners who keep the grounds impeccable, and also welcoming to a profusion of God's creatures. Last evening, she and I relaxed on a stone bench by the fishpond, sipping a glass of wine each and watching the sun set. Over the course of an hour or so, more than one thousand Abdim's storks came in turn to roost in the gum tree, high above us.

"Do you know, over the period of a year, forty-two species of birds pass through here?" Ann said.

"Listen, a purple-crested lourie, it will be here for about two weeks." She went on enthusiastically about which feathered visitors appear through the seasons.

In the few weeks I've been here, I feel a sense of purpose and inclusion. The guesthouse needs a brochure designed, which I've begun to do on my Macbook; this results in a discount for my accommodation. After that, comes a re-write of their web-site text, as well.

But just at this moment, the screen dims on my laptop. The electricity has gone off, another unpredictable power cut. The regional grid, the infrastructure, is overloaded, so the authorities just shut everything down, intermittently, with seemingly whimsical timing. I look up at the sound of footsteps approaching the verandah.

"Good morning, lovely day. I'm Charlie Davies from up the road. What brings you to a guesthouse in Borrowdale?"

"Horses." I reply. "And, I've fallen in love with Zimbabwe—and will be going north to the Mavurdonha Wilderness to volunteer with some horses soon. The cultural landscape up there just called me to come last year. So I went. You know, the spirit in the atmosphere."

Oops, I wouldn't normally say this in a first conversation.

"You must meet my wife, Mel, then. I'll bring her 'round, you'll get on famously. She can take you to a Shona community in the rural area."

"Lovely, Charlie, thank you. I'd like to meet your wife."

True, too. I could do with a kindred-spirited woman's perspective.

As he walks away, I check my laptop power cord light and it's clear the electricity is still out. No problem; uploading photos for the guesthouse brochure can wait. This afternoon, in the outdoor dining area, the regular Sunday art group is about to begin. The elderly watercolour students greet me in turn.

"Are you new, I haven't seen you before?"

"These chocolate biscuits are so good, do have one."

"Don't sit there, my friend always sits beside me. She isn't coming today."

"Hello dearie, that's a very pretty...oh, what do you call the thing around your neck?"

Ann initiated the art-making group for people with Alzheimer's who live in a nearby seniors' home and for her husband Roger who has become uncharacteristically forgetful. The activity of watercolour painting benefits their mental condition and sociability in general. As well, the instructor cuts the paintings creatively into postcard size pieces of paper and makes remarkable note cards as a fundraising effort. I've bought several packets to take home and have been invited to join the class. The unabashed painters are fascinating company; some continue their bantering while others work in absorbed silence. I follow the instructions for creating light and shadow in a still life.

The next day, Charlie Davies turns up with his wife Mel. She and I set out on an excursion to Shingirirai Trust, the health and education project she co-founded in a community on the outskirts of Harare. Once out of her car and making our way on foot, the tin-roofed kindergarten is our first stop. From the edge of the outdoor classroom I notice right away the little girl is different from the other kids—a little lopsided, but moving with careful deliberation, shuffling her feet, making her way over to where I am standing. Observing the child approaching me, Mel suggests I just relax and see what happens.

"We don't have any agenda or formal role today," she says quietly beside me, "so just enjoy yourself, and the children." As Charlie predicted, Mel and I have become immediate friends.

Before I know it, the young one has reached me and we sit cross-legged on the ground facing each other. Perfect's mouth is wide open and she does not blink, keeping eye contact with me. I admire her snow-white teeth, perfectly spaced, and talk to her about their brightness, their size and evenness, guessing all the while how old she might be. She couldn't be a preschooler like the others, though she is as small; her front teeth are big with no gaps indicating missing baby teeth. Her response to me is silent. She beams and makes small gurgling noises.

Perfect takes hold of my index finger and touches it to the sandy ground, moving our hands together, making a curved line. With my free hand I brush another patch of sand clear and draw two parallel lines; Perfect reaches for my finger again and draws an arc to cap each end; grinning, she shows those teeth—brighter than the morning sunlight.

A sweep of my palm erases the images, and with her warm grip on my finger Perfect traces five small spheres until a larger circle is formed by them: a solar system in the sand. I add a fingertip dot to the centre of each small sun. She repeats the entire complex image exactly, several more times.

Mel tells me later that Perfect's mother brought her to the Early Childhood Development Centre in a tentative gesture of curiosity, never imagining inclusion for a child so different. On the spot, Perfect was included naturally by the other kids in their play, and her mother wept with profound relief and gratitude—any of us with children or grandchildren know her story in our bones.

Perfect may have a future in design and painting on fabric, on ceramic tile and handmade paper—products of the Shingirirai Trust community arts project. Turn me inside out, and you'll see an invisible tattoo, the unforgettable image of the little artist's Perfect-ly made circles.

Later, when Mel and I walk into the nearby craft studio, a pile of folded cotton tablecloths catches my eye. Before I know it an apron is tied around my waist and a giggling teenager, with intriguing tufts of hair forming a dark halo around her smooth face, lays out a length of white cloth and hands me a potato block cutout of an elephant.

"Choose your colour, and just start," she advises.

Blue, it will be a gift for my mother, who loves hand-printed fabric. More giggles and encouragement as I stamp out a procession of blue elephants on the white fabric.

On the way home from Shingirirai a friendly clerk in the grocery store gave me a recipe for the world's simplest scone biscuits, so I bought the ingredients. Farai, the guesthouse cook, is curious about everything new to do with food. He and I stand side by side in the outdoor kitchen. First of all, I need an apron.

Then:
3 cups self-raising flour
1 cup Sprite (yup, the soft drink!)
1 cup cream

Mix the Sprite and cream lightly, so as to keep the bubbles. Fold the liquid gently into the flour. Softly pat the dough into two circles, then, cut into wedges. Place the dough triangles in a large cast iron pot and cover with the lid inverted. Put the pot in the midst of coals in the cooking fire and cover the lid with more glowing coals. Wait about fifteen minutes.

Farai sets out butter and honey on a tray and makes a pot of tea. I take off the apron as Ann happens to walk through the kitchen gate. The scones turn out to be fluffy and delectable, though a bit too crumbly for spreading the honey. Farai accepts the scone I offer, a taste test, but will not join us for the cup of tea.

Ann has asked Clemens to move my things to a cottage, near her own, on the far side of the guesthouse grounds. The horse stables are clearly visible from the sitting room window of my new home, the Dairy Cottage. The evening mealtime has me at the cooking fire of Stephen and Hambani outside their room beside the stable. Hambani makes *sadza*, of course, with an accompanying stew of butternut squash cubes cooked with a leafy green vegetable, like chard or kale, finely chopped. The side dish is called relish, whether meat, fish or vegetable. The meal is eaten with one hand, finger food. I reach for a tin cup of water and a small plastic basin.

*The Geography of Belonging*

Stephen says, "No, Hambani can do that!"

I remember from meals with Stephen's family last year that etiquette requires the youngest able person to wash the hands of their elders before anyone eats—by pouring a thin stream of water over our hands into the basin. How this makes hands clean, I have no idea. Never mind for the moment, the food tonight is delicious, though I can never finish the huge mound of *sadza* that is always served despite my groaning protests. I think my leftover is warmed over the fire for their breakfast.

Stephen is quite fixed in his way of doing things, I notice. He prefers tidiness and order—everything in its place, every person in their place—which is a valuable asset around a tack room and horse stable. But this quality becomes a bit tedious when my way of doing things inadvertently contravenes his expectations and the social norms of his culture. Not to say I don't enjoy the traditional customs that show respect, there is real pleasure in knowing what is correct in different situations anywhere in the world.

For example: the little handclap, slight curtsy, and greeting "*Makadii?*", when meeting someone in their home for the first time makes a big impression, smiles of acceptance from the Shona hostess. In Stephen's world, acceptable appearance for women in public means wearing a skirt or dress, especially in *kumusha*. That's easy because I love wearing skirts and feeling feminine, especially in Africa with the other women; except, I should add, on location in the bush when wearing jeans brings out a different kind of self-assurance. And my long hair—it took a while for Stephen to point out matter-of-factly one day that wearing it loose in public looks like "bedroom hair," and that it would be better to pin it up, or tie it back, when I'm out and about on my own.

On one hand I confess to enjoying the feeling of belonging I have with him, in some primal way. On the other hand, at this stage of life, it's entirely foreign for me to behave solely to conform to a man's preferences. How to discern between what is culturally prescribed in Shona tradition and what is Stephen's own penchant—and then to make respectful choices based in my own values and morality? I think what truly matters in not forsaking my sovereignty, and respecting Stephen's, are the consciously examined ethics that govern each of our lives. Are these conversations possible between us? That's a good question in any relationship.

"Hey, baba, where is that music coming from?" I ask, plastic plate in hand. It's coming from a different direction than church last Sunday, and has an altogether different kind of singing.

"Oh, across the way, a funeral." Stephen replies, "You can go if you want, if you like that music. Anyone can go. But myself, I am not going to church things."

"No, thank you," I say, "It's dark and I can hear it from here."

I ask Hambani, "If you don't go with those Christian people or your Shona spiritual ceremonies, what is your church?" Hambani takes the single earbud, attached with a cord to his cell phone, out of his right ear.

"Music is my church. Can take it anywhere you go." He grins and puts the earbud back in place. Stephen nods approvingly and then puts the question to me. I think about it for a minute.

"Remember riding in Hwange?" I say, "Out in the wilderness all day on the horses, sleeping under the stars at night? That's my church, same in Canada. Nature. And what about you, baba, what is your church?"

"My church is doing right by every person. Not only Sunday, every day, I am good to all people. That's it."

"Mr. Hambani, this way please."

Stephen and I get up from our seats in the waiting room of the lab downtown to follow the white-coated technician down the hallway, as we did last year. Half an hour ago Stephen had his quick-results-blood-test to check for hiv/aids and the results are ready. We both had the test last year when I arrived, it seemed only fair for me to do it too. But this year I brought my paper with me from Canada that confirms the negative-status results. I had prudently been tested for everything under the sun that might have come home with me.

"Excuse me, Madam, but you must wait here," the technician says.

Stephen looks back at me apologetically.

With that, the floor drops out from under me and I plummet into darkness. Last year we were simply handed plain brown envelopes in the waiting room, with our good-news tests results inside.

What news do they want to give Stephen in person, alone?

My hands fumble to find the chrome arms of the chair behind me. I grip on for dear life, sit down and fold myself forward to keep from fainting. No one else in the room takes any notice of me. The hum from the fluorescent light drills my brain.

"You may come now."

I follow the white coat along the hallway to an open door. A pleasant-looking woman decked out in an urban Africa dressy-occasion outfit sits behind a dark wood veneer desk. The chair beside Stephen is empty.

"Please sit down. I am the sexual health counselor."

Barely hearing her, I slide into the chair and push my spine against the straight wooden back. Stephen reaches for my hand in my lap.

"Shall I tell her?" The woman looks at Stephen.

"Yes," he says.

"We didn't allow you to come into the room with Mr. Hambani because only he had the blood test. So, we presumed you are his employer, because you are white. And, in that case, it is not your business to hear the results from us."

I feel pooled on the floor.

The woman goes on, "When I explained this to Mr. Hambani, he told me we were wrong. That you are his fiancée, that the two of you are intimate. It is very unusual for us to see a mixed couple. This is most special."

I cannot collect myself, and don't want to hear any more.

"Would you like to know the test results?" she asks looking down at the paper on her desk. I feel played out, like a small rodent in feline paws, and try to sit taller in the straight-backed chair.

I don't want to know.

The fancy-haired woman smiles, "The results are negative. He is fine, safe."

I don't hear her tell us she was on holiday last year, and that's why we didn't see her personally to receive our blood test results.

"Please, enjoy your time together in Zimbabwe. And Mr. Hambani," she looks pointedly at Stephen, "be faithful to this woman and treat her well."

What does that mean?

"Are you excited about going up to Mavuradonha and returning to the horses you loved last year?" Mel asks in the car as Charlie drives us to Avondale to buy our passes for the Harare International Festival of the Arts, which runs the first week of May every year.

"Well, wait till the opening night of HIFA, that's something to be excited about too!"

She goes on to tell me about past years' performances and describes a phenomenal week of the best in African and international music, dance, and theatre. Zimbabwean performers share billing with opera stars and music legends from around the world. The tickets are not expensive for the calibre of the performers. At the Avondale ticket kiosk, a charming young man, Amos, attends to us and promises to reserve a t-shirt for me to take home for Devon. I wish my son were here and coming to the festival with us; music is a special bond we share from his musician father. Devon himself is an accomplished drummer, both kit drum and hand drums

"Come home with us for dinner," Mel offers, "I'm cooking Asian chicken stir-fry with brown rice."

"It might be a nice change from *sadza*," Charlie adds, with a chuckle.

Early next morning in the office of the guesthouse, I check on-line news for Zimbabwe, since the internet is working. AllAfrica.com has published a story about Theresa's situation in Chiredzi. No wonder she emailed me that this is not a good time to come and stay with her and the elephants. The article describes how settlers have pressed closer to the enclosure around her house and farm buildings; they remain outside the tall wire gate, day and night, threatening.

There's only one thing to do right now before Janine arrives to collect me for the drive to Siya Lima. In the heartache and helplessness of Theresa's plight, I return to the Dairy Cottage and sit quietly in the overstuffed armchair. Let my heart fall open in the face of her oppression; Metta, lovingkindess meditation, as I did in the mornings with her and the elephants of Wasara. Of course, one hopes this makes a difference to the recipient, but for the moment defusing the anger and anguish I feel ensures that I won't inadvertently act with irritation, annoyance or unkindness today.

And after returning to Canada, I will create a tribute to Theresa's fortitude, as part of my presentation of stories, videos and music that my friends have come to anticipate after my pilgrimages to Africa. This time their cash donations can support "Water for Wild Elephants," Theresa's effort to trailer tanks of water in the dry season to the troughs she's built across the fence for the wild elies.

# Come As You Are

Late afternoon the Land Cruiser turns up the long driveway to Siya Lima farmhouse. Douglas opens the yard gate and I'm out of the vehicle almost before it stops beside the stable.

"Welcome back to Siya Lima, Oriane," he smiles.

"How very nice to see you again, Douglas. I have missed Zimbabwe."

After unloading our gear and groceries, mostly mine since Janine will be returning to Harare tomorrow, she suggests a walk in the field to counteract our long road trip.

"Let's go through the stable and put some horse cube treats in our pockets," she suggests, and off we go in that direction.

The sea of pale-ale grass is taller than I am. A rolling wave in the middle of the pasture is not the wind, but discloses the location of grazing horses. I enter the quiet expanse, navigating my way down to the pond on the far side, guided by the position of the surrounding trees. Janine hollers from higher ground in the distance reminding me, "Talk to the horses loudly enough to be heard. They can't see what's moving toward them in the grass, predator or friend; they're standing alert, they'll be anxious."

"Hello, you beauties, how blessed is this day," I say into the air. "What a relief to be out of town. How's the grazing? Any new babies?"

And then more quietly I sing to them, no words in particular, sounding the elements in the atmosphere: bird song, hoo-whill, hoo-whill, whirrrrlll; cloud trails, heyahhhh; peace, mmmm.

Up close, the slim stalks of grass have seeded tops, and sway slightly in response to a wisp of wind, a gesture of greeting from the unseen spirits. A rustling by my shoulder and as I turn, one beautiful big soft brown eye.

"Hey there Munhondo, gorgeous buckskin boy, how wonderful to see you. My goodness, look at you!"

He's got a zebra, indie, haircut. His shiny black mane, clipped short, stands straight up, much cooler in the heat and easier for the grooms, and shortly for me, to remove the ticks that lodge at the bottom of the hair shafts. I had better check my own hair at bedtime, too, after this cruise through the high grass. Munhondo nibbles at my jeans pocket, I pull out treats for him and then off he strolls, one grazing step at a time.

I reach the reeds at the edge of the pond and see three mauve water lilies afloat on the smooth surface. I remember this. Lie down on the damp ground and take some deep breaths, relax, and fill my lungs with the scent of the earth. The air carries, too, a faint trace of the alluring fragrance of night-blooming flowers falling open with the waning light. Up above, a slender crescent of new moon imprints her promise on my homecoming to Mavuradonha.

Jecha, the young palomino mare, is clearly balking at the lunge line's heavy brass hardware that Douglas is trying to attach to both sides of the horse's thick leather halter. What the hell does he need this gear for? For training he must believe, while grappling with Jecha in the round corral at Siya Lima Farm. Old-school training in a European tradition, the way he was taught many years ago. The weight on her nose, the discomfort, and her growing agitation are not the best start to a productive outcome in learning to carry a rider. Jecha remains jigging by the curved rail, tossing her head and switching her tail as Douglas walks to the center of the corral determined, with lunge whip in hand.

Outside the rail I turn away and let my eyes rest on the towering rock dome of Nyambare in the near distance, sacred mountain, abode of the Ancestors. Cloud streams rift rows in the blue sky above.

*The Geography of Belonging*

"May we try something different, Douglas?"

"Yes," he says, "please show me. I want to learn the new things."

"Okay, how about go to Jecha, take off that halter and those lines, and talk to her quietly, stroke her, just help her relax. Become her friend again."

This time when Douglas returns to the centre of the corral with Jecha at the perimeter, parallel to the rail, her unbridled ears are cocked toward him. He casually sweeps his right arm toward her hindquarters as if he is imagining coming up behind her. "Trot," he says firmly and off she goes in a dignified trot around the ring. Douglas remains in the center with his attention focused lightly on the now-willing mare. After she's made a number of consistent laps around the corral, Douglas relaxes his posture a bit and says, "Walk," and Jecha slows to a purposeful walk. Then Douglas simply bows slightly and steps back from her, as if inviting her toward him. And indeed, Jecha turns into the middle of the corral and walks toward Douglas, stops a foot or so in front of him, lowers her head and blows. Her honey-blonde coat is gleaming under the bright morning sky, her flaxen mane and tail seem spun of sunlight. Douglas seems at peace as he strokes her neck talking softly; I am near tears.

This is not a new way of being with horses for Douglas I have noticed, it's what he does naturally when left to himself. Another horse comes to mind, in Canada, her name is Sage; as I passed by her one day at Healing Heart Farm, considering what approach to take with a new client, she looked up at me and I heard the silent words, "It's not rocket science, just come as you are."

"Douglas, how can I distinguish the four white horses from one another until I know their character better?" What appear to be white horses are actually termed gray, in the equine colour palette, if their skin underneath is black. When the skin beneath the hair coat is pink, you have truly a white horse.

We're inside the stable with a wheelbarrow half full of mash—morning feeding time. Douglas gestures to each horse in turn. "Fundungwe, Fundi for short, has a pink nose, the one truly white horse. Waterspot has a shadowy patch on his right hip. Apache is the biggest and his nose is a bit darker than the others. Sixpence is the smallest."

I ask about Moonlight, that memorable white, gray, horse and find out that, happily, both she and Basera were retired a few months ago—given to a girls' school in Harare to live out their lives in safety and comfort, adored by the resident students.

"You can ride Fundi today," Douglas says, handing me the gelding's bridle. Douglas tacks up the spunky adolescent Gizmet for himself; the horses need to be exercised in rotation, different ones each day. Outside the stable, the day is varnished bright and I follow Douglas' lead as we set out on a leisurely two-hour circuit through the treed woodlands that will pass beneath the imposing cliff face of Nyambare Mountain. By the time we reach the mammoth building-sized boulders at the foot of the colossal monument, shafts of sunlight pierce the tree canopy highlighting patches of rock surface.

When I reach out and touch the glittering stone, it is warm, alive; my body wants to press against it. All the while Douglas quietly talks about the Ancestor spirits who live in the mountain, and how one must not trespass on the heights without asking permission of the spirit medium who answers to them, or else some misfortune will befall the intruder. The elder man who inherited the life tenure of spirit medium, lives not far from here, Douglas tells me.

"We can go there one day and pay our respects," he says.

Fundi stays close to the warm rock wall as we curve round out of the trees into the full sun on the eastern side.

The next day I suggest taking our horses into the round corral, one at a time, before we head out, to practice some groundwork before riding—just like Douglas did with Jecha. I can get the feel of my horse that way, how is she showing her temperament today? Is she compliant, defiant, restless, fatigued? This is the way I learned to be with horses when I first followed the call to their wisdom, at age fifty-two. The energizing rush of being on foot, moving on the ground in sync with a powerful and responsive horse, sealed my fate. Douglas proposes I ride Gizmet, saying he is a horse who likes to learn.

Out in the sunshine, after walking Gizmet into the corral and repositioning the poles across the rail opening, the horse stands attentive as I untie his rope halter, or head collar as they're called in Zimbabwe. The morning sun glints off the golden hairs on my tanned forearm. A fly alights on Gizmet's nose, translucent bronze wings motionless, just for a second. Gizmet stretches his neck with a yawn then licks his loose lips, and I walk into the centre of the circle picking up a slender branch that has fallen into the corral. Grounding myself, feet lightly planted on the earth, I gently swing the branch toward Gizmet's hindquarters and he moves off at the walk around the rail; a little stronger whoosh of the branch and he speeds up with an energetic trot. When I confidently request, "Canter," Gizmet slips into an easy, rhythmic canter, circling around the inside of the rail with poised collection. Douglas has done well in training the horses and later confesses that he doesn't use the lunge lines when no one else is around. And will never again; the art of liberty horsemanship. "At liberty" means no halter, nothing to inhibit natural movement, unbridled freedom. Gizmet and I have something in common.

As I stand in the middle of the round corral, cowboy hat shielding my eyes from the sun, Gizmet circles the rail clockwise with perfect composure. When Douglas gives the thumbs up for "enough," I ask Gizmet to slow down by relaxing my body posture and saying, "Trot" and then "Walk." When I shift my weight to step backward, away from the horse, and lower my head slightly, the attentive young gelding turns into the corral and walks toward me in the centre. He stops within arms' reach and it's time for a rub and hug around his neck.

Okay, now we're partners and ready to ride. Douglas has done a little groundwork with Apache in the dirt driveway before stepping up into the saddle. He holds Jecha's lead rope in his free hand; more training for the young mare as she follows him on our morning ride. I take Gizmet's saddle from the rail, lift it onto his back, buckle the girth and adjust the stirrups to my height. I'll circle him another lap or two, then tighten the girth before mounting and settling into the saddle for our morning exercise ride, into the hills.

Much later, after an afternoon of grazing for the horses, I open the metal gate of the pasture. The beauties come running in their usual order and make a beeline for the stable, hooves clattering on the worn stone floor, each of them trotting into his or her own stall straight to the feed basin, just like at Mary's Farm at home in Goldstream. Over our own evening meal—Douglas cooked the *sadza* after I had chopped the tomatoes, onions and leafy greens then braised them for a long time in a cast iron pot on the fire— our upcoming assignment is laid out. Preparing the horses for guest riders in bush camp next weekend, and my own return to the Mavuradonha Wilderness bush camp. I have yet to sprinkle my offering of thanks—the earth from Mary's farm pasture and the water from the ocean estuary—to the land and Ancestor spirits here in Africa.

Next morning Douglas and his second-in-command, Shepherd, who lives nearby the farm in a collection of mud-walled thatch-roofed *dzimba*, have hooves to trim and horseshoes to replace. That leaves me to groom each of the twelve horses. I take particular care with Hugo, coming into his stall last of all. His back is in bad shape following a heavy bouncing-in-the saddle rider a month or so ago. The client had, of course, claimed an expertise he did not have that didn't show up until the safari was well out in the bush, and now Hugo is shuppering, a Zimbabwean term for suffering. I remember an equine hands-on healing practice that my colleague Michelle designed for a group of massage therapists who came to Spirit Gate Farm. The effect on a horse of the chi energy coming through the practitioner's hands is more tangible and visible than with humans who can be resistant, caught up in their minds, overly talkative, or spaced-out. Horses respond instinctively to healing hands and are uninhibited in their responses. Lowering the head, blowing out his nostrils, shifting her weight, pooping, and other physical expressions that show the horse is coming into ease.

Standing by Hugo's neck, facing him, I place one palm on his forehead and the other between his ears, and breathe, staying aware of the contact of my hands on his head. I imagine the energy of the earth coming up through my feet, flowing upward and through my hands to the depressed-looking horse in front of me. As well, with each inhale, imagining the healing energy of the universe enveloping Hugo and I, and penetrating his swayed back.

Hugo's head drops down a few inches, a release of tension, and I slide my palms side by side past his ears, cupping them across his mane. As I move incrementally down his neck Hugo begins first to lick his lips and then yawns a long stretch of his throat, mouth wide open revealing his teeth, waggly pink tongue reaching forward.

"Thatta boy, Hugo." I begin to hum, such pleasure in being calm like this.

Hugo's ears pivot between the sound of my voice and the clinking of metal outside in the courtyard as Douglas ping-hammers horseshoes onto freshly-rasped hooves. I have another, different, perspective about shoeing horses and have brought a copy of Barefoot Trimmer magazine for him, and Janine, to read, sent along by my mentor in all things equine, Frances, herself a professional barefoot trimmer. But I'm not about to impose my thoughts right now, in unfamiliar riding conditions like this where I am not an expert. Respect for the Vardens and their safari horsemen take precedence over all.

When my hands complete the length of Hugo's neck, I slide them a few inches below the centerline of his wither and continue along just beneath his tender swayed backbone, again, incrementally in synch with his signs of tension release in the body. Mostly he shifts his weight, as if to realign his spine. Once my hands have curved down his rump beside his tail, it's clear that Hugo is much more relaxed and comfortable; the muscled flesh of the top of his tail is slack rather than held tight against his anal opening. I walk round to his other side and repeat this progression from shoulder to hoof; the whole sequence from forehead to hoof follows the bladder meridian, which affects all the energy pathways in the horse's body. The stone floor of the stall is strewn with clumps of horse manure. As I lead the chestnut gelding out of the stable into the sunlit morning, Douglas remarks that Hugo is walking with more fluidity and natural movement.

Riding the familiar upslope of tall-grass that crests just before the Raphia Palms Botanical Reserve, my back is tingling, my belly aflutter. We've slowed the horses to convene the herd, in case, true to Douglas' christening of the protected swathe last year, a fawn-coloured reedbuck leaps up suddenly and sprints across the open grassland, the vlei, startling the horses. Munhondo takes command of the assembly with Douglas in his saddle expertly trailing four other horses, their lead ropes held in his left hand. I'm on Manini, trailing two more. We're taking eight horses to Kopje Tops camp to settle in before the guest riders arrive tomorrow.

"You know, Douglas, in western Canada the cowboys and horsewomen who work with horses like this are called wranglers."

"Okay, we are two wranglers in African bush. One of Canada, you, and one of Zimbabwe, me," he says, pleased.

The herd moves forward collected, Munhondo in the vanguard. Passing over the crown of the hill and dipping toward the reedbuck vlei, the sunlight intensifies and I think my sunglasses have fallen off. Looking down, they're not underfoot on the ground. Oh, I haven't been wearing sunglasses—we've just entered the lucent domain of the Raphia Palms. The copper-coloured fronds that skew downward from the tree trunks are dead ones, sloughed off in the heat of the dry season. But now, March, rainy season just passed, the remaining resplendent soaring fronds appear supernally green in the fresh pure air. Indeed, the whole biosphere shimmers with jewel treasures—elemental shades of southern Africa in her native finery.

The meadow grass before us spreads a rich coverlet of emerald and topaz; a woodland canopy interspersed with citrine and jade borders the far edge of the vlei. When Manini and I reach the Tingwa River and ramble along its low bank, the flowing stream of water reflects an opalescent ribbon of sky. The two horses I'm leading match Manini's pace, content to meander alongside us and occasionally reach for a few mouthfuls of grass, the lush stems sticking sideways out of their mouths as they chew.

The palms fronds above rustle-sigh in the warm west wind, and their undersides mirror the undulating patterns of light beaming upward from the moving water. The tingles in my back are streaming now, just like that light, between the crown of my head and root chakra in the saddle. And when I slip my feet from the stirrups to let my ankles and knees relax, my legs seem to stretch down into the earth. The burnished bronze branches of Msasa trees glow from the opposite hillside. Gold reflections and mercurial silver mirages are flung across the landscape by the sun, radiant overhead. Douglas and his fan of horses are threading their way, lit up in front of us. My friend is quietly singing, a Shona tune I don't know.

Once we traverse the botanical reserve the horses pick up their pace and raise their heads, knowing that Kopje Tops camp is just another half hour away. When we arrive, Shepherd has travelled in before us, on foot, and filled the cement water trough in the paddock. The horses are impatient to be unbridled and left to drink, to be unsaddled and free to roll in the familiarity of their field in front of the thatch-roofed stable.

The Easter bunny came to camp this morning so everyone, clients and staff, had chocolate for breakfast. Our VIP guest is six-years old, here with his dad and grandparents for the holiday weekend. Pension is busy making him a coconut-covered bunny-shaped cake for this evening, no easy task in a fire-powered bush kitchen. The boy is an impressive pint-sized rider on gentle Manini, the immense bay gelding who was my horse on that Hwange safari. Yesterday the little equestrian was enthusiastic and at home in the saddle for the entire daylong ride. It seemed odd to me, though, that the other adults rode in front of him on the trail, where they couldn't keep an eye on him. I couldn't help but ride at the back of the line, behind him. He reminds me of Devon as a boy, inquisitive, independent, and affectionate. He fell asleep in his father's arm by the campfire after dinner. The young one had been telling me about learning the sport of polo cross, which I had never heard of. It's classic Zimbabwean, played like polo, the team players ride horses, but instead of mallets knocking a ball along the ground, the players have lacrosse sticks with nets and hurl the ball through the air. The little guy is apparently a stellar junior player.

The boy's grandparents are here, as well, and the family's conversation at mealtimes gives me yet another point of view about Zimbabwe. Resilience, resourcefulness and passion for life are the mainstay of these Zimbabweans, who remained in the country despite losing their farm businesses and all their assets.

As we relax after breakfast, the boy's father tells me about present-day Zimbabwe as a land of opportunity for those with an entrepreneurial spirit, so different from the first world in North

*The Geography of Belonging*

America and Europe, he says, where substantial financial backing is needed and there is so much regulation. Here in 21$^{st}$ Century Zimbabwe there is no viable credit, the interest rate for mortgages and loans is 30%.

One must buy outright whatever is needed, or rely on being able to reciprocate the generosity of friends. This family call themselves traders, importing for resale what the people need: frozen chicken in bulk from producers in the U.S., manufactured goods like appliances from South Africa, truckloads of maize from Zambia in years of poor crop yield at home.

"Losing the family farm was a blessing, really," the young family man confesses. "Now I'm not tied to the burden of being responsible to the bank which fronted the investments for crops till harvest time, nor responsible for the community of workers that need to be supported to run the farm. No rat race—only ingenuity, adaptability, and money in the pocket," he continues. "If leaving Zimbabwe became the only option, I would stay in Africa and move northward into English-speaking countries beyond the Zambezi and Angola Rivers."

I had expected to be put off by the grandmother, likely my age—her dress and hairstyle look classic-colonial from what I've seen in the movies, and match her efficient bossiness. But she proves to be lovely: warm, soft-spoken, and appreciative of the camp staff, speaking Shona with them. I'm drawn in by her straightforwardness and bountiful humour. She is business savvy, too, I've heard from her son. She's also curious about the tarot cards and wants a reading when we're both back in Harare.

Earlier, at sunrise, before feeding the horses, I'd walked with Douglas to sit underneath a big-leafed Mahobohobo tree. Once our shoes were off, we clapped our hands in greeting to the Ancestors. Douglas sang quietly in Shona while I shook the tiny vial of loamy North American soil onto this continent's dry red earth and then poured out the other vial, of Pacific Ocean seawater, and silently spoke my thanks for being welcomed here as the water seeped into the ground.

It was an Easter Sunday long ago, when my agnostic father conceded to my baptism in the place of my birth, Ocean Falls, on the wilderness coast of western Canada. He wanted me to have the option, without pressure, of choosing the Anglican religion of my grandmother when I got older. Then, another Eastertime two years ago, came my personally-chosen baptism—in the wild, on a horse, under African rain. And now, another Easter in a place of falling water—this time, the sacrament of Confirmation, when one assumes from one's godparents the responsibility for one's own spiritual life.

Rather than riding this afternoon, I walk with Mafusire, just the two of us, to a special location I haven't seen before, the sacred cave of clay pots. Many visitors are guided by Mafusire to the "Pot Caves" but it isn't until we're bundu-bashing through dense shrubs that he tells me the story of happening upon the ancient site while on a personal exploratory walkabout; the entranceway, camouflaged by foliage near the top of a steep rock *kopje*, had eluded him before. Neither did I know that Mafusire has trekked most of the topography of the Mavuradonha Mountains, either on anti-poaching patrol or in his own free time. He was the first person of record to come across the caves in modern times, and the archeology team from National Museums and Monuments last year were most impressed by his find.

The opening in the rock is a tight squeeze, even for me. Mafusire who's a tall slender Ndebele man, has climbed behind me onto the high stone ledge, a kind of doorsill, which is inside a cavern hung with trailing vines and tiny yellow flowers.

"You must hold onto the rocks above you, find some footholds to help you climb up and then twist around onto your stomach," he says, muffled from below.

Okay, I now lie on a gritty surface in the dark as Mafusire hoists himself effortlessly up through the narrow portal. In a flash the chamber is lit up, he has turned on his flashlight. We're eye to eye with a scattered collection of clay vessels, most about the size of a five-gallon bucket, but shaped in elegant curved forms. Reddish-gray clay, bottoms blackened by fire and time.

"These were not everyday pots," Mafusire says, "not for cooking or food storage or carrying water. These are the sacred pots of the chiefs and the spirit mediums for their ceremonies with the Ancestors, ceremonies in this cave. Asking for guidance in hunting, praying for rain or healing, revealing a leader—many purposes."

Here we are millennia later, sitting on the same ground, breathing the same air, the same smell, the same spirits, the same. A whiff of herbal smoke, my imagination? I suddenly see skins of leopard and lion on the floor of the cave, feel the sharp rock wall against my back. A low growling gravely sound. A spirit medium talking to his lineage? Now? Or then? When Mafusire turns off his light, the sanctum is not in total darkness, an opening to the side lets in veiled daylight; the holy vessels seem to glow, embers of the Ancestors.

After showering for dinner under the canvas bucket suspended behind my thatch-roofed chalet, I'm back inside leaning against the African print cushions on my bed. Through the wide doorway, the panorama of distinct individual treed hilltops layering into the distance gradually slips into a single continuous dark silhouette, overshadowed by the fiery throes of the sun's departure from Easter Sunday. Alone in my *imba* with the evening's numinous stillness, Mavuradonha once again begins to sift inside me. What remains foremost is the imperative to preserve the archetypal African wilderness. The cultural landscape, the spiritual ecosystem, this "Place of Falling Water."

# PART THREE

HARARE, ZIMBABWE

# Mbira Stairway

The Book Café is a legendary music venue, a hot spot for culture in Harare. Ann and I are the only white people in the packed club, seated at a table with her friend Saki Mafundikwa who is the director of ZIVA—the Zimbabwe Institute of Vigital Arts, a graphic design school he founded after his heart was called back to Africa from a successful career in the U.S. Elegantly dressed in a dark collared sweater, an obviously custom-designed denim turban conceals the shape of his head. Beneath full cheeks that round when he smiles, a soft-looking beard, kind of wild, tinges grey along his chin.

Across the table, Saki inhales a pinch of cardamom-coloured powder. He offers the tiny gourd-container to me and I decline what I later learn is snuff, *bute*, specially-cured finely-ground tobacco. His companion is quiet, wearing a top hat above thick chest-length dreadlocks, a black motorcycle jacket, and tight leather trousers; then, without a word, this intriguing man disappears.

Suddenly the stage turns electric. A stream of performers snakes into the spotlight and begins to create a polyphonic otherworldly musical sound I've never in my life heard. With a startle I recognize the lead player as the man in the top hat. He's now outfitted with a minimalist animal skin around his hips, a leopard-skin loincloth; the black leather must be backstage in the dressing room. Ankle bracelets adorn each performer and armbands drip with multitudes of clacking shells, while sticks and feathers embellish elaborate twirling hair. Curved gourd shakers say *che-te-che-te-che-te-che*.

Chest-height hollow-log drums reverberate in the floor under my shoes. A huge dried gourd shell is suspended by a guitar strap from the neck of each of the main musicians, their hands hidden inside.

This is Mawungira Enharira, Zimbabwe's acclaimed mbira band, plugged in, playing their version of their traditional music. In this exhilarating moment there's no knowing that the unusual instruments and entrancing music will later come to touch me in a deeply personal way.

The tallest and most animated of the dancers leaps from the stage onto dance floor and into the audience. Oh, no! Me?

He grabs my hand and pulls me up from the chair—there's nothing to do but follow his lead despite feeling hot, inhibited, and apologetic for every introverted bone in my body. Hours later my night dreams are perforated with snakes and waterfalls.

A few days later Saki comes to the Dairy Cottage in the early afternoon, so that I can do a tarot card reading for him, to help sort out some family matters, he wouldn't mind me saying. He's pressed for time and leans forward in his chair. When the tarot divination is complete, as he is leaving, Saki turns to me from the doorsill.

"I have a friend I want you to meet. On the way over here today I had a strong sense that you must meet him. He works with spirit, not throwing bones or doing showy things, but truly a healer. Not that I think you need healing or a consultation, but I am just guided to introduce you. He lives an hour or two away from Harare. We will go there to see him."

"Yes, I would really like that, Saki. I brought a set of divination sticks that I carved in Canada before I came, but I didn't know who they were for."

Later, Stephen laments mournfully, "When that guy Saki comes into the house, you chase me away and give him tea, not me. You are not respecting me."

I see Stephen's point because Shona culture is pretty much an open-door way of life. Yet, in my world the tarot consultations are private and my visitor didn't have time for socializing. I sigh to myself, knowing it's fruitless to remind Stephen that when he came by the Dairy Cottage on his lunch break, I'd said he was welcome to rest in the armchair for half an hour then I'd have something else to do in the house, a visitor was coming. It felt awkward and I knew he'd feel disregarded; the undertone being that this is not a home we share, where he is man of the house, but my domain in which he is an invited guest. I know that jealousy is a theme for Stephen, from betrayal in the past. He claims that bad *juju* from long ago relationships can threaten to put his heart in harm's way again.

Chipunza, the archeologist, and I have been in touch and have a meeting scheduled at the NMMZ headquarters downtown. I'm eager to hear about progress toward securing National Heritage status for Mavurdonha and the timing of submission to UNESCO for World Heritage status. I'm also curious to know the extent of foreign mining prospecting along the boundary and of the encroachment of new settlers on the fringes.

So far in Africa, it seems that trying to speculate how events will turn out, even in the short-term, is not productive at all. Nevertheless, the experience last year of riding with the horses beyond the veil of surface appearances, and into the enchanted domain of the ancient rock paintings and sacred sites, remains a potent touchstone in me.

Is there something I can contribute toward Mav's preservation? We'll see what comes of talking with Chipunza.

Besides this prospect, Janine has proposed we do a weekend program together with the horses, at bush camp in Mavuradonha, for horse lovers in Harare who'd be intrigued by a new approach, the Equine Guided Learning I've demonstrated to her. We set dates for mid-May after the HIFA festival and designed a flyer. Today we're talking about the logistics over an informal lunch at her house in town.

"Four people have signed up so far," she enthuses. "And by the way, there's a new booking for an Explorer Safari in Mavuradonha next month for seven nights. You're welcome to go along at base price. You'd probably have to ride, let me see, Fundungwe or Water Spot, and help set up camp at the end of the day."

With her words, something unzips in my chest—just like that, a long-held yearning is materializing. Seven days and nights out in the northern wilds of Zimbabwe, in the furthest reaches of the Mavurdonha Mountains, the southernmost point of the Rift Valley, bordering the escarpment of Zambezi River Valley.

Much later that day, I turn out the bedside lamp.

"Stephen, guess what?" I gush. "There's an Explorer Safari in Mavs next month and I'm going! And after that, the HIFA music festival, you can come on your day off!"

"That's good. After that we can go to *kumusha* near Kadoma. You can meet my mother."

Stephen wakes up in the night with a dream of a funeral.

"But I'm not tell you the dream now, in the night, or the dream won't be coming to finish."

That's all he will say. I pull the covers up around his shoulders and think no more about it.

At lunchtime the next day, we sit together on the grass in front of his room by the riding arena.

Hugging my knees to my chest I manage to say, "My father called from Canada this morning. My mum is not well, very sick in the hospital." Curiously, the previous week I had emailed my travel agent, just in case Dad himself took a turn for the worse.

Stephen is eating a perfectly ripe guava fruit. The skin is yellow. Broken open, the inside looks like a tomato with light-coloured small seeds. The flesh of the guava is dark pink and exactly matches Stephen's gums and tongue, the inside of his mouth—in contrast with the glistening black of his lips and chin.

"I'm shoo-ah it is her heart, thinking about your father."

It is her heart. She has a ruptured aortic aneurysm. If she doesn't die within a few days, she'll be moved to a chronic care facility to wait. I know she won't be tolerating that prospect well. While listening to my Dad on the phone, everything slowed to an underwater without time. What shall I do first? I think. Nothing, right this minute.

I choose a tarot card to reflect what's happening with her, with mum, my mother. The Knight of Cups: a red-haired knight, emerald green suit of armour, astride a white-winged horse, shimmering in the rarified high-sky atmosphere. Her heart is returning to God. She is being lifted up, soul returning to heaven, spirit carrying her home.

I need to talk to my mother. Thank God I'm not in the bush, and the electricity has come back on in Harare today. Thank God the internet is working, so I can find the phone number of the hospital that holds my mother. Thank God I have airtime left on my cell-phone SIM card.

"Hi Mum, it's Lee, how are you feeling?"

"I don't feel very good. A big pain in my gut."

She sounds terrible, and weak, but clear, and she knows it's me.

"Thank you for coming," she says, oddly.

"You're welcome. How are you feeling?" I ask her again.

"I am really tired out."

"Okay, I'll let you rest, Mum, and I'll see you soon as I can. I...love...you."

"I love you too, dear. Bye-bye."

That was the conversation. Stephen has finished eating the guava fruit and lies down on the grass facing me.

Softly he says, "*Isa moyo wako pandiri.* Put your heart to me."

"Do you mean 'Give my heart to you?" I ask.

"No," he says. "Give is *kupa*. Different. Put, your heart to me. *Isa moyo wako pandiri.*

I let go of my knees, lean back and turn toward him. My left temple rests on his bicep as I lie in the cradle of his arms. His palms curve to fit my back, one across the tension in my shoulder blades, and the other on my sacrum, that soulful spot. I feel the slight pulse of his heartbeat on my breast. After a time, my breath falls in with his, as if we are one breathing body.

That evening comes one of the toughest conversations of my life, sooner than I want to have it. But I cannot, in fairness, leave Zimbabwe without voicing to Stephen what I'd been thinking, before the call came about my mother.

How to say to Stephen that our dream of marrying might not work in the everyday world of distance and difference, in the disparity of our circumstances?

Now, unexpectedly, my father will be alone before long—and in the African way, I won't abandon him. Instead, I will leave Stephen, abruptly, with no time to find out whether we're able to build a life together. A wrenching separation, too soon.

We lie on our backs, side by side in bed, and I turn to lay the palm of my hand on his breastbone. How do I own up to doubt, in the face of love? How do I say that we don't know each other well enough to make a promise for a future on hold?

Stephen's words will haunt me.

"You are suspending me. You are saying 'No' and returning me."

I lie awake into the night, listening to the soft exhalations of his breath as he sleeps. A Rumi poem slips into my mind:

Pale sunlight,
pale the wall.
Love moves away.
The light changes.
I need more grace than I thought.

Two days later it's my parent's sixty-fourth wedding anniversary, a Friday. I'm awake very early. My sister calls.

"Mum just died," she says. Silence.

I don't know what the word "die" means. How to comprehend this? How can my mother, on the other side of the world, be gone from this earthly life? I want a bedtime story, a long poem, some powerful music.

When I text Saki with this news, which means I'll be returning to Canada, he understands what must happen. He will take me tomorrow, Saturday, to meet his Spirit Guide, Samaita, of the Zebra clan.

In the meantime, Ann proposes an impromptu farewell soirée this evening, to honour my mother and my unexpected departure on Monday. My friends gather on the Dairy Cottage verandah—Roger with Ann, Mel and Charlie whom I've begun to adore, and dear Janine from the horses in Mavs. It's comforting to sit in their company, to have some food and drink, and to talk a bit about my mum; it's also a relief to listen to the others' comings and goings of the previous week.

I invited Stephen to join us as well, and he arrives later than the others after meeting someone about farrier work. His presence at the far end of the verandah is comforting, too. At least initially, then it dawns on me that he's had too many glasses of wine from the cardboard keg, and talking fervidly to Charlie without pause. I suddenly feel bone-tired, alone, and aching for sleep. Soon Ann and the others get up to leave, and Stephen goes off to find the night security guard who will open the driveway gates for the vehicles to exit. I walk with Charlie and Mel to their car on the other side of the property, they ask if I'll be all right.

"Yes, I'll be fine, no problem," I assure them and head back to my cottage.

When I return to the cottage Stephen is wavering by the door. Every night that I've been in town he has slept here with me. But the door is locked at the moment and he blames me for causing him to fall down and smash his eyeglasses by turning him out of the cottage. Oh, crap, I know there'll be no dissuading him. Looking back, I was surely too exhausted to think of going and finding the security guard.

Just help him into bed, I calculate, and once he lies down sleep will overtake him. But he sits on the side of the bed not shutting up, talking on and on incoherently, and pulling at me when I turn away. I don't know this man. I beg God for silence and comfort.

I feel oddly detached, watching as an observer, curious, wondering why this is happening on the very day my mother has died on the other side of the world. Not overly concerned at this point, I just want to be alone and out of his cacophonous madness that presses in on me. About to finally lie down under the covers. Stephen abruptly decides he wants a cigarette and has none, as usual.

"Let's go to your room and get you one," I say, picking up his jeans and throwing them in his lap.

Outside in the opaque black night he lurches and staggers toward his room by the stable. I'm angry, on the edge of losing my temper, but can imagine the outcome of that. Summoning a patience beyond what I humanly possess, I continue walking beside him knowing that if I turn away he will follow me. The thought of being chased, even with my agile sober advantage, is unbearable. At the door to his room I knock sharply and call to the boys; Emeesh and Hambani are asleep inside. Emeesh opens the door and Stephen crumples onto the floor.

"Your father is drunk. I am afraid of him. Please keep him here for the night. Make sure he does not come out."

Back in my room, I phone the guesthouse office. The night receptionist is supposed to be on duty, the one meant to answer calls and summon the security patrol. No response. My bedside light is still on. Oh, no. Whispers and quiet tapping at the curtained window, "Eh, bebe…"

The demand escalates, "Eh, eh, bebe!"

Insistent banging on the cottage door. Needing to collect myself, the seemingly safest and least visible spot is on the floor on the far side of the bed. I reassess its distance from the door and lie down flat on my back, knees up, palms down. Get grounded and pray for intervention. Let me find strength and fortitude in the earth, a few moments of stablizing comfort. I can hear that Stephen has moved to the other half of the double door, which is not dead-bolted but held closed by a bent nail on the inside. It can't hold now that the thumping has turned into full-blown pounding.

Rather than be found lying on the floor, I can think of nothing else to do but calmly get up, walk to the door and lean hard against it, my back to the planks, feet braced on the floor. The sound of splintering wood. My bare feet slide into the room and I'm swept with alarm, as if my breastbone pierces the surface of my skin—the only time in Africa I have been afraid.

Stephen's palm and fingers clench my forearm but I single-mindedly cross the room and reach for the phone. This time, dialing Ann directly.

"I'll send Clemens, he is the most conciliatory," she says evenly.

"Security is coming now-now," I say to Stephen, looking him straight in the eye, then, stride forthrightly toward the splintered doorframe and outside into the unconfined night, safe in the open space of the garden.

Stephen is backlit, standing in the doorway, when the beam of Clemens' flashlight snakes across the grass. I move to stand silently behind Clemens and imagine myself invisible to Stephen. Many words pass between them, in Shona, before the two men, who are friends, start off in the direction of Stephen's room. The night guard settles himself into a lawn chair by my ineffectual door; he gives a brief salute as I re-enter the cottage and touches his hand to his heart. I will be safe.

When Saki picks me up at dawn, I see for the first time his shoulder-length dreadlocks, held informally back from his face with a worn blue kerchief that matches his jeans and plaid shirt. I'm wearing a vermillion-coloured cotton gauze tunic from India, found in a thrift store long ago and now soft with wear. Stephen calls it the bedroom dress, which is where he first saw it on me; I think he means nightgown. My mother values beautiful fabric and dressing up for special occasions, and feels very present with me, more so than if she were here in the everyday.

Saki's sister, Hessy, is beside me in the backseat of the car; I haven't met her before, and she is very quiet. She wears a long, straight, gray knit skirt over her jeans. Women don't wear trousers in a village, I know. When I gesture to my knee-length tunic, balloon trousers underneath, Hessy nods. Their friend Stanley sits in the front with Saki; he talks about peace and love and sings softly all through the two-hour drive to Samaita's homestead in the rural area. When the car stops at the only collection of *dzimba* visible in the flatland, it's impossible for me to tell which direction we came from, or where on a map we would be.

Six young men sway under a thatch shelter as I kneel on the cement floor. Each holds an enormous, hollow, bowl-shaped gourd shell. Inside the gourd resonator is a handmade musical instrument—metal tines fixed on a square wooden board—and the young players pluck the tines, articulating a doorway into the realm of trance. This is an Mbira Orchestra—Shona music of Indigenous Zimbabwe, welcoming us to their village. I close my eyes and put my hands across my chest as if holding my mother, pure mbira-spirit massaging swollen heart. The burnished, harp-like melodies, honey and silk, thread a stairway to heaven and open the way for her, mum, to go.

A hand touches my shoulder. Samaita. He's not an old man, maybe in his forties with short dreadlocks, wearing a western shirt and trousers, unusual patchwork fabric vest, and a well-worn cowboy hat. He accepts the small, frivolous gifts I've brought—a gourmet chocolate bar, a bottle of fruit juice and some biscuits. He opens the little zip brocade bag I offer and examines the set of divination sticks I carved, each finger-length twig with an intuitively-felt pattern inscribed into the bark. He addresses me in Shona. Saki translates.

"You are powerful; a seer, with more contribution to make, yes? Why are you not doing that in a bigger way?"

Without thinking I reply, "What would my mother think?" And then, "Oh. She has passed away now." After a pause I continue, "Well, recently, there have been concerns of self-diminishment."

"Never mind this self of yours," Samaita counsels. "It is not about you. It's about the Ancestors and the spirit world. You are simply the medium. Yes, it's fine that you make prayers and offer-ings, but you must celebrate the spirit world—singing, dancing, laughing, and thanking them. You don't have to tell people it's for the Ancestors, but you must tell the Ancestors the celebrations are honouring them."

Samaita leaves the pavilion with Saki, Hessy and Stanley for their healing treatments, I imagine. I'm left alone with the Mbira Orchestra. As the young musicians play on and on, the spiraling streams of golden-sweet sound reset my nervous system. I am being unwrapped and tenderly held in an ocean of loving-kindness. And it seems that my mother's presence, so palpable in the car and upon arriving here, is dispersing.

Another hand on my shoulder. Saki invites me to come into the Spirit House. I haven't noticed the structure before, although it's in plain sight. The warm tawny colour of the thatch roof means it's quite new. My friend motions to an empty place on the circu-lar earthen floor beside Hessy, who sits on a black animal skin, mbunzi, goat. Saki walks across the light-filled space, about five metres, to sit beside Stanley on another black goatskin. Samaita sits opposite the door on a low Tonga stool, a zebra skin covering his place on the floor, a basket of other animal skins, leopard, nearby.

The spirit guide fixes his attention on me; his instructions are very clear, perhaps the same for everyone:

"You must wear black and white beads when working."

The long strand of seed beads given to me by Stephen last year encircle my wrist.

"You must have the colours yellow, green and gold visible when doing your work."

A tiny polished deer bone nestles in my medicine bag—it's wound in a shiny yellow satin strip, then wrapped with a green Tibetan prayer flag and tied with gold thread. My hand moves to my chest where the medicine bag is tucked into my bra, since I have no pockets today.

"The guidance of our Ancestors is part of that wilderness preservation project you are asking me about. The dream will come true only if you, and the others, are aware of the spiritual significance of the place and act accordingly.

"You will return to Zimbabwe," he tells me.

"The stories you are writing, they are not your stories but messages from the ancestral spirits that want to be heard—a book is the beginning and there is a big contribution to make if you understand this."

I ask about a special friendship, without naming Stephen, and my desire to act with integrity.

"It is not for you alone to determine," Samaita says. "There are two involved. If you are aligned in spirit, it will be a life-long friendship; if not aligned, then it won't go anywhere, but it is not up to you alone."

Sometime later, all of us rest on worn, upholstered furniture in the household sitting room eating brown beans on enamel metal plates. Kids of all sizes peek at us through windows and doorways. In the car driving back to Harare we're silent, until Saki invites me to meet his parents at their home.

*The Geography of Belonging*

Dusk settles in the walled garden as the four of us get out of the car and enter from the driveway. Hessy's young daughter stands beside a marula tree laden with golden ripe fruit and she drops the aromatic plummy balls into an enamel basin. I follow Saki along the stone walkway onto a dry lawn bordered with broad-leaved shrubs. Saki introduces me to his parents, along with the news from my own family in Canada, the news of our loss. He asks me to sit down in a wire garden chair beside his father. The elder Mr. Mafundikwa extends his right hand in welcome. Frailty, so like my own father, as he struggles to rise up from his chair. I reach out to hold his offered hand and can't help but kiss the gnarly, veined top of it.

The softness of Baba Mafundikwa's skin is a surprise, his palm, smooth and slightly cool, rests on mine. Then, his left hand mirrors the slow motion of an imaginary butterfly alighting on the back of the hand I hold; he pinches a fold of his skin and releases it, marveling at the loss of elasticity.

"It's painful," he says, "the changes that come with old age."

I hear the soft click of Saki's digital camera and notice that my cheekbones are wet. Baba remains in his chair and leans closer to me.

"Your mum is gone; she is home with the Ancestors. Your father is alone, and in your care. This is God's plan; you must look to the future and know you are guided—just follow the path before you."

Being in the company of a precious elder on the threshold, I find the pressure under my breastbone eases a little, and weariness floods in. Hessy brings out glasses of pale, amber-coloured tea and hands them around. On the stone walkway as I leave, Saki's mother gently takes hold of my arm and guides me toward the car saying over and over, "I am so sorry for the loss of your mother. Shame, shame."

This is our first time in one another's company, yet she is the one weeping. When Mama Mafundikwa turns to me and opens her arms, I rest my whole self on her wide, soft body. My breathing deepens with the amber fragrance of her skin, and my feet feel stable on the ground.

In the early evening back at my cottage, Roger, who hovers on the cusp of dementia, comes to the outside of my open window.

"Everything seems gentle," he says, addressing the sky, the flower in his hand, the trees and the birds.

Shortly after, Stephen comes by and asks if he might speak with me. We sit on the verandah chairs under the fluorescent light, purposely visible to all. He is ashamed, repentant, almost broken. I'm not taken in by his profuse apologizing, which is standard in the aftermath of a drunken episode. At the same time, I feel a neutral open-heartedness, as with kids who've misbehaved. And I wonder, again, about this event coinciding with my mother's passing away.

As the black and white storks fly overhead, coming to settle in the gum tree, Stephen begins a story:

"Today, early morning, when you go with Saki, I myself go to Mrs. Hamilton King to talk. She orders cups of tea. Clemens and the other manager too, four of us sitting together. Mrs. H. K. says to me, "You intimidate Oriane and you are drinking my wine, so you can pay for that wine." I say, Okay, I pay for the wine. But I didn't pay and she never asks me. That white guy I met for talking yesterday did buy me three strong beer, then three glasses wine. Yes, I was overdrunk when I came to your party. I was already overdrunk from that guy. I am very shame. You can go to jail when you drunk like that. It's a police case. But the staff here, they know me, so didn't call the police.

"Mrs. King says to me if she tells my boss, the horse madam, I can lose my job. But I tell her after-work hours is not part of job. When Oriane needed accommodation, I haven't got house for my friend to stay, so I bring my friend to your guesthouse."

*The Geography of Belonging*

Stephen shifts in his wicker chair, adjusting the cushion behind his back so that he is facing me. He continues.

"In our culture when my mum dies, I am supposed to stay alone, not go with people, bad systems coming if not alone after mum die because the wind from passing away of the dead person can come to you, and it can get bad from other people around.

"Yes, the very day your mother passed away the bad wind came to you from me. When your relatives die someone can be harsh to you, so you must stay to the home. That bad wind causes bad things to happen. Like what I did. But, you know, then people can talk after and make friends again. Like now.

"When that wind comes and it's bad, you are not supposed to give it power. Don't talk and talk and make it bigger. Say thank you, and go away. Like you, go away with Saki this morning after that bad wind I brought. All day you are not here so I am thinking—what I did yesterday is not good. So, when you come back, we can sit here now and I listen to your bad wind story about what I did. Say very sorry for what I did. Because if I didn't say sorry to you, when I leave my mum's house when she is serious sick something bad can happen on my way home, then I know my mum pass away because of my shame, I will know."

Over the weekend, before my flight home on Monday, the yard enclosing my cottage is the scene of extravagant flower arranging for a wedding on the guesthouse grounds. White calla lilies and creamy iceberg roses, scented jasmine, vines of greenery, all soaking in the oval pond. I think of my sister at home taking care of practicalities, while I'm immersed here in the spiritual passage of my mother, bathed in beauty. A soft tap on the doorframe—Zoni, one of the staff, holds a huge bowl of brilliant orange and purple bird of paradise blooms, one of my mother's favourites, for my verandah table.

Emeesh and Hambani, Stephen's sons, come by too. "Hallo mama, we have come to say good-bye to you." I invite them in.

"Your father will be sad after I go, please care for him well," I say. "He has always looked out for you, and now you are grown men who can look after yourselves and your own families. It's your turn to look after Baba."

To Hambani I give my headlamp and extra batteries, much easier to see into the cooking pot than by the flitting candlelight that drips by the fire. To Emeesh I give a small solar-powered desk light with a socket for charging cell phones. His wife can earn a little money by recharging phones for people in their village.

With an hour to myself, I need to repack my big, rolling duffle bag and the smaller black carry-on. The vivid red and pink of my mother's headscarf flares up as I empty everything out of the two bags. Mum gave it to me when I was last with her, and I had decided to give it to Stephen's mother. He and I were supposed to go to his mother's homestead in a village near Kadoma so I, "the last wife," could meet her. We haven't gone yet, nor have we gone to Chinhoyi or Chiwiti to see the rest of his family—where he is highly regarded—as we did last year.

We've only been together here in town where madams and bosses draw the lines in Stephen's life. Have I been naïve to imagine being able to reconcile our deep place of soul meeting, with my continual wrangle in the day-to-day challenge of finding common ground with Stephen in an essentially segregated society?

On the way to an equestrian competition with his horse owners, for instance, I rode in the car while Stephen stood in the horsebox towed behind. He stayed with the other grooms in the showground stables, had white bread and coke for lunch, while I sat in the stands with the white competitors and horse owners and shared their midday chicken sandwiches. I took Stephen a hamburger from the food concession in the afternoon, then felt badly that I hadn't brought hamburgers for every groom in the stable block.

It was an awkward walk back and forth between the grandstand and the stables.

Yes, there is the black and white divide, but even more divisive is the economic hierarchy delineating those in material poverty and those with financial means. They don't mix, in Zimbabwe, just as they don't most everywhere. I have not managed to bridge the two worlds, hand in hand with Stephen. Nor has he stood beside me when we are in white company together; he stands behind, defers to anyone with more…more what?

I've plunged into the tragedy of this 21st century polarized world: the disparity between "haves, and have-nots"—whether of education, money, inheritance, or power. And equally true, haves and have-nots of generosity, benevolence, compassion, inclusion and kindness.

I stand with my feet on two shores, legs spread wide, about to collapse. Yes, I can step into Stephen's world and feel at home, but for months, or years, on end? And it's achingly clear that Stephen is unable, in himself, to stand equal beside me in a world beyond what he knows. Would this be different in Canada?

Beyond that, how can we make a life together when so much that I value is not part of it—even the simplest of things like written correspondence, conversation about world affairs, awareness of time zones? Can the deepest intimacy—feeling known in the essence of my being, entirely at home in myself with Stephen, the trust and safety we have established—override the shadow and light our way?

I feel heartsick with failure, and about leaving Zimbabwe with these questions hanging. I run across to the stable and find Stephen sweeping the last bit of manure from a stall. He straightens up, and I tuck the scarf into the pocket of his baggy work trousers.

"For your mother, a gift from mine."

In the evening, I walk in the dark with a small bundle in my hands toward the smell of wood smoke, and find Edward, the guesthouse security guard, warming his hands. Garden debris blazes within a circle of stones. Log stumps are spaced at intervals around the fire pit and Edward sits on the one nearest the hedge; he motions to a seat near him. This is my final night in Africa.

"Evening, madam." Edward takes his baseball cap off and holds it across his chest. "God bless you in the big loss of your one mother. May the Ancestors welcome her and may your mama rest forever in peace, in heaven."

I show him the creation in my hands: the now-dried flowers, handwritten notes of sympathy, a green prayer flag folded into a thick ribbon—all tied with maputi-bark twine around the cream-colored pillar candle that's been burning over these few days since mum left this world. Edward appraises the collection and nods; I lean over the heat and place the offering in the fire, step back, and watch as it begins to flame. A slow burning of candle-wax, flowers, fabric and paper; a curl of smoke rises in a lazy spiral, like the cigarettes my mother exhaled when I was a kid, but this time, the fragrance of woodsmoke and roses.

On the morning of my departure day, I keep the scheduled meeting with Chipunza. We were to sketch out my role as an international volunteer documenting the Mavuradonha Wilderness Heritage project. He has arranged a desk for me in the office, in addition to extended time out in the field in Mavs. In the rawness of losing my mum, I can hardly bear the prospect of not being involved in what matters most—preserving the wild. But I collect myself and tell Chipunza of my mother's death. Then, I put this to him:

"Given that I'm going home to Canada now, what is the next step?"

I imagine he'll come up with something I can do, remotely, by email and Skype. Chipunza, however, leans over his desk and looks at me, his short dreadlocks backlit in the bright window behind him.

"What you must do for yourself—and for us—is to go home and honour your mother's passing. Attend to her Ancestor spirit. Reconstitute yourself. And come back to Zimbabwe reconstituted."

Returning to the guesthouse, I stand by the little pond in front of the Dairy Cottage, deep-pink roses in my hand. One by one I loose each petal from its stem sending it in a slow drift onto the clear surface of the pond. And, I remember. Sitting in my car on the ferry, two months ago, sobbing into the steering wheel, overtaken by a crushing shadow.

Stephen comes by on his mid-morning break from work and accepts the fragrant flower I hold out to him. He delicately detaches a single rose petal, then, opening his thumb and forefinger lets it fall to float on the water. Rose petals drift onto the pond, and my throat goes sore, hearing him softly repeating *Hambani, mushe*, Mama. *Hambani, mushe,* Mama. Months ago, I found the English translation for Stephen's surname, *Hambani*: fare well, it means; go nicely. *Mushe* means all that is good and beautiful. Fare thee well, good Mama.

Mel has come with the car to take me to the airport. Ann, waiting by the cottage gate, says to me, "Look behind you."

All of the groundskeepers, gardeners, security guards and stable grooms are walking together up the sandy drive toward us. Each in turn, hat in hand, bows his head, wishes me well and offers condolences for my mother. Tears slip from my cheeks onto the red earth path. Ann beams tenderly, and with a slow sweep of her arm includes everyone,

"This is Africa," she says. "This—is Africa."

# Dorje Ling and the Stardust Ballroom

"We'll have to get rid of your mother's ashes when your sister comes back"

"Okay, Dad, what would you like to do?" I ask.

"She liked the water, we could put them in the ocean. Maybe we'll drive to Port Townsend and dump them off the pier."

"I'll check the tide tables, Dad, it would have to be an outgoing tide."

"Oh, that's right. We wouldn't want her coming back to shore. Maybe a boat would be better."

I can't quite tell if his sense of humour is showing or not. The liquor cupboard is still fully stocked; the exotic or large bottles are at least seven years old, packed from Arizona when mum and dad moved to Sequim where they didn't know anyone. They were tired after the move, their energy significantly diminished, and their social life just didn't pick up.

Tactfully I ask, "What should I do with the alcohol, Dad, pour it down the sink?"

My father hasn't had a drink since 1976, another story.

"Oh, no. I'm going to take it to the Lodge. I might have people over!" I'd better retrieve the ice bucket and the crystal tumblers out of the thrift store donation box.

"You never know, I might get married again."

"Any prospects at the Lodge?"

"No, they're all old ladies over there. Except for that attractive blonde on the front desk, she's nice. But she has school age kids, I think she's married."

My sister Tracey has been back with us for a few days, with her welcome efficiency. We've got the paperwork under control and she's going home later today. The weather is overcast and windy. Dad seems restless.

"Where did you put that box with your mother's ashes?"

"Right here, Dad, beside the tulips, under the stack of sympathy cards."

"Can you find Captain Charles phone number on the internet? Your mother and I went on some boat rides in his water limousine last summer."

A few minutes later I hear Dad at his desk, asking Captain Charles how long ahead he needs to reserve a trip. "Oh, two weeks? What about this afternoon?"

He comes back into the living room. "Tracey, you bring the ashes and the dog. Lee, you go buy some flowers, a bunch of them, colourful ones." Dad's little Yorkshire terrier, Wild Bill Cody, is panting by the front door.

Within an hour, Dad is safely wedged in a high swivel seat beside Captain Charles as we leave the John Wayne Marina. It looks pretty rough out there. Tracey sits at the back of the boat under the zip-on rain awning, holding the dog in her lap. I'm standing up in the centre of the boat, hand on a rail, with knees bent, bracing in anticipation of a bumpy ride. As soon as we hit the open water the powerful outboard motor surges, propelling us at high speed across a very choppy ocean passage.

The thrill of riding the tumultuous green-gray peaks and troughs of seawater brings back memories of our ocean adventures as a young family. Dad opens up to Captain Charles, telling him about the scary rides around Ocean Falls in our open dinghy with the small outboard engine. He was scared, he says, because he can't swim; mum loved the boat because she'd been a champion competitive swimmer. Today Dad says, grinning, "Your mother would have hated this ride!"

By this time Tracey is queasy and clutches the dog to her stomach. Dad sits upright, beaming and energized. Captain Charles is intent on finding a protected spot calm enough to stop, so we can release mum's ashes to the wind and water. I'm in a little conversation with mum to steady myself on the stormy ocean of today.

"Thank you, mum, for having two children so I don't have to do this alone."

I'm grateful, too, for her quick and clean death—and to be honest, for going before Dad. He's so easy to get along with, and much easier to please.

"Thank you, Mum, thank you, *Meitta bassa, tatenda.*"

Thank god, too, that I had the foresight to stuff a pair of scissors in the square black plastic box that holds Mum's remains. The plastic bag inside is thick and fastened with a metal clamp. The boat is idling now, though still rocking precariously. Tracey stands up, lurching beside me, Cody in the crook of her arm.

"Just dump them out!" she cries, "Hurry up! Here, take the flowers, throw them over too!"

I lean over the side of the boat to pour the sand-like remains into the water—but the wind blows the particles back into my face like a dust storm, covering my hair and shoulders. Dad chuckles in his quiet way, and seems to be having the time of his life.

What I had imagined as an orchestrated holy ritual is over before we know it. The words I'd rehearsed, unspoken. Captain Charles abruptly opens the throttle, the bow of the boat spears up and we plow through waves again, a cloud of mineral ash and tulips trail on the ocean surface receding like a party that's over.

Back at the boat dock Tracey hands over the dog, accepts the Kleenex I offer, wipes her eyes and sets off on the drive back to Vancouver. I try not to cry my way through dinner at home with

Dad, and when I say to him, "I feel sad right now, how are you?" He says just what he usually says, "Fine."

I miss Africa intensely. Dad, on the other hand, lives pretty much in the present moment, and is not looking back. His mind is as finely-tuned as ever, and our next steps are in place. He seems to be looking forward to his move to the seniors' lodge, though when we find early photos or their marriage certificate or something like that, he willingly tells a story or two in a matter-of-fact reporting way. Marge, their wonderful neighbour across the street, bless her heart, thinks he'll continue to be fine.

Mother's Day. The park is quiet in the late afternoon, fragrant with springtime and open to the sky. A delicate green weeping willow tree shades a shallow pond, merganser ducks and Canada geese cruise lazily on the surface. Cody, the dog, has ridden with me to the park in his carrier bag that I have strapped to hang from the bicycle handlebars. After I lift him out and we walk for half an hour, I lie down on the grass while he intently sniffs a four-foot radius around me. I'm trying to come to terms with the fact that I do not have a home, or a lifestyle with routine and order, into which I can welcome my father. I wonder, if I'd been immersed in African family-centered culture sooner, would I have planned differently for this stage of life? The waning sun warms my shirt-front and fatigue slips into the day. More tears come.

Devon turns up one day after a long bus trip to get here. I hear him in the den with Dad.

"What are these, Grandon? They look like war medals."

Indeed, they are, the ribbons and crosses from my father's service in the Royal Canadian Air Force in World War II that my sister preserved in a handmade frame one Christmas. After some conversation I can't hear, Devon comes rushing out to show me a brocade box in his hand.

"Look, mum! Grandon's given me the Porritt family seal, for his surname. The crest with the stag head that means to bear wisely and bravely! Do you know how much this means to me?"

I do. Devon's father is adopted and has no family history.

The house sells, I move across the street to Marge's. Tracey returns with her husband Rick and all five of us enthusiastically produce a festive Saturday morning garage sale. How different it would be if Tracey and I had to do this sometime in the future, after losing Dad, too. Instead, freed of our mother's at-times-dampening presence, we enjoy ourselves immensely and I can feel Dad's former emotional reserve melt away, How to describe the feeling of no resistance, no obstruction, between us? A prayer from my spiritual friend and mentor, Thomas Atum O'Kane:

My heart has become an ocean, Beloved
Since thou hast poured
Thy love into me.
And for my father:
Since thou hast received my love for thee.

One day, Dad announces it's time for me to leave for a while, so we can see how he fares on his own.

## CORTES ISLAND, CANADA

It's good to be back in the familiarity of Cortes Island, staying at Dorje Ling, a modest dharma meditation centre in a forest hillside clearing. A little rustic and haphazard, it was built by my friend Kenny who used to work on movie sets and has traveled in Asia. The mainland mountain range, visible across the ocean strait to the east, is reminiscent of the Himalayas, he says.

At night I sleep on the roof of the meditation hall, climbing the narrow steps flashlight in hand. I lie on a pile of cotton quilts with the quivering dark sky a raven black blanket sequined with stars. Tattered prayer flags swish-rustle in the gentle wind and brass bells echo softly from the cedar trees in back. Every dendrite in my body thrums, as the star sequins sew themselves onto my skin.

One mid-morning I happily recommence work on the text revision of Borrowdale Manor's website with my laptop on a plank table by the open balcony door. My cell phone rings, a call from Dad's seniors' residence:

"Your father has fallen, he's conscious and on his way to the hospital. His dog is with a neighbour, Marge."

Stay calm, I say to myself, stay put for the moment and see what is called for. I cannot get to Sequim from Cortes Island leaving at this time of day, besides, tonight I've planned a fundraising presentation for the horses in Africa. I phone the hospital, the same hospital in which my mother died. Dad is stable. Closing my eyes, stilling my heart, it seems right to carry on with the day here, to keep checking in about Dad's condition, stay in touch with my sister, and leave early tomorrow morning.

When I walk into the hospital room, Dad is propped up in the metal-railed bed, earnestly reporting on his long night lying awake, immobile on the wooden bench of a speeding train. That fits with ten hours on the bathroom floor of his suite and the disorientation of an ambulance ride. His body seems to be unbroken however, so he'll be transferred to a nearby rehab centre to regain his balance and improve his mobility. Let's keep this as normal as possible, I think to myself. "I'd like to take him in the car." Good, the physician agrees. We'll stop and get a raspberry smoothie at Dad's favourite drive-through take-out on the way.

A few days later, Dad is enjoying round-the-clock attention at the rehab centre, with the goal, he says to the physical therapist, of walking his little Yorkie to the marina again. Cody has been a lifesaver for Dad, a bundle of doggie love and purpose; when my

*The Geography of Belonging*

parents moved in their early 80's to Sequim from Arizona, they gave up golf. In the new community, their social life now had no source, so Dad found Cody, a one year-old Yorkshire Terrier, the cutest four pounds of fur we'd ever seen. They went to Pet Therapy training classes and joined the Olympic Gentle Paws Therapy Dog club.

Today is Tuesday and the weekly activity sheet posted on the wall shows the Gentle Paws group is scheduled to visit the rehab centre this morning, serendipitous timing—a once in every two months rotation. How will it go with Dad on the receiving end this time? I wheel him into the activity room with Cody on his lap, setting them in the semi-circle of eight other residents, waiting.

The padding of soft paws coming down the hallway. The tinkling of metal dog tags.

"Oh, Don, how wonderful to see you!"

"Cody, we've missed you, little buddy!"

A golden retriever trots straight over as Cody bounces up and down on Dad's lap. The two of them sniff and wag their tails in a delighted reunion. As the other dogs settle, Cody seems anxious to resume his usual Gentle Paws duties, and I lift him down to the floor. He makes a beeline for a child-sized white-haired woman crumpled sideways in her wheelchair, her eyes are closed, hands tied into white cotton gloves. When I lift Cody lightly onto her lap, he lies down there, and I kneel on the floor beside them. Only her hands begin to move, slowing finding their way to the curve of Cody's warm and tiny form. He begins to lick her naked wrist. Dad has nodded off, the sweetness of a faint smile lifting the ends of his thin moustache.

When I return to the rehab centre in the afternoon, Dad is resting in bed after the morning exertion.

"Dad, Tracey and I want you to come to Victoria, we need you close by. There's a place for you in the Lodge where mum's old friend Isabel lives. I'll find a home for Cody in the neighbourhood, he'll be able to come and see you. You can go to the dining room, or have meals brought to you, someone will bring your medication and vitamins every day. Your extra health insurance is valid in Canada—you'll have more personal attention through the day and someone to help with all the little things that are tough for you to do."

Dad looks up at me. "Do you think my reclining chair will fit in Tracey's car?"

After dinner, having phoned our family with the good news of Dad's imminent move to Victoria, I return to the rehab centre. Dad is tucked up in bed wearing a white T-shirt, he looks child-like and content resting on the three pillows arranged beneath his head and shoulders. The curtains are still open, the muted glow of early evening watercolours the walls. Some unnoticed tension in me softens, and tenderness blooms in the room.

"Hey Dad," I say, gently holding his hand, supporting his palm on mine.

"Everyone is over the moon you're coming to Victoria. It means the grandkids who don't have passports can see you, your sister Oriane Jane can get there easily too, from Vancouver. Tracey and Rick can take the seaplane over from Vancouver in twenty minutes, and I'll be close by on the farm in Goldstream, half an hour away. All of us are thrilled about you being closer.

"So next week I'll go home to the farm for a few days and get everything in order while you're in good hands here continuing the physical therapy. It'll be easy. Then we'll come and get you."

Dad pats my hand and doesn't let go, "That's great. Thank you."

He who has kept everything together for the sixty-two years I've been around allows me now to care for him. The television on the bureau is tuned to the country music channel. Dad loves it because he finds the perfectly turned-out women so attractive, and I love it because the guys sing romantic songs with tremendous conviction. An hour passes with me in a comfy chair beside Dad, my feet up on the bed. We're still holding hands.

"I guess you can go now."

"Okay Dad. See you in the morning. I love you."

"Me too."


In the morning I wake up with the happy purposefulness of having a plan. It's a beautiful morning. Cody and I are on our way out the sliding patio door. The phone rings.

"Dad died."

Why is Tracey telling me this on the phone from Vancouver? I'm right here in Sequim. The stream of early morning sunlight into the living room brightens, dust specks float in the still air. Cody looks at me intently from the doormat outside the patio door. A young woman in brown overalls is cleaning a lawnmower in the courtyard.

"Let's go, Cody."


Dad rests in bed with his clothes on, a pale blue blanket up to his chest. The collar of the new plaid shirt that Tracey mail-ordered, with velcro under the non-functional buttons, is open at the neck, his white T-shirt peeks from underneath. Lifting Cody onto the bed, I lie down beside Dad, gently slide my arm under his head and put my other hand on his heart. Only Cody and I are breathing. My forehead rests on Dad's temple. Does he know he is gone? Cody licks my father's face.

A long while later, a soft tap on the door and the nurse, wearing pastel mauve wrinkle-free pants and blouse, comes in.

"He was up and shaving in the bathroom this morning. We had his clothes laid out, a different shirt, but he wanted this new plaid one instead, the gift from your sister. The nursing aide wheeled him to breakfast, he was eating bacon she remembers as she glanced over and noticed his head falling backward. She brought him back here and we laid him in bed. I held his hand and kept my other hand on his heart. In a few breaths he was gone."

*Dorje Ling and the Stardust Ballroom*  225

The nurse's hand has been resting on my shoulder. Cody curls up on Dad's stomach and the nurse quietly leaves us.

Dear Dad. How—I—love—you. How I love you, how I love you...

Thank you for these beautiful timeless days, allowing me to love you, pouring your love into me. Thank you for gifting Devon with the family crest, and staying around for Mum; taking care of business so Tracey and I wouldn't have to sell the house and all the other legal affairs by ourselves. You're free now, no more junk mail to answer, no more weekly blood tests, no more prescriptions to fill. I miss you now, I will miss you and miss you and miss you. I am here for you, however long your passage takes. You're not here, on earth, anymore Dad, you know.

I close my eyes and the pillow soaks under my cheek. The room is adrift in the dark shimmer of timeless deep space. I want to stay here forever, just here. Eventually Cody stretches and puts his nose to my ear, sniffing. My eyes open and I notice the tube of organic massage cream on the bedside table beside the tiny moustache trimming scissors. Carefully I slide the signet ring with the Porritt family crest off Dad's right ring finger. Undo the strap of his wristwatch.

One last time, I tenderly caress my father's papery-skin hands, still supple and warm. And then his feet, his soft and precious blue-veined feet, just as I've done every day we've been together over these few months.

After carefully putting his socks back on and smoothing the blanket, I move about the room gathering his things. His two bags fit easily into the basket of the walker with wheels. Cody rides on the seat and we head down the hallway to the parking lot. The sky is cloudless blue outside. The petals that have enclosed us all morning fall open in the warm sunshine. Cody hops into his bed in the car and I go back into the building to my father.

I slide a thick square of foil-wrapped chocolate, his favourite ultra-dark, into the breast pocket of his plaid shirt. I tuck into the pocket as well, the straight slender stems of fresh lavender, fragrant with remembrance of Mum. I lean over and press my lips to cool forehead, lay my head on motionless chest. Close my eyes. Through the open patio door, two birds in song. Their melody fades and I rise up, hands on my heart, and bow to my father, "Bye Dad, see you around."

It's been a few days and I'm still staying in Dad's suite in the seniors lodge with Cody, attending to the prescribed arrangements that follow death. Tracey has come and gone, needing some time at home to regroup before returning to clear out the suite by month's end. Devon, too, brought solace for a few days.

This hot summer Sunday afternoon finds me at the local casino, in the cabaret, shiny silver mirror ball seeming to set the dark ceiling in motion. Dad's tablemate in the Lodge dining room has invited me to come dancing. Why not? Charlie is 92 and his lively girlfriend is 83; this is the weekly gathering of the Stardust Dancers. Onstage, a live 18-piece big band plays Dad's favourite kind of music. I feel perfectly at home, in a happiness infusion, all the tunes are familiar from my years with Devon's jazz musician father. At first, I hesitate when invited to dance.

"I'm afraid I don't know the steps."

Charlie, undeterred, offers his hand and waits for me to stand up. Darn, I'm wearing jeans; all the other women are spiraling the room in flowing skirts and dancing shoes. Charlie is a little unsteady on his feet, so we do a smooth sway-shuffle in place, mirror ball glittering off his glasses.

Seated again, sipping my cranberry and orange juice soda, I sense another approach— baggy jeans, short-sleeve white shirt untucked—another hand extended in invitation.

"May I have this dance?"

"Mmmm, I don't really know the steps."

"May I teach you?"

Tom is a fantastic dancer and my body memory does know the steps. Fifty years ago, Dad, a very classy dancer himself, would put the vinyl LP's on the turntable, lower the needle and I'd stand in socks on his feet. He had natural elegant rhythm and timing, whirling, dipping, slowing down—enthralling meld of music and motion. The basement rumpus room turned into girlhood heaven.

Here I am again, spinning around the ballroom, the guiding pressure of Tom's hand on my back, the leaning in or yielding of his shoulder against mine, my right temple brushing his jawline, a streaming blur of colour as other dancers swirl by. In this comforting universe my eyes close; a slow sigh, the aching tension in my face evaporates. Somewhere in the ballroom, joyous giggling overlays "Fly Me To The Moon". Eyes wide open now, it's clear that I'm the one laughing, my sure-footed dance partner twirling us with measured abandon. I'm not dizzy, I am ecstatic. Ecstatic!

As I slide onto the leather banquette seat beside Charlie, Tom responds to my enthusiastic "Thank you! Thank you! That was so much fun!"

"My pleasure," he says with a familiar wink that crinkles his silver-gray moustache.

"Your harmonic balancer assembly has fallen apart."

"I beg your pardon?" I respond into the speakerphone, glancing around to Marge with exaggerated horror. I've come to stay with her in Sequim, across the street from my parents' former home, while taking care of some estate legal affairs. Marge whirls her dishtowel in the air.

"Your harmonic balancer assembly has fallen apart and all the drive belts have come off. It's a good thing you didn't keep on driving the car last night or it would've been toast."

The mechanic carries on about torsion and stress, friction, vibration and resonance, all leading to potential crankshaft failure. The crankshaft is the part that drives the car.

Over breakfast Marge suggests that I've been driving myself, not just the car, rather relentlessly. It's true I've been going between Cortes, Vancouver Island, Seattle and Sequim for a few months; but I hadn't recognized this as unwarranted busyness—to relieve the desolate dispossession that faces me when I stay still. And last week I'd been in the doctor's office, only to find that minor surgery is needed to repair a tear in my upper abdominal wall. He put me on a six-month hospital waiting list.

"Have you been doing any excessively strenuous lifting or anything?" he'd asked. "Nope," I answered, putting my hand on the tender area and not considering the dismantlement of my parents' house. "But a few times, sobbing so hard it hurt, here."

"Oh, that wouldn't do it," he said. I disagree.

So now the car is being repaired, but how do I restore my own stressed harmonic balancer? Three days with Marge and Cody while the car is in the mechanic's shop is a good start. Marge sits down to breakfast, knits for pleasure, reads in the afternoon, and relaxes with a glass of wine at 5 pm. And in the evening she especially enjoys hearing my stories of horses in Africa.

I begin to tell her about riding Gizmet to the dam at Siya Lima, with Douglas on Apache trailing Jecha for training.

I'm back in Zimbabwe.

When the horses reach the dam, which is a lake-reservoir constructed for irrigation purposes by the farm owner decades ago, Jecha balks at the water's edge and won't budge. Up till now she's been contently walking beside Apache through the bright green spray-topped reed grass along the shore. Then Douglas turned Apache toward the sparkling water, as if to enter the shallows of the lake. The astute horseman knows Jecha is scared to walk across, or into, any shiny surface in front of her, whether rain puddle or flowing stream. Her head and neck are raised, hyper-alert.

"Come on girl, no problem here for you." Douglas is patient with her, loosening pressure on her taut lead rope with the slightest forward inclination on her part. When she takes a tentative step, he praises her "Good girl, good girl," and slackens her lead rope. Jecha lowers her head and blows out indicating a release of tension. Apache starts to walk again, leading the way and Jecha follows him, tentatively stepping into the water.

As if by silent agreement, all three horses bend their heads to the sun-shiny surface of the lake, lips curled open, and slurp a long guzzling drink. Two blue dragonflies spiral, in tandem, among them. A white cattle egret takes flight from the back of a cow on the far shore and glides above us. When the horses are rehydrated, Douglas lifts Apache's reins and pulls gently on Jecha's lead rope.

"*Unde*, let's go," he quietly commands.

Gizmet lags behind, pausing for a longer drink, and I take my feet out of the stirrups to stretch my legs. The thirsty boy keeps his head down and begins to paw the water with one front hoof, then the other. How wet do I want to get? He's about to lower himself down and roll over.

"Not today, Gizmet!" I burst out laughing, swiftly raising the reins and pressing my heels to his belly asking him to move on, "*Unde!*"

The lakewater sloshes noisily around his knees and soaks my boots as we cruise through the wetland reeds. Veering toward shore and trotting to catch up with Douglas, my trusty buddy Gizmet carries me through the green-bordered footpaths back to the farm. Outside the stable, hovering over the morning's manure pile, tiny butterflies are palest moon blue. The delicate pink bougainvillea petals scattered under the tree in the courtyard seem poised to take flight.

Looking around Marge's living room, I feel envious. It's been a few years since I've had a home to myself—a place to call my own from which to come and go. I imagine sitting in my favourite wingback chair, now in storage at Goldstream Farm, curled up with a pot of tea and a book. My round kitchen table covered with the soft Indian print cloth from my mother and serving salad in the wooden zebra-striped bowl from Victoria Falls. My baskets from Morocco, from France, from southern Africa, and the ones I've made myself.

Talking with Marge, it dawns on me—there just may be the means to do that, thanks to my sister's generosity in apportioning our modest inheritance. And on Cortes Island, unbeknownst to me, my friends have decided to list for sale, next summer, their hand-built cedar home in a light-filled forest clearing.

Mid-winter I'm back on Cortes Island, once again house-sitting my friends' lodge overlooking Desolation Sound. Upstairs, in the bedroom with a view of the bay, I wake in the gray dawn, acutely aware that I have only the natural world for parents. I'm concerned, too, for Devon whose life in Vancouver seems to be unraveling. I picture his goodness as a boy and ask the *vadzimu* to help him stay true to himself. Absorbed by my own loss, I won't understand for another two years that Devon put aside his own grief to be present for mine.

This morning, I rouse myself and sit on the bed, facing the ocean's high tide and begin a meditation practice called Dissolving with the Outbreath. Before long, at the end of each outgoing breath, when I really pay attention, there's a moment, a pause, when nothing happens. And then, the in-breath comes sailing back on its own, as if from the sea. After a time, with each slow exhalation, some essence of me really and truly does deliquesce, and disperse into the ocean's mass.

An odd primeval sound, though the windows are closed, curiously in synch with my breathings. Something. Opening my eyes, a log slightly offshore, a limb or two protruding into the sky.

Carefully putting on my glasses, I see it's not a log—the limb is a dorsal fin!

Orca whales, just beyond the rocks in front of the house, arcing and surfacing in the same slow deliberate gathering and releasing rhythm of my breath—a pod of maybe eight or ten linger. I slip downstairs, pull on a coat over my pyjamas and go outside to stand on the ocean's edge. White-bottomed tail flukes flip slowly upward, dark dorsal-finned backs submerge and reappear.

Suddenly, an up-rushing of water not five metres out—an entire head rises straight up, out of the water, white underbelly glistens. One Orca eye takes me in, then, sinks down. I feel the empty space she leaves in the air, as if half of me is gone; the granite foreshore under my feet seems to swell and trough with the motion of the whales and the waves. How does this synchrony come about? With whom does the entrainment begin?

As the sheening oceanic bodies curve away and traverse the bay toward Mary Point, I clutch my coat around me and sit down on the rocky shelf, otherwise it's too tempting to slip into the deathly cold water, lured by the Orca's call to the deep and the wild.

*Nhemamusasa*: Shona. The place we make our home.

*Nhemamusasa* North: a week-long immersion in Shona musical culture, close by, on Vancouver Island. Mbira and marimba players and teachers from Africa, the North American diaspora and local aficionados; joining them will be my consolation for not going to Zimbabwe. The year has been fatiguing: settling my parents' affairs, fulfilling the spiritual rites of their passage, recovering from the small surgery, then, purchasing and moving to the cottage on Cortes Island. Light comes with the birth of my stepdaughter's darling baby girl—and with settling into my new home in early summer.

On the way to the music festival I pick up my niece's 12 year-old daughter for company, just for today. Mia takes my hand as we walk in to the circular yurt gathering space; smiling faces brighten the room, a woman wearing an orange-patterned zambia gestures toward cushions on the floor.

Who is that striking young man, with feathers in his shiny black dreadlocks, and the voluptuous woman beside him, colourful headband around her wavy long golden-brown hair? Gourd rattle, *hosho*, in hand, Tafadzwa Matamba opens the ceremonial portal this morning, welcoming the Ancestors of every tradition into our musical community. He explains that the Mbira music, our raison d'être this week, is the conversation with the Ancestors, with their unseen presence—a sharing of blessings and offerings between us.

Tafadzwa introduces his Canadian wife, Amy, then passes the *hosho* to her and picks up his mbira.

"Traditionally, we play this song, *Nhemamusasa*, for housewarming ceremony. We are saying to the spirits of the land, and to our Ancestor spirits, that we put our home here. So please take care of us, look after us, and we will take care of you."

Beside me, Mia raises her eyebrows and smiles the question, "Really?"

I nod, "Yes, true." She leans against my shoulder; washed in the mbira sound that spirals 'round us and I remember her as a baby, softening into my arms.

Later, I hear from Amy her story of meeting Tafadzwa in Zimbabwe only last year—when I was also there, listening to an mbira orchestra for the first time, at Samaita's homestead. Amy and Tafadzwa fell in love over the mbira lessons he gave her in their cultural exchange, one music teacher to another. I'm fascinated and we agree to stay in touch.

"May I join you?" It's been a long time since an attractive man about my age, smooth silver hair and warm handshake, has turned his attention to me.

"Yes, please do," I say indicating the chair across the picnic table from where I sit with a lunch plate of *sadza* and beans.

Later in the afternoon, on a moss-covered bluff away from the festival events, we sit with two mbiras. I learn a simple melody in tandem with my charming tutor. Then, unexpectedly, his playing streams off with harmonies weaving in and around, under and over—into the pure pleasure of feeling airborne, the lift-off that happens when the mind puts itself away. Two eagles spiral above the bluff, wings spread, on an updraft of summer wind.

He listens to the story of the Mbira Stairway that lifted my mother to heaven. I hear about the passing of his own mother, her head cradled by his sister as he wove the mbira melodies that ushered his mum across the threshold. He offers to massage my neck.

"No, thank you." I say quietly.

"Why not?" The velvet green moss underneath us is thick and furry soft, luxurious underlay.

"I have an unresolved love affair in Zimbabwe."

The day after arriving home from the music festival, I lie down on the grass in the shade of the turquoise-blue hydrangea bush. I look up at the sky and try to clear my mind. The moss-bluff mbira tutor has offered to make the trip to Cortes Island to see me. I will decline. It's the one-year anniversary of my father's passing and a few months more since my mother's.

Overhead, wisps of summer cloud drift to the northwest. Two squirrels scurry and chatter in the cedar tree across the fence.

A shivery tremor against my spine pulls my attention to the ground. What on earth? Instantly, I know. The impulse is coming from the cedar tree across the fence, roots shallow and wide underneath me. Cedar—lifeblood of Indigenous, original, culture here on the west coast.

I've been learning more and more about the history, and consequence, of European colonization on this continent, but it hasn't taken hold in me, viscerally, till now—I am making myself at home on the ancestral territory of the Klahoose, Homalco and

Tla'amin people. The ground I lie on is un-ceded land; no treaty agreement in the past transferred ownership, stewardship of this property, to any white predecessor of mine. What does it mean, today, to "honour aboriginal rights and title" when a newly-signed paper names me as owner of this three-acre parcel of land?

When I first came to live on Cortes Island with my young son, three decades ago, I mainly felt like a trespasser, having grown up under the reproachful eye of my don't-bother-the-neighbours mother. Despite being at home in nature and grateful to be on the island, as a newcomer, one with no home of my own at that time, I imagined I was intruding on the people who were here before me: the First Nations, primarily. With hindsight, indeed I was. And I was preceded by four generations of homesteading families since the late 1800s, back-to-the-landers in the 1970s, and more recent transplants from afar. Who, or what, said I deserved to be one of them—to live on this beautiful and sane rim of the wilderness?

One morning, feeling particularly un-rooted, unworthy even, with no family tree on Cortes to claim me, I went for a walk on the beach, feeling quite blue. From above, I heard a commotion, a multitude of familiar raspy *kaw-kaw-kaw*. A throng of crows in the treetops along the shore, keeping pace with me. I continued walking. Were the birds really moving alongside me? Yes.

Were they trying to get my attention?

The blue-black winged-ones were not flying away and when I moved ahead, they moved too, and persisted with their vocalizations. Were they giving me a message from the trees, from the ebb tide, from themselves?

It was June or early July, because I picked a handful of red pearl huckleberries and ate them. I meandered along the beach, threw a few stones in the water, sat on a log—the crow companions above me in the trees, raucous *kaw-ing*. I lay my forehead in my hands and tried to be still, the beach pebbles were warm on the soles of my bare feet.

Then, clear as anything, I heard: "This is your home. Keep listening. Ask the salmonberry if you may pick her, the oysters if you may have them for food. Make friends with the deer."

I stood up from the log, waded into the ocean and looked back at those trees and those birds on the shore. Sunlight shimmered up from the ocean surface, gilding the green cedar branches.

It was after this gesture of inclusion from the wild ones, I think, that I started to grow a garden, to plant seeds for food, to sprout roots.

A few days after lying under the blue hydrangea nearby the cedar tree, my son Devon phones from Vancouver, listens to this story then reflects:

"Mum, what allows us in a place, even claims us—alongside people whose genealogy resides in the rocks and the trees—is a respectful everyday kinship with that place. Like you have with the island."

He sounds wistful as he talks about Cortes Island compared with the demands and limitations of living in a city.

"You know what I miss, most? In the city, the people I know, you can't tell your friends you love them, even my best friend would think that's weird."

My heart aches for him. He tends to underplay himself, and won't accept a promotion at the hotel where he tends bar, not wanting to succumb to the corporate ladder, he says.

Later in the summer when Devon comes home for a holiday, I tell him about my conversation with the mbira player and arrive at: "I have an unresolved love affair in Zimbabwe," he is quick to reply.

"No, you don't. It is resolved. It was resolved when you came back from Africa when Grandma died. After what happened when Stephen was drunk, it's very clear you are not going back to that story."

*The Geography of Belonging*

Ah, the veracity of youth. He's right. Still, there needs to be some further resolution. I cannot miscarry the fruition of this *affaire d'coeur*—in whatever form it comes or however long the ripening takes—whether with Stephen, or with Africa herself.

The Zimbabwe national elections were held last week, July 31st, 2013. The outcome: Robert Mugabe's return to power with a majority vote. This surprised even his own political supporters, according to credible international news sources. Mel and Charlie, back in their family home in Spain, had sobbed in each other's arms, she relays by Skype this morning.

"The Zimbabweans' response," she says, "appears to be dispirited resignation to more of the same despotism in the upper echelons and disintegration of the economy and welfare of the people, on the ground."

I wonder aloud, "What good are sanctions against Zimbabwe by key players in the international community when those leave more room for China's invasion?"

That foreign self-serving plunder of resources—diamonds, gold, chromium, platinum—and desecration of land also fills the pockets of Zimbabwean officials without regard for reparation to the habitats, wildlife and people whose way of life is destroyed.

I wonder, too, with the status quo outcome of the election, what awaits in the monumental assignment of trying to keep the Chinese mining interests out of the Mavuradonha Wilderness protected area.

Mandy Retzlaff is prolific with Facebook posts for Mozambique Horse Safari, and now, too, for her just-released book, One Hundred and Four Horses. One evening in the fall, morning time in southern Africa, I read another of her posts and am seized with concern—their devoted head groom Jonathan Mazulu has returned home to Zimbabwe, very ill. I remember the gift of heart wisdom he gave to me on the beach that first time in Africa.

"I live each day with all my faith and all my love." I have tried to be true to that.

A scant month later, at the same time of evening, Mandy makes a new post: Jonathan has passed away. Gone, for good. I cannot grasp the import of her words, but climb into bed, my face pressed to the pillow in a long-drawn howl. For days I feel this loss acutely, on the heels of my parents' passing. Jonathan, too, enters the realm of the Ancestors. Scores of Facebook comments show how enormously valued he is, was.

I'd anticipated seeing Jonathan again, and something important feels incomplete—so different from the loss of my parents in which I had participated. I imagine a visit to Jonathan's wife and sons at their family home, if it feels right, when I return to Zimbabwe in a few months.

*The Geography of Belonging*

# Africa's Finest: a Disappearance

A third time, I cross the world to meet Stephen in Zimbabwe, and the fourth to affirm my relationship with Africa herself.

"Welcome home, Mrs. Johnston!" smiles Clemens on the Borrowdale guesthouse veranda. The two of us walk together through the gardens to the Dairy Cottage, my home in Harare, led by Stephen who came to meet me at the airport and now carries my big duffle bag and hefty backpack to the doorstep.

Fortuitously, given my conundrum of whether, or how, to navigate our relationship in a different direction, Stephen's work is down the road now, rather than across the lawn. His employers moved their horses to a different stable a short walk away, and Stephen sleeps in a room on the grounds of their residence, in worker's quarters, a half hour uphill bike ride away. I wonder if I'm just overly self-controlled or self-centered, in not asking him to stay the night. But it seems right, to sleep alone these first few nights. He, too, seems to know change is afoot and makes no presumption or demand.

Dinner, *sadza,* the next evening is at Hambani's house, in a laneway nearby the stables. He continues to work with his father and the horses. I follow Stephen along a path off the road bordered by shoulder high green grass, until we come upon the most basic of two-room cement cubicles, where Hambani's unofficial wife is bent over a fire on the concrete porch. No electricity, no running water.

"Tsungi, say hello to *gogo* Oriane," Stephen instructs his four-year-old granddaughter as he crouches to her level on the cement stoop and beckons me to sit down. As soon as she reaches her little hand toward me, and whispers "Hallo, *gogo*," I want nothing more than to be in her company forever. *Gogo*: grandmother. Tsungi's dark eyes, bashful and bright, hold an invitation that swells my heart and opens my arms. And here she stays, on my lap, while neighbours come by and join us in the dusky evening to say hallo to the new lady. Tsungi is not Hambani's daughter, but is the daughter of Emeesh, and she is visiting from their home in the rural area. Almost reverently she examines my pearl earrings, my Buddhist pendant, my eyeglasses, and then, when *sadza* is ready, she slides down onto the ground to share a bowl of food with her cousins.

Stephen and I walk back to the guesthouse when he pauses a moment on the path.

"You are blessing to me, to my family."

"As you are, to me," I sigh.

My God, the ache of a heart on the precipice of loss.

Within a few days of landing in Harare, I go north with Janine to Siya Lima Farm. She stays overnight then returns to town in the morning, but first she lends me a brand-new book that is the most comprehensive, thought-provoking, optimistic and pragmatic analysis of present day Zimbabwe that I've come across.

"Africa's Finest: The most sustainable and responsible safari destinations in sub-Saharan Africa," is a weighty photographic and journalistic treatise by David Bristow & Colin Bell. Preserving the wild as wild is how ethical safari outfits can have a positive influence in 21$^{st}$ century Africa, the book authors propose.

Varden Safari's Mavuradonha bush camp is one of the destinations included in the survey. Settling into residence at the Siya Lima farmhouse, I pore over the book—it responds to all the "why is it like this now?" questions I've accumulated since first coming to Africa. It puts my new friends, Zimbabwean both white and black, in an historical perspective that deepens my understanding of how their lives have gotten "this way." It comes down to land entitlement.

On my first ride out with Douglas, through the grassy hillsides from Nyambare sacred mountain toward the Raphia Palms Botanical Reserve, an eruption of new homesteads along the way look familiar: each with a sleeping *imba* or two, plus thatch-roof cooking shelter, lush green vegetable plot, rows of maize, and foraging goats. When I ask Douglas where these new settlers have come from, he tells me they grew up here and are the now-adult offspring of the families who resettled these agricultural lands during the farm invasions. The next generation has its own young families now.

This time in Africa, less blinded by love, and as I return to the book pages and photographs, something fundamental becomes clear: there are too many people who need, or desire, too many competing things, the least of which is a little scrap of land to grow some maize. And not the least of which is chromium strip-mined from the Mavuradonha earth to bedeck an ostentatious SUV with sparkly bling.

When I turn to the section about Varden Horse Safaris and the Mavuradonha Mountains, the pages are filled with historical and geographical facts about this wilderness, beyond what I've heard from James, or Marvin, or Douglas. I feel especially grounded reading about the sacred nature of the eco-systems, as old as time, and about the present-day spirit mediums, men and women, who maintain the *rushanga*—shrines.

I wonder how the archeologists of National Museums and Monuments of Zimbabwe are progressing in their work to secure Heritage status for Mavuradonha. Douglas tells me he guided the team further into the Cultural Landscape last year in their quest to create an inventory of the natural and cultural sites. He lowers his eyes, and his voice, when describing how the expedition fell short due to unseasonably heavy rains making river crossings on foot or horseback impossible.

Janine reported, with relief, that she and James have a partner now in the lease for the wilderness concession, one who brings badly-needed resources to the cause against the encroaching illegal mining. Their new partner has a viable plan to deter prospectors and poachers, and to restore wildlife in earnest: it starts with a perimeter fence patrolled by game scouts, and later, reintroduction of plains game animals native to Mavs habitats. He intends as well, to invest in upgrading Kopje Tops camp by rebuilding the kitchen-dining room and the tree-level lounge that had burned down.

As I stay longer in Zimbabwe, the contrast between those who live here with optimism, and those who don't, becomes more and more apparent. Some are despairing and hopeless about the state of Africa, and the whole planet, but many I meet savour the beauty of creation and the love in humanity. I ask Ann, when I return to her guesthouse in Harare, what accounts for hope and cheerfulness in her countrymen and women, rather than discouragement and depression.

"People who feel a sense of purpose and accomplishment each day," she replies, "have a more positive outlook, perhaps not about the future, but about today, which leads to the future.

"Of course," she adds, "this is true everywhere, not just Africa."

One warm morning Douglas and I ride our horses through the community lands, this time to check some bee hives, and there's something I haven't seen before. Most of the home sites have a freestanding chimney, maybe five metres high, atop a brick firebox that blazes today with tightly packed logs.

It's tobacco harvest time in the arable regions of Zimbabwe. Those beautiful lush green fields around the homesteads are not food crops, but large-leaved tobacco plants ready for harvest. In the former glory days of agri-business, white farmers operated massive thriving farms that produced premium quality tobacco for domestic use and for export; finely-timed, seasonal plantings, efficient irrigation systems and fertilizer, ensured a profitable return on their substantial investments. At harvest time, the broad tobacco leaves were stacked on racks in two-storey brick drying kilns with a firebox at the bottom. Fires were stoked with coal brought by rail and truck from Hwange. Farm owners and their managers were in attendance throughout the days and nights of the process, to maintain precise temperature so that the leaves were cured to perfection. Never mind one's own ideas about the deleterious effect of tobacco smoke on human health—this was a primary agricultural product and international export for Zimbabwe.

Tobacco farming is a sensitive subject nowadays—post-land invasions—and I tread cautiously with my foreigner curiosity. Initially, in the early 2000s, the new land occupiers mostly had no skill in growing crops, and tobacco production plummeted. Within a few years, contract buyers invested in the new farmers' production costs in advance and provided agricultural training, then paid net proceeds to the growers.

Still, in more remote rural areas like this one, many patched-up or hastily-built kilns are tended by local village farmers and labourers, who squat through days and dark nights around the glowing orange hearth at the bottom of the tall stack. Witnessing this first-hand looks movie-romantic as we ride by this morning, but the reality is chilling. The tobacco kilns are fired with wood from trees cut down for that purpose, ravaging the countryside of irreplaceable prime woodland. It's illegal to cut down Indigenous hardwood trees in Zimbabwe, but some areas of the country observe the law and some don't.

Massacred limbs and trunks lie on the ground as we ride; I try to imagine the compounded volume of firewood used every day for cooking on this continent, and the labour of women and children who collect it from further and further afield. Of course, it's often deadwood, but the ratio of wood fuel needed per family, per day, grows greater with each new generation that overlaps their longer-living elders, while the remaining wood stock diminishes. Now, when I hear the thud of machete on wood while we walk or ride on the land, I'm reminded that the ongoing destruction of remaining native-species woodlands—without living tree roots to bind the land to itself in extremes of wind and rain and drought—portends desertification over time. Where, then, are the habitats for future generations of humans, of animals, insects, and birds?

Douglas brings me back to the present; he takes a pinch of loose tobacco from his shirt pocket and a small scrap of paper that he rips into a rectangle.

"Little bits of tobacco leafs everywhere around, leftovers," he says. "We can roll our own cigarettes. Some guys take this tobacco nobody wants to Mozambique to trade for fish, along the Zambezi River to Cabourra Bassa." He carefully slips the slender twisted roll back into his pocket; with no matches on hand, he saves it for later.

All the while that we've been on horseback this morning Douglas also talks, with real enthusiasm, about his bees. I share his passion—bees everywhere make international news as agrochemical corporations pressure the developed world to legalize pesticide toxicity that will decimate bee populations. Bees, the most prodigious food-plant pollinators on earth.

"My bees know me," Douglas says, as he points out an oblong rectangular wooden box suspended in a mopane tree on a nearby rocky slope.

"If someone else goes to my hives, the bees will sting because that person's smell is different than me. The bees don't want to smell a strange person smell. I wear my clothes from work with the horses so my bees will smell horses and know me."

By now we've ridden to the gate of a well-kept homestead bordering the dam, a verdant and bountiful garden extends to the water's edge. Douglas introduces me to the mature woman who straightens up from her planting and wipes her hands on her faded orange cotton tiered skirt. She wears bubblegum-pink plastic slip-on shoes.

"Oriane, this is Stella."

I hop down from Munhondo and recognize a kindred spirit in her unabashed smile and beautifully articulated English.

"Welcome to my homestead, Oriane. I have been waiting for a friend like you from Canada."

Douglas, too, dismounts, and addresses Stella, "Oriane wants to buy some vegetables from your garden."

Stella picks up a pitted enamel washbasin, "Yes, please! Tell me what you want. I have got tomatoes, green beans, rape, onions."

Fortunately, I know that *rape*, pronounced rrrep by Stella, is a leafy green vegetable in the kale family. Those three years ago when I first went shopping in Harare, it took a while to become used to the hand-lettered signs for rape in the grocery store produce section.

When we've transferred the bounty from her basin into my saddlebags, I look at Stella inquisitively and she says, "I don't know the price. Give me what you want."

When I reach into my pocket and bring out a $20 bill, she glares at it with distaste and says, "I am not a thief! That is too much."

Our eyes meet, then I suggest, "How about I come again another time for more vegetable, and maybe another time, until we agree we are even?"

"Yes, that is good, come back and see me. I want to hear about your country."

"And I want to learn more about yours."

Douglas is not ready to leave and asks Stella to show us her beehives. He continues with his tutorial.

"When I come to inspect Stella's bees, I wear a bee suit, because her bees do not know me. I sit down and observe the hives and the bees, to see if ants and spiders bother them. A spider traps the bees and sucks them; the ants get inside the hives and eat the combs and the honey. So I put old engine oil on the wires that hold the hive in the tree, too slippery for spiders and ants to climb. Then, check for honey, but can't harvest the honey if you see babies. All these things I learnt from the workshop of Honey for Money project."

Janine initiated the "Honey for Money" project last year by securing a funding grant to alleviate basic humanitarian hardships. An immediate benefit is that trees, woodlands, can generate more revenue as bee habitats than as firewood fuel for tobacco-curing. Especially if beehives constructed from recycled planks are suspended in the trees, to replace hollowed-out tree trunks that are usually cut down for that purpose. Honey is a cash crop on the rise in rural Zimbabwe. Together Janine and Douglas enlisted the Siya Lima community in a blossoming enterprise.

A few weeks later when Janine comes up to the farm, the three of us spend a day driving the Toyota Hilux along the backroads to homesteads tucked here and there, to buy honey. I'm especially touched by the quiet pride of one elderly gentleman as he pours the golden liquid honey from his spotlessly clean plastic pails into a five-gallon bucket in the back of the truck, honeycombs and all. And by his gratitude as Janine hands over his cash. Back at the farm, Janine places a pint-size clear plastic jar in my hand. The front of the orange-coloured label, decorated with hand drawn bees, reads:

"Honey for Money. Sustaining Livelihoods Around Wildlife Areas in Zimbabwe."

And the back: "100% Natural Wild African Honey. The Sweet Taste of Africa."

Janine will take an order to Harare when she returns there tomorrow. I buy three jars and will pack them in my riding helmet to protect them on the flights to Canada. And some months after that, it turns out I will hold them up for auction during a presentation of my Zimbabwe stories and videos to raise funds for whatever needs our support here.

"Elixir from the wild of Africa," I will announce with a flourish, "From the bees and flowering trees of Zimbabwe."

Alice, who keeps the Siya Lima farm household in order, brings tea and wash water to my room each morning at 7 a.m., before I go out to the stables. Through the day she and Pension, the cook who after these few years is now a familiar friend, fetch water in the donkey cart, collect firewood, visit neighbours for vegetables or chicken, bake bread, cook for us horse wranglers, do dishes and laundry by hand, and keep the dilapidating house from succumbing to the elements and little critters. The kitchen fire dominates an alcove of the once elegant farmhouse courtyard, blackened pots line the dented cement patio. Greenery of every description grows out of the red clay Spanish-looking roof tiles. Wash water is collected in rain barrels, or in the dry season like now, the borehole pump is run by two mules, who walk in circles around it. Otherwise a little solar power helps: each morning we set out micro-panels to charge in the sunlight. They power portable lamps to cook and read by, seldom-used cell phones, even my laptop.

This homesteading is a lot of work, but it's luxurious-seeming and safe, the feeling of being "somewhere," with the horses outside, the community nearby, and Mavuradonha Wilderness over the hills. We're dry and protected in the farmhouse during the intense thunder and lightning rainstorms. And most refreshing for me—an absence of self-criticism, which highlights how ensnared I am by that, in the familiarity of Canada.

In the evening after dinner, Alice brings hot wash water up to my blue bedroom. She sets the steaming plastic bucket into the middle of the oval non-functional soaker tub, where I can splash myself clean and pour the soapy remainder down my back. Though I've felt uncomfortable in the past with all this household support, there's just too much work required in a day to worry about who does what chores. The argument that this arrangement provides jobs for people, both here and in town, is true enough, but I cannot make peace with the impossibly low wages, yet don't want to skew the local economy by excessive over-tipping that would create expectations of later visitors on the part of the staff. For now, I take a turn at the chores beyond horse care, express my sincere appreciation for others' work and think about how to show this in more tangible ways before I leave.

Today, Alice makes s*adza* for lunch. Usually the vegetable accompaniment, called relish, is pumpkin leaves, or some other kind of greens stewed with fresh tomatoes. The pumpkin leaves are delicious, softer than the chard or kale we eat from our gardens in B.C. But today's green vegetable relish is made of bush okra leaves she collected, which, when cooked, become gelatinous, even mucilaginous. All I can say is that it's exactly like a small bowl of hot nasal snot with bits of chopped up spinach. I try...but can only eat the *sadza*. That's lunch.

By dinner time I've ridden into bush camp to have a night in the wilderness for a change, accompanied by Shepherd who leaves me here and returns to the farm. As the sun drops behind the hills, I join Mafusire, the camp manager, and his crew in the kitchen shelter. Just five men and I sit quietly around the fire in the dark. Dinner is delicious, *sadza* and butter beans. Mafusire, who made dinner, is fluent in English—classical colonial English with words like "whilst we do this" instead of "while we do this."

The conversation around the fire is mostly in Shona, though, when out of the blue Mafusire says to me in English, "What is this thing in your culture called Viagra? I have just heard this word sometimes and don't know what it means."

Hmmm...well...let me see. Umm...okay...well.

"Viagra is a tablet, *muti*, medicine."

Tablet is a big word here; it means any kind of medicine from a clinic.

"Sometimes men in our western culture, as they get older, well... how can I say this...umm...can't make love; they have a problem."

Problem is a big word here; there are so many problems. I practically sit on my hands to keep from gesturing what I mean.

"A man can go to the doctor and get Viagra tablets and take one to fix the problem each time, and then their woman is happy and they are happy."

"Oh," says Mafusire, "in our Shona culture we can just go in the bush and get some plant *muti* for aphrodisiac. In Canada are there tablets for women?"

"No, Mafusire, not tablets to eat, but tablets or cream to put where the problem is. Then everything is good." I pause. "Good like bush okra relish."

The other four guys, aged from around twenty to forty, lower their heads and look sideways at each other.

"Okay, thank you for explaining this to me." Mafusire carries on eating his *sadza*.

Later, alone in bed, I'm thankful for being in a mature stage of life and unfazed by such conversation in their company. The windows and doorway are open to the night sky, full dark with no moon; the Milky Way and the Southern Cross mark our place in the universe. Usually there is the sound of horses snuffling and snorting in the night at Siya Lima farm. Tonight, in bush camp, zebras.

Back in Harare next month, when I tell this story, I will hear a different perspective on the same subject: that for some men in the social fabric of southern Africa the preferred *muti* for a woman's condition would be a drying agent such as ash, rather than a lubricating one. The sources of this information are a mid-life Shona woman who is happy to be widowed, a nearing-retirement-age white gentleman foreign aid diplomat, and Stephen, who affirms the practice and says, "Is not good, that way some people do, not kind."

Swesh-swash, swesh-swash—the sound of scythes cutting grass in the nearby field; the second story windows of my blue bedroom in the Siya Lima farmhouse are open wide as I sit in the afternoon light with my notebook. Cowbells conkle-jangle beyond the garden wall, young herd boys chatter and wave their long sticks to keep the mooing *mombes* moving across the field toward the shade trees. That coughing bark in the distance is not a pack of dogs, but baboons asserting their whereabouts. A vine of creamy scented jasmine flowers threads further through the window into my bedroom each day.

A month now since I've been here on the farm in the company of Douglas, Shepherd, Alice and Pension while the Vardens have gone to Australia to visit family. Janine stays in touch momentarily each day via sketchy satellite internet, to check on the horses. For me, it's a time of staying in one place—the complexity of beauty and shadow deepening with each new day, and night.

Inadvertently, I am on retreat, a mindfulness retreat—slowing down into an organic flow day-by-day. There's a purity and simplicity with immersion in an unfamiliar language, too, as if others' conversations are simply background humming, or bird song, or goats bleating, or wind in the trees. It's a relief not to hear English unless I'm specifically engaged in a conversation—no familiarity of words to distract from my own perceptions or attunement to place. And writing, too—polishing the language of the stories that ask to be written in my notebook comes so much more easily here than back in Canada, where I feel separated from their source.

No peace for Alice though. She hears through the grapevine that her husband is sick with malaria. She must go home to her village, which means four hours on foot across the bush hills. I wonder about the malaria—she told me that last year he took another woman into their home for six months; he missed a woman in the house when his wife was away at work in camp. Alice is dressed for her bush trek in a white pencil skirt, black lace blouse somewhat tattered, and the ubiquitous fancy flat shoes, too big. A short while later, I'm hanging laundry to dry on the pasture fence when a line of five young women, each with a bundle or basin on her head, walks single file through the tall grass, hips moving in curvy wide-flung rhythm. I fall in with them, mid-point in the line. The woman behind gives me a small sack of rice to carry on my head. Behind me someone who speaks English laughs kindly.

"No, no, your body is too straight," and I gamely try to exaggerate a hip-flinging saunter. The women in front turn around to giggle at my efforts. Then they turn off toward their homesteads in the hills and wave.

"*Zvakanaka*, Oriane. Bye-bye!"

I'm alone under the mid-morning sun, deeply content in this community life. The other day Douglas brought his new, pregnant, wife, Rachel, to Siya Lima to meet me. A year after his first wife passed away, he and Rachel struck up a conversation on a bus. She's an early childhood educator, less tradition-bound than her predecessor. Now when I cross paths with Rachel in the village, where she stays with her aunt when Douglas is at work, she waves her arm high.

"Hallo, *maiguru*!"

I wave back, "Hallo *mainini*!" *Mai-nini*, wife of my younger brother.

Janine left the Hilux 4WD truck for me to drive to the nearest little commercial centre for diesel generator fuel, toilet paper and in case of emergency. Behind the wheel on the twenty-minute drive to Ruyamuro I negotiate the truck around mule-drawn carts, goats and cows crossing every which way, and people appearing at the side of the road out of the tall grass. It's a good thing Douglas or Mafusire always come with me, too, because Zimbabwe traffic drives on the opposite side of the road from Canada, and an attentive navigator is a good safety precaution in all these distractions. Besides, I feel more accepted in the local community, my projection perhaps, with a black companion.

I hear intriguing bits and pieces from Douglas, Mafusire and elders of the community in response to my queries about Shona cultural traditions, spirit mediums (actual people), spirit of the land and the Ancestors. I learn that white farm owners in earlier decades, and the original horse safari outfit in Mavuradonha in the 1990's, acknowledged the traditional cultural practices by sending one of their employees, usually a manager, to visit the homestead of the local spirit medium once a year to present the requisite offerings to the Ancestors. The farm workers assumed these were requests for rain, good harvest, health for their families and harmony on the farms.

My friends' stories of more recent times—encounters with the supernatural in the form of weather, animals, and so on—affirm the existence of the spiritual eco-system in Mavuradonha Wilderness, which holds true for all more-or-less intact Indigenous cultures worldwide. However, most white Zimbabweans these days apparently don't take that to heart—why would they in 21$^{st}$ century Zimbabwe?

I've grown curious whether this could be a factor in no one signing up for the two-week horse safari in Mavs, scheduled for next month, that Janine and I put together: "Immersion in the Cultural Landscape of Mavuradonha Wilderness."

Of course, I questioned whether I had done my bit regarding marketing and publicity, but I do think Janine and I made a good effort. We publicized it to my North American contacts and to Varden's clients, but no one has reserved a spot so far. I am aware, now, that the Ancestor spirits of Mavuradonha had not been acknowledged or consulted before we made the plans. We haven't asked permission of the spirit world to bring visitors into their domain, so may not have their blessing. A deeper consideration emerges, now that I think about it: to invite Canadian riders to come to Mavs would be presumptuous and unethical if the region's spirit medium and chief had not been consulted and paid respects to beforehand, with the purpose of asking permission of the spirit of place. What was I thinking? This omission contravenes the values I've learned, practiced and written about even before I first came to Africa.

"Douglas, do you think I could meet the spirit medium for Mavuradonha?"

The two of us sit cross-legged and barefoot on a rounded rock *kopje* a half hour trek from the farm. The panorama below lifts us out of the ordinary: scattered homesteads and tobacco fields fan raggedly to the south and the west, the sacred Nyambare Mountain protects in the east, and to the north, smaller *kopjes* rise toward the mountain wilderness.

Receiving no answer, I begin to hum as Douglas fits a tiny beeswax candle I've brought, into a crevice in the rock surface, then lights it with a match. The flame burns unmoving in the stillness of the afternoon. My friend quietly claps his hands, while I shake some earth from Canada out of a little glass vial onto the rock, then, sprinkle maize meal I pounded myself, and lastly, pour seawater from another little bottle. I smooth the muddy offering over the rock with the fingertips of my right hand.

"Hello, it's me again," I say quietly, "called by something more than I comprehend. Thank you for the blessing, really, of being welcomed here into your spiritual home. *Maita basa*, thank you."

Douglas and I stretch out on our backs on the rock, some distance apart. Oh, the bliss of drifting off to sleep, outdoors, when one is drowsy in the afternoon.

A tree branch snaps violently, startling me awake. No, it's the electric crackle of lightening behind the mountains, then the booming rumble of thunder. Opening my eyes, I see a huge herd of zebras that look miniscule far away on the plains. A few minutes pass before I realize, I'm not looking down on the earth, and it's not a herd of zebras. I'm looking up, overhead, into the leaf pattern of the mu'unze tree above me. The silhouette of millions of tiny feather-shaped leaves in a mountain acacia tree does indeed resemble a massive herd of zebra seen from the sky. The ruffling of leaves in the wind mirrors the grazing movements of a Lilliputian herd—pattern language.

Douglas sits up, "The Ancestors have heard your prayer, the spirits have accepted our ceremony."

Raindrops soak our shirts and our hair.

"Tomorrow," he says offhandedly, "we can go to the homestead of the *svikiro* for this area, and ask him about a ceremony for your purpose."

Translation: *svikiro*—spirit medium, the human who becomes possessed by Ancestral guiding spirits.

A black-cloaked slender figure emerges from an ochre-coloured *imba* carrying a reed mat. He unrolls it on the swept packed-sand ground and sits down, legs stretched out, one foot crossed over the other. He wears a wide brimmed sunhat woven of thinner reeds; two silver bracelets gleam on his left wrist, a single strand of raisin-sized black beads circles each ankle. A profusion of necklaces covers his chest, one is a thick rope of plied bead strands, another is a medallion the size of a tin can end with a spiral design. Otherwise he wears a thin black cotton shirt and wrap-around zambia, sarong, and the cloak over his shoulders. The *svikiro* is perhaps in his forties, and when he looks up his face is open and kindly. His name is Chabvuta.

Douglas and I sit on a log rail, about half a metre off the ground. Now, with a little bow and clap we greet the *svikiro*, "*Makadii?*"

With a nod from Chabvuta, Douglas introduces me and begins to explain in Shona the purpose of our visit. Beforehand, I had asked him to please tell the *svikiro* that I understand if some of the things I ask about are none of my business. Douglas does this, and Chabvuta motions him to continue.

Douglas says that first of all, his visitor, me, wants to pay respects to the spirits of Mavuradonha in the traditional way and to give thanks for having been welcomed here. It's clear from Douglas' hand movements that he adds his own commentary, about the gifts of soil and water and maize I bring from Canada. He asks, on my behalf, whether the Ancestors would allow small amounts of African earth and water to return to Canada with me.

Chabvuta continues to listen. The second enquiry is about the new settlers in the community and the loss of trees on land that is meant to be preserved and undeveloped. And also, what does he know about the NNMZ project to protect Mavuradonha with Heritage status?

I feel on very thin ice, asking about this as a foreigner and as someone who has not been actively involved in the conservation plan. Do I have a right to care this much? And why do I? For now, I keep these doubts to myself.

Chabvuta doesn't wait for a more formal ceremony to respond. He reminds us that Nyambare Mountain is sacred, and that no one must homestead on the surrounding land—things won't go well when people move onto that land. He has talked to the Guruve and Muzurbani chiefs about this. They will find new land for those settlers, he says, but it will take some time, two or three years. He knows too, of course, about NMMZ's field surveys in Mavs as part of securing national heritage status for the wilderness. Chabvuta says the big Guruve chief would do a ceremony for harmonious resolutions.

Douglas then presents my third and last enquiry—about bringing visitors, friends from Canada, to Mavuradonha. Friends who would want to learn from the people themselves about culture and traditions, historical and present-day, and to experience the value of the spiritual eco-system first-hand. May we have permission from the Ancestors to come for this purpose? I also mention friends in Canada who have been successful in preserving wilderness, who advocate for the value of intact eco-systems and will be heartened to know about this parallel preservation project in Mavuradonha.

Chabvuta names a date, a few weeks hence, for us to return for a ceremony in the spirit house, when the ancestral spirit will be asked to speak through him about these things. The impression that remains with me after we leave is the low timbre of the *svikiro*'s voice when he talks at length or when he responds after listening to Douglas with the occasional "aye, eh." This resonance is felt in my body, rather than heard, and it pops into my mind that my son Devon will be here by the time of the ceremony. The other day a text message came through from him.

"Flights confirmed to Harare. I can stay for a month, all of April. I need to see your life in Zimbabwe. What is it, about Africa?"

Later, back at the farmhouse as we wait for dinner, Douglas says, "Do you hear it is raining? Do you remember our ceremony on the *kopje* under the mu'unze tree? Then, the lightning and thunder and big rain after? Today we had first talk with Chabvuta—it is now raining. It has not rained since that time we were on that *kopje*."

Just after sunrise the air is fresh, barely warm, purified by the nighttime of rain. A month-old foal breathes on my cheek as I crouch in the dewy grass beside the wire fence. Horses wait for me to unlatch the bent metal gate. The little filly doesn't move when I reach to stroke her downy soft mane. She is the result of a villager's lone stallion, who jumped the fence when three rescued mares arrived on Siya Lima farm. He had quite a time of it—there are three foals—and has been sent to a more secure property near Harare.

Surrounded with horses—their pastures encircle the farm-house—I am rooted. I hear them nickering or running in the night. In the morning we open the stable doors and they trot in, each to his or her own stall, for feed, grooming and tick removal, and first aid treatments. Twice a day each animal is checked all over for wounds, bites, scrapes, or swellings. I learn how to sense these things by working alongside Douglas and Shepherd, who take care of every little detail in the horses' care and are so willing to include me. Shepherd, who speaks Shona only, answers "yah" to everything I ask him, especially either/or questions.

"Shall I groom Mawari or clean the bridles?"

"Yah," he grins.

This morning the two men brush used engine oil on the horses' hooves to prevent them from becoming brittle and cracked.

"We will not ride Munhondo today," Douglas says, "his leg is swollen, an abscess it seems."

He squats beside the horse's left hind leg and gently runs his hands over the lower section above the hoof, feeling for tenderness.

"A small puncture wound we can't see," he reports, "from the last time we rode him in the bush, maybe a sharp thorn. I will find the medicine in the tack room for treatment. For today, you can ride Gizmet. I will take Apache."

An hour later, Gizmet and Apache traverse the rust-sand drive-way of a nearby former farm, alongside a high brick wall. A flash of colour catches my attention and I nudge Gizmet over to the mortar wall overlàin with bush and vine that is decaled with magenta-coloured five-petal flowers, open rounded stars, with ultra-long deep yellow stamens that beckon bees—Hibiscus rosa sinensis in full bloom. Less visible, peeking out of the greenery, are pastel sun-set-coloured silky offerings, voluptuous bud shapes, a variety of hibiscus I've seen once before, that saves its unfurled beauty for nighttime. Hibiscus caesius. Gizmet stands steady as I reach out and pick one of those closed flower buds and slide it into my shirt pocket. At bedtime, the furled bloom rests in a small teacup of water on the table beside my bed.

In the earliest glow of sunrise next morning, just visible in the pre-dawn, the teacup is an overflowing froth of ballerina pink. Finely rippling layers of blushing petals, the innermost are smooth and glow deepest red at the very centre where the petals join the calyx. I'm flushed with remembrance of Stephen's gift—the flower bud in Hwange when we first met—and the unfurling in me when I returned to Africa, and to him.

When I go back up to the bedroom to wash after the horses are groomed, the rosé splendor is still lush in the bright light of day. In the evening, before I blow out the candle, a little bow to my frilly friend. The second morning, though, the pink flower has drawn in its extravagant display, as if the fluted petals are snuggled close for comfort, faintly wilted, keeping to themselves, never to open again.

When I arrange myself cross-legged on the bed for meditation and close my eyes, the very same flower appears inside my chest, as if it's my heart, pink and silky fresh. When my breathing deepens, the bud falls in with that rhythm—furling up with my in-breath, blooming open with my outbreath. Furling up, blooming open, furling up, blooming open; and then the flower seems to envelop the room, the earth, the universe—everything.

It was less than a week ago that Munhondo's seemingly minor injury appeared. Today, the two grooms carefully load their beautiful boy into the horsebox. Douglas is behind Munhondo, gently entreating the lame horse to step slowly up the sloping ramp, while Shepherd holds a rubber pan of feed at the top. Munhondo, whose ears are perked back toward the sound of Douglas' soothing voice, tries to move but winces with any pressure on the inflamed foot. Finally, he is halfway up the ramp. Douglas directs me to hold the feed pan while he and Shepherd stand behind Munhondo on the ramp, link their arms at the shoulder, hold on to the metal rail on either side of the horsebox with their free hands, and lift their fragile friend up into the mobile stall.

At the veterinary hospital in Harare, the front wall of the horsebox opens forward and becomes an offloading ramp and Munhondo is able to make his way gingerly down.

"Who's in charge here?" the woman veterinarian asks, looking at me expectantly.

I respond, "Douglas is the head groom and knows the horse best, please explain directly to him exactly what you are doing, and your assessment. He wants to understand the situation so he'll know for other horses in the future."

The vet is wonderfully efficient and informative during the proceedings. Seated on a low stool in the stall, she light-handedly shaves Munhondo's lower left hind leg with an electric razor and injects a local anesthetic so Munhondo can bear the touch of the scanning probe attached to the portable ultrasound machine. Then she withdraws fluid from the affected area with another needle.

"Here, hold this." She hands me the liquid-filled syringe for the lab—clear fluid with streaks of blood and pus. The results are serious and concerning, infection in the fetlock joint. None of us at Siya Lima knew, until the veterinarian tells us now, that even the slightest puncture wound or injury around a joint is a dire emergency and calls for immediate medical attention. She surmises that arthroscopic surgery may be the only option. The alternative is what you'd guess, though I can't imagine a choice being made to put Munhondo down.

It's tough for James and Janine, who are in Australia attending to urgent family matters. They are unable to stay in touch at first, with the undependable internet and cell phone signal at Siya Lima farm. Within a week, though, the two of them get off a plane after a fifteen-hour flight from Australia and come directly to see

Munhondo at the veterinary clinic, and to hear the prognosis. The primary care vet, now back from a field trip, is one of the best in southern Africa, in all of Africa, according to Janine. He has never seen a full recovery after surgery for this condition, infection of the fetlock bones; the x-rays clearly reveal the crumbling bits. The vet recommends they put him down right then.

"No, we're exhausted," says Janine, "and cannot contemplate this. Keep him as well and comfortable as you can for now."

Her voice quavers and her knees tremble through her jeans. Munhondo is named for an Indigenous hardwood tree native to the savannah woodland of southern Africa. Douglas agrees that when he returns to Siya Lima, he will place a small branch of the tree in the horse's empty, for now, stall.

A few days later, Munhondo shows a very slight improvement after the week of intravenous antibiotics and "bute" anti-inflammatory pain medication, so the beloved horse goes into surgery. The operation is done with him held in a sling, standing up, under a high-four-point nerve block, a local anesthetic, because post-op recovery from general anesthetic can be perilous; the horse may wake up and attempt to stand before he is fully conscious, then panic and break a limb. I have emailed horse-lover friends in Canada to request healing prayers for Munhondo. It's all I can think of to do, that and imagine him strong and active again.

One week post-surgery, Munhondo nibbles vanilla biscuits from Janine's palm. She and I groom him carefully, one of us on either side. His glorious thick black mane is dull and hard to brush. He is not weight bearing on the bandaged foot. Beautiful spirit, he is attentive to our humming and we feel badly that he is alone so much of the time, horses naturally live in herds and the equine clinic has no other patients at the moment.

Munhondo is about fifteen years old James reckons, a scrawny young stallion when they found him. That was in the early days of the farm invasions, when white farmers still thought they might get their property back. Seven buckskin horses, creamy tan coats with black mane and tail, had been left to run wild on a grass-covered fenced citrus orchard. It had a dam, a water reservoir, bordering one side, from which they could drink. The horses had been on their own for a year because the farmer had not returned.

Janine got a call from the Zim SPCA that the horses were destined to be shot if someone didn't come and take them away within twenty-four hours. Zimbabwe's Society for the Prevention of Cruelty to Animals played a pivotal life and death role in the rescue of injured and abandoned farm animals throughout the land takeovers in the decade following 2002. The farm's new occupiers expected to grow food on the land and to build mud-hut homesteads for their re-settled families, they had no use for crop-eating horses. The horse rescuers must be women, they decreed, no white men—bosses—allowed.

"I gulped," Janine remembers, "called a girlfriend and drove up there with a horse lorry. We went into the treed pasture with feed to look for the horses and they wouldn't come anywhere near us. It took a few hours till we were able to approach one mare close enough to put a halter on. We led her to the gate, but the gate was in the middle of a long stretch of fence, not in a corner where we could round up the rest of the horses from behind. The curious herd followed the mare to the gate but stayed dispersed and uncollectable."

"We were able to halter another one or two at a time and take them out the gate to the cattle kraal (corral). There was a chute at one end, sloping up to the back of the horse lorry. The horses were pretty scruffy and scrawny and covered in ticks. All in all it took about seven hours. Two of the mares and one older gelding with a displaced hip had to be put down right there."

"Munhondo has been the standard bearer of our herd," Janine says wistfully, "if we'd known he'd grow up to be such a fine horse we would never have gelded him. He'd have a few generations of offspring by now."

Lifting her beloved's forelock, hairbrush in her other hand, Janine kisses his nose.

She projects into the future, "Even if he needs to rest for a year after surgery, we can take him back to Siya Lima farm."

The veterinarian says ideally Munhondo needs a water pool for his recovery, a world-class rehab facility like one he's seen in Texas. There isn't any such place in Africa.

"What keeps you here in Zimbabwe," I ask the vet, "frustrated and disheartened as you must be at times, when you don't have the facilities to treat a horse as you could elsewhere?"

Running a hand through his smooth gray hair, he says, "I'm an African boy—couldn't live anywhere else. I've been to America, worked in a state-of-the-art hospital. If I could, I'd work in America, eat in Europe, and have weekends in Africa. That would be perfect."

For some, the expense of Munhondo's care would be better allocated to human need, for others all sentient beings are valued equally. In any case, Munhondo's well-being ensures the safety and education of wilderness safari clients, and thus generates revenue which supports the safari business and surrounding community.

# Kadoma *Kumusha*

It's pouring rain in Harare today and I've brought some peanut butter and tomato sandwiches to the stable where Stephen works now, at the different facility, down the road from the guesthouse in Borrowdale. We sit side-by-side on a trunk inside the tack room, which is a portable metal-clad trailer on blocks. The downpour is noisy on the roof. Without prompting, Stephen begins talking to me about his idea for changing work.

"Can I tell you about my plan for my business?" He pronounces it "bismiss."

He's been thinking about a small shop, a bottle shop in Chegutu, where his sister lives, that would sell alcohol, staple foods and meat. He knows the premises he wants and has a friend, the barber in Harare, who has solar panels and a generator, a big refrigerator and counters, all unused at present. Stephen needs cash to pay for permits and civic bribes, to buy the merchandise until some credit is built up, and for the initial operating costs. Stephen himself would live in the back of the shop. He explains to me the people he knows for supplying goods, the means of transport, and his plan to reinvest revenue back to grow the business.

I can imagine a thriving shop, a social gathering place really, as he describes music playing, powered by solar panels and car battery in the daytime and by a generator at night, and allowing a woman to cook on a fire out front.

"Take-away food," he says, "or, customers can stay at the shop, sit in chairs outside. Must close the shop by 9 p.m. or *totses*, thieves, come drunk later, if shop is open to midnight."

He goes on to tell me the purpose of this change and the way he intends to accomplish his plan. His reasons are compelling—first of all, he wants to do work that will support him when he is older and not physically able to work with the horses. I know that his back aches all the time, even now in his early fifties. And he wants to build something to pass on to his children. With the miniscule wages paid to a horse groom, he is unable to make any progress on building a house in *kumusha* or providing education for his last dependent child, or helping his extended family. As the oldest adult son of his elderly mother, he feels dishonourable not being able to provide.

"I didn't manage to buy Teneyi school uniform, no shoes or sweater. So Teneyi, my last-born son, is not going to school this term, not good. I pay the fees but still he cannot go because no uniform."

Stephen looks up from unwrapping his sandwich, "The boss say to me if I want to be paid more money then go get another job. When I go to get a new job, he will be telling the new boss that I am not good groom because I go with a white woman."

I wonder if Stephen's perception is correct—that the white bosses won't tolerate any departure from colour-coded rules of conduct.

"Myself, I want to be my own boss now," he says.

This is a monumental statement—from a man who has been in dutiful and conscientious service of bosses and madams since birth.

"I will hire someone, give a fair wage to trustworthy person. I keep training horses six or seven months, mind my business in my off days. When shop going nicely, quit job with horses, and stay with shop. Sometimes go—by contract, not job—to do farrier work or training horses."

He pauses and puts his sandwich down on the lid of a feed bin.

"Will you lend me money to start my business?" he asks. "Two thousand dollars, I need."

"Let me think about it a while," I say, knowing some threshold has been crossed.

Suddenly Stephen stands up and puts his hands on the sides of my ribs, under my arms, easily lifting me up—and there is nothing in me that can resist the touch of his lips on my throat, his open mouth on that tender neck spot under my ear.

Thunder cracks overhead, as if a lightning rod flashes through me. A bang from the outside, on the metal door—Hambani has returned after lunch—and Stephen sets me briskly down with a low-rumble laugh.

That evening the two of us sit across from one another at the kitchen table in the Dairy Cottage. Stephen has brought fire-cooked chicken and ready-made *sadza* from the roadside vendor. I press a shred of chicken inside a clump of *sadza*, my fingers glisten with chicken grease in the glow of candlelight. Stephen talks about his younger brother, the mechanic, as he often does.

This time I ask, "How many younger brothers do you have?"

As always, something new, something I didn't know. Stephen has five younger brothers and four sisters. I thought there were just six siblings, altogether.

He says, "My mum has ten children and only one who passed away, makes eleven."

He goes on to list all eleven noting their names, birth year, and current place of residence. The customary term is "first-born," "second-born," and so on. Diana is first-born, lives in Chiwiti where I first went to *kumusha*. Stephen names himself as third-born child, first-born son.

I know that Stephen himself has six children, four he has raised and two who stayed with their mothers as babies when he divorced.

I ask if he has seen Olivia, his youngest child, since she has grown up. "Did she find you?"

"Yes, she find me and come with two children to stay with Hambani and his new wife in the workers' compound here, at the guesthouse. Two weeks she stays here with her two boys. I am very happy!"

Then I ask him if his last wife, the one who died in 2006 when they'd been married for three years, had any children of her own when they married.

This is the wife Stephen referred to when we first met on the safari in Hwange, when he said to me, "My wife she died, 2006."

I didn't know then that she was the fourth wife. He tells me now that they lived in the village homestead of his mother, the *kumusha* near Kadoma, several hours south of Harare. His wife had seen him off on the bus to go back north to bush camp in the Mavuradonha Mountains.

"She was fine, strong, when I see her, but she was getting a headache that day," he remembers. She had unknowingly contracted cerebral malaria and passed away three days later.

"I am out in the bush," Stephen says, "and comes a messenger on a horse, tells me to come right now to see James in camp. If you ask James, when he tells me my wife passed away, he can see me crying."

A white neighbour of his wife's parents in Norton was helpful and generous to Stephen and his family; she provided food for the funeral, a vehicle for him to use and money for the burial. Every so often over the time I have known him, he mentions her name with gratitude. "That woman, very kind to my family."

"Your wife, your last wife, did she have any children when you married her?"

Stephen licks the chicken grease from his fingers and wipes his hands on the dish towel lying on the table. He lifts the water glass, puts it down without drinking and looks at the candle flame.

"Yes, she have got two child. One stays with grandmother, that *ambuya* want that girl, it's fine. And one girl born few years after we marry—that baby girl passed away, her name Sharon." He pronounces the name, "Shehdron."

Oh, that means it was Stephen's baby. A seventh child, when he was in his mid-forties.

"How old was that baby girl when she passed away?"

"Four months old."

"Mmm, how old was the baby when her mother died?"

"One month old. I give that baby to my brother's wife after my own wife passed away. I myself am working in the bush and give everything for the baby, milk, cloths, blankets. My brother's wife gave the baby cold milk, not warm milk from a mother. So that baby getting swollen, arms, legs, not good, and passed away. I was in the bush and didn't know, so Emeesh and Hambani my sons bury that baby girl, their baby half-sister. Buy the coffin, organize the funeral, everything."

Emeesh and Hambani were in their late teens.

"Yes, I love that wife and that bebee girl."

Reaching across the table to touch his arm, I ask Stephen, "Tell me again, the name of that wife you loved."

Stephen presses his forehead into his hands. He sits very quiet, trembling. After a minute I get up from my chair and walk around the table to lean behind him and wrap my arms around his shoulders, lay my cheek on his head.

"Emma," he says. "Her name, I know, Emma."

Tonight, Stephen doesn't bicycle back to his own room after dinner. When a story, a revelation such as this one, is followed by a night together, our first this year, then it will be sweet and mature and tender. Which it is. His smooth body is more slender now, his touch less urgent. There, it has happened, the bed. And just this once.

The cell phone wake-up alarm comes on at 4:30 a.m. Stephen has to get on his bicycle and go load horse feed into his madam's car. Through the open bedroom window, the low sounding of a bird in the pre-dawn.

"*ZeZe*, in Shona," Stephen says, "Owl."

Later that day, on Stephen's lunch break, we squeeze into a jam-packed mini-van commuter bus and go to the shopping plaza to buy the shoes and sweater ($40 USD each) for sixteen-year old Teneyi. In the shop Stephen holds up the dark blue sweater; he is beaming and grateful, "Thank you, thank you very much." My heart wrenches, anger flares. How the hell could he ever afford anything like this on $250 a month wages? After work he will carry the package on his bicycle, an hour ride each way, to Emeesh who will deliver it to Teneyi tomorrow.

After that, we go into the plaza supermarket for a few groceries. Stephen will only accept one loaf of sliced bread and one jar of peanut butter.

"Otherwise," he says, "one day if there is no food that is a big problem, makes a big pain in the body. Better, not get used to too much food."

The fluorescent-lit grocery aisle turns cavernous and dim. I stand motionless in the chill, washed with the rag of despair—until two little girls circle around me, giggling. I let the ashen feeling go and pick up my spirits, so I can be good company in this brief time we have together today.

Curiously, as we reach the checkout counter, the manager, a woman with braided hair that looks like an exotic snake, comes up to the till to key in a discount for our purchases. On the screen she clicks on the line "promotions discount." On the line underneath I notice "senior citizen discount" and I ask her how old a senior citizen is in Zimbabwe.

"Sixty years," she says.

"Oh, I am older than that! Next time may I ask for that discount?" I say with a smile.

She looks me up and down in disbelief, "What! How can you be old? You look like a teenage girl! How can you look so young?"

I hold her gaze, put my arm around Stephen's younger waist and raise my eyebrows.

"Agh, no!" she shrieks, slapping the counter, then raises her hand high to slap my palm. She is bent over now, hollering in Shona to the other cashiers who are all hooting, brilliant white teeth. The whole front of the market laughs uproariously, except for the dour shoppers who wait, sighing, in line. Stephen and I walk out the door, me practicing that sashaying African woman walk.

Stephen lowers one eyelid and says slyly, "Don't walk like that when you are alone." And laughing, he takes my hand as we run through the parking lot.

A few days later Stephen gets my attention, by saying, "In my culture, no money; in your culture, money. I need money, so I am thinking, thinking, how can I get money? Now I have plan for a shop, that one I told you. Then I will have money, you can ask me for something and I can give to you."

"You are my friend, equal beside me," he continues. "You care about my family, not thinking I am poor black man."

Indeed, Stephen is right; it's clear he is valued by his peers and community as hard-working, fair-playing, humble and generous. Add to that his easy-going grace and laughter, and I do feel the fortunate one in our friendship.

As proficient as Stephen is in his job as a horse trainer though, it seems his employer sees him as just another black worker. But now, when this employer, the horse owner, talks to him harshly, Stephen is determined.

"When the boss is angry, he must not call me *shamwari*," he declares. *Shamwari*, friend.

I have not given Stephen any substantial amount of money in the past—and Mel assures me, when we talk about it, that handouts are just not productive and don't result in anything long-lasting.

Stephen says he will pay me back. I'm sure he would, just as he repaid the amount I lent him to buy a new cell phone for each of his children. How he managed to do that is a mystery, though;

roadside commerce I imagine. I think a more productive thing than him repaying the loan, however, would be to re-invest the money—in the unlikely event of profit beyond Stephen's cost of living—in education for the family kids or in market farming that would generate revenue to pay for seeds and fertilizer the next year.

Before this shop idea goes any further, I have a confession to make somehow to Stephen. I don't like the idea of a bottle shop at all. How could I, in good conscience, participate in something that contributes to drunk and disorderly behavior, public intoxication that carries over to disruption in the home and undermines family safety and community cohesion?

I have walked by bottle shops in the small towns and rural areas, men hover around the premises like wasps over fallen fruit.

"Stephen, I've been thinking about your business plan and how it can be successful. I know your idea is to start as a bottle shop because that brings the most cash right away. What do you think about stocking the dry goods and household necessities first, before the alcohol? That way the women in the community become your friends first of all—good customers of the shop. You don't want the women mad at you for selling only alcohol, they won't come to your shop later when you stock other goods."

"Good idea," he responds agreeably, "then in few months when customers come, and I have music in the shop, sell beer too."

Done. We have held the delicate balance of being both optimistic and pragmatic. Now, for myself, I will trust Stephen and let go of any attachment to the eventual outcome of his plan. This is the true test of the sincerity in my contribution.

Let's stay open to some sign, I think to myself, evidence to show this is a good idea, not necessarily the actual shop but the investment in Stephen himself as an entrepreneur—the opportunity to be his own boss. The first affirmative sign is that Stephen's request, and the amount, line up with a pledge I have already made to myself.

Before coming to Zimbabwe this year, I'd felt it seemed time to offer Stephen and his family something of value, something tangible and enduring. In the vicinity of $2000 came to mind, and I had just that amount in a dormant savings account. I wondered about a borehole in his mother's village: that is, a deep well with a mechanical pump powered by hand to raise the water up with two or three people on the handle at once. Or, I'd wondered about a maize grinding mill, a diesel-powered motorized machine that pulverizes the dried corn, to replace the arduous daily task of pounding the hard kernels using a stand-up hardwood mortar and pestle. Or...I didn't know what, really.

Tafadzwa, my Zimbabwean musician friend in Canada, had counseled against a borehole and water pump because neighbouring communities who didn't have one would come. First of all, there may not be enough water for all who wanted it, especially in the dry season, and it would put Stephen's family in the unfortunate position of having to keep watch on the borehole and turn people away, neither of which is desirable nor culturally acceptable. Secondly, that investment wouldn't generate any income for the family—water is not a commodity to be purchased in that setting. So Tafadzwa recommended I invest in something that would contribute to the livelihood of Stephen's family. His own father had been a successful shopkeeper, with several different premises around Magunje. When we talked, Tafadzwa was also helpful in regard to my more personal question about Stephen: how to shift from lovers to friends, and if that is possible.

I remember Tafadzwa saying, "We Shona people live in the present. You cannot make a plan for another person ahead of time. Trust your self, when you get there."

Both in town and the rural areas, it's apparent from every Shona man I come across that a wife is the most important thing in his life. A man without a wife has no home, no ground, no place of belonging. Home or homelessness is the measure of a man and the foundation of a purposeful life. Family. Land. Home.

It's time for a conversation with Stephen, about the two of us. One evening, we take a walk along the dusty roadway on the flatland below Borrowdale Brook subdivision. Please, I ask the Ancestors, let me find how to say what is possible in the future, not what isn't going to come to fruition between us, or why our love affair is not going to mature any further. I do not want to bruise his pride, nor diminish what we have experienced together, nor negate all that I have received from being with him in his culture and his geography. Quietly and earnestly, I begin.

"Stephen, my prayer for you now is a new wife—not me—a wife who can grow crops in your garden and take them to market, who can cook your food and wash your clothes and carry water to your house. Someone who will allow you to help with these things. A wife who can talk-talk-talk in Shona with you, make plans for your homestead and for your future. A wife who will manage your plot in *kumusha* when you are away at work, make a home there where your children and grandchildren can gather. A woman who will take care of you in the traditional ways when you are an old man."

"Oh, you mean a permanent wife."

Gathering more courage, I say, "You know my heart has been to you, Baba, and you know I thank you deeply, but that wife is not me. Do you know, that?"

"Yes. I know." Stephen's sterling earnestness. "It is big loss."

It feels wise and correct to imagine Stephen with a new wife, a real one, not the part-time lover, friend-of-the-heart that I have been. Despite everything that is good, there just isn't enough common ground, shared values and life experience, or ability to communicate, to build a "whole" life together in either of our worlds. I suspected that was true the last time I was in Zimbabwe, the year my mother died, and had tried not to let it show when

I would become frustrated, impatient and irritable with the limitations. Not to say this disengagement is easy, particularly when body heat remains. There may be a transitional period, I recognize. My God, it's a good thing I'm at this stage of life and not decades younger, I think, hoping some spark of mature wisdom will guide the way.

Stephen and I sit at the kitchen table in Dairy Cottage, as is our custom after dinner together, before he bicycles back to his room in the backyard of his employer's walled yard for the night. I have brought up, once more, the prospect of him finding a new, permanent wife.

"I don't think I am doing that," he says.

"Why not?"

"Because African woman, you marry, then they go with someone else, too." That has been his experience, twice before. "And a new young wife want sex all the time, and I am getting old man."

"Can you imagine a woman who will be true to you like Emma, your last wife, and like I have been? A woman close to your own age, not too young?"

"Yes, I can think that."

Stephen has been planning a week away from work when he would take me to his mother's *kumusha*, a long-held wish of his. Of course, I want to go and meet *Amai*. She is the revered matriarch he worries about and is the only one left of her generation in the family. But how honourable is that, now?

Stephen, and a Shona woman friend, assure me that it's not a breach of Shona propriety to visit his mum, even though I'm likely not the woman to become the rest-of-his-life wife.

We start the journey early in the day, joining commuters on the crowded kombi, with a short ride to the veterinary hospital to see Munhondo. Stephen, along with everyone I know, is especially fond of Munhondo and has wanted to visit his trusty friend from horse safari days. As we arrive, Dr. Karl gets out of his truck and greets us cheerily. I explain our purpose and he waves us toward the low stable, a row of stalls across the courtyard. Munhondo is the only horse in residence.

Stephen unlatches the wooden half door and steps inside. He begins to talk softly to his friend, and I watch from the doorway. First thing he does is run his hands slowly and lightly all over Munhondo's weakened body. He alights most gently on the injured, now bandaged, hind leg.

Then he straightens up and asks, "Take photo, please."

Standing quietly on the straw beside the horse, Stephen closes his eyes. I shift position to just outside the stall and rest my elbows on the half door, camera in hand. Munhondo turns his head slightly, to rest his broad cheek against Stephen's chest. The tip of his soft buckskin ear just touches the outer rim of Stephen's ear; the two of them listen in the silence, and breathe together.

We're quiet on the kombi into central Harare, and I wonder if Stephen is imagining himself back in the bush with Munhondo, as I am. Next on our agenda for the day: kissing babies. Torai, the younger brother, the mechanic whom Stephen often talks about, lives in Budiriro, a "high density" suburb southwest of Harare. He and his wife have three beautiful little girls. The youngest is just a few months old, and when Stephen kisses her tenderly from heart to the top of her head, little giggles of baby pleasure brighten our spirits, while her sisters laugh and clamour for a turn. Before long, the oldest, four-year-old Tanya, leans shyly against my skirted legs as we all go outside to sit down "for visiting" in the shade of a tall hedge. To my utter contentment she snuggles herself into my lap, as if I've been her auntie forever.

I'd noticed a familiar-looking vehicle when we first walked into the yard and now Stephen wants to show it off—the derelict

Volkswagen beetle he'd wanted me to buy two years ago. Torai has apparently brought it back to life. He turns the key in the ignition and blue smoke shoots out the rear exhaust pipe for only a minute or so as the engine sputters then turns over. The two brothers high-five each other and give me the thumbs up. The sad news is that no one can afford to pay for petrol and the car stands unused. Nevertheless, it seems from Stephen and Torai's handshakes and backslapping, that proud ownership is a reward in itself.

On the old intercity bus, heading southwest on the main high-way between Harare and Bulawayo, Stephen gives me a running commentary of his early life as seen through the dust-streaked window. We pass by fields of sunflowers, scattered homesteads, small-scale subsistence farms, forlorn storefronts and, always, people and *mombes* on the move. For the entire body-roasting three-hour trip, he points out and talks about what has been sig-nificant to his family—an eye-opening retrospective of Shona farmworker family heritage—the flip side of what I've heard first-hand, and read, of the white former-farmer perspective about the same land. The window beside the seat in front of us is wide open, hot wind bakes our faces.

Just before Chegutu, he waves an arm to the west and says, "There was the clinic where I was borning. That big tree, my father's house on the farm was under that tree."

I can see the silhouette of a huge spreading canopied tree a kilo-metre or so in the distance, across the flat dry grassland. Making the most of a five-minute rest stop in Chegutu, I dash into the fast-food chicken diner and return with four chilled Sprite, the classic green glass bottles. One I drink straightaway and one I clasp to my cheek. Stephen downs both of his while they're still cold.

It's dark by the time we step wearily off the bus in Kadoma. The warehouse wall across from the bus yard bears faded lettering: Golden Star Ventures. (Pvt.) Ltd. Great Things Don't Change.

Grinding Mills. Peanut Butter Machines. Candle Moulders. Bees Wax. Oil Expellers (for sunflower seeds, maize, and peanuts.) Stephen is enthusiastic. I'm exhausted by our journey, but there still remains the prospect of meeting at last, face to face, the woman who means so much to Stephen. *Amai*, the mother. Reminded of our purpose, my flagging energy revives when a late-model Toyota sedan pulls into the bus yard. Stephen's niece, Shorai, and her young husband jump out, leaving the car doors open. Heavy-duty rap music erupts into the night.

Once Stephen and I settle in the backseat, the young man turns the volume down after Stephen says something in Shona that includes my name. The car turns off the paved road and onto a wide, sandy pathway. Tall grass brushes the doors. The young husband drives the car slowly, taking care of his owned vehicle and his community's land. It feels weird, though, to ride in a car, as I think back to my first entry into a *kumusha*: we walked the few hours to Chiwiti by moonlight three years ago. Tonight, too, the moon floodlights the land and the small settlements at rest for the night. Stephen's hand lies across my thigh, I lean into his shoulder and close my tired eyes.

When Stephen opens the car door and takes my hand to help me out, his mother is beyond formality. She rushes toward me, arms outstretched, the two of us caught in the car headlights. She hugs me vigorously; I take her hands in mine and kiss both her cheeks. Then, I step back and greet her more formally—my hands in the vertical clap with a little dip of the knees in curtsey.

"*Mamuka sei, gogo?*" I say, addressing her as grandmother.

Mama Hambani responds, with the customary, "*Tamuka, mama,*" and then she starts to laugh, a quiet deep rolling chuckle, so familiar, and I see she has a dimple in her right cheek, just like Stephen. Sevillia was named by her father, who was Mozambican. Born around 1930, she is in her eighties now. She looks ancient to me— missing teeth, reed-thin, regally erect, wizened yet strong.

We follow her into the main circular *imba*, the food storage-dining room and general gathering place. Meals are prepared in a separate smaller shelter, with half walls for better ventilation of smoke from the big fire in the centre. Two younger women, introduced as wives of her nephews, lay blankets on the packed-earth floor—Stephen and I are to sleep here this first night in *kumusha*. Candles are blown out when the others leave and we're left alone in the dark; by the time I grope in my backpack for a towel to fold under my head, Stephen is snoring.

Early morning under the blankets brings talking-talking with Stephen, or for me, listening-listening, to his life stories. The farm that he pointed out on the bus trip belonged, in those days, to a White Rhodesian farmer, of course; Stephen's family, along with the other farmworkers, had thirteen hectares, or thirty-two acres, of that for their own food crops and self-contained neighbourhood, or compound, as workers locations are still called. Then Stephen left home and, after Independence, forged his own way as a horseman—a groom, as his employers refer to his profession.

"This homestead, here in *kumusha*, is ours today, not owned by anyone else, but no money to pay for tractoring or to buy fertilizer and seeds."

My hip and back hurt from sleeping on the hard floor and I have to confess, by now, my interest and my patience have waned for hearing the same stories from Stephen again and again. Have I been attentive enough that he feels heard? Yes, I've been enthusiastic, and able to repeat, later, the details of what he's said to me.

As I emerge into the morning sunlight, a young woman with a baby bound to her back by a blanket, hands me a bright yellow five-gallon plastic bucket.

"*Maiguru*, come, let us go fetch water at the borehole."

And off we go into the tall grass, following a line of three women in front of us, each with a brightly coloured bucket. The familiar term for addressing me as "our brother's wife," *maiguru*, does not necessarily mean that Stephen and I are actually married. He has explained it's simply a relational way to identify me in the constellation of family in *kumusha*.

"Not girlfriend," he said. Girlfriend can be one of many.

"And you are not my permanent wife to the future, you are my half wife now-now."

After a breakfast of deep-fried doughnut balls sprinkled with sugar, Stephen and I return to Kadoma for supplies with Shorai and her husband. The young man's most important purchase, he announces in English, is a case of plastic-bottled water for me, so I won't get sick from drinking borehole water in *kumusha*. His thoughtfulness is touching, in an entirely different way from the traditional water purification I'd received in Chiwiti *kumusha* a couple of years ago. Within an hour, the car overflows with food: mesh sacks of potatoes, onions, and squash; ten kilo bags of flour, mealie meal, and white rice; smaller bags of sugar, salt and tea; a two litre bottle of cooking oil; bundles of leafy green veg and tomatoes.

With the continuously arriving extended family that converges for my visit, lunch prep is an assembly line of white bread slices scantily swiped with peanut butter or margarine, then stacked on communal plates and passed around. A big cooking pot of tea is filled to the brim and saturated with heaps of white sugar and Cremora, synthetic milk substitute. Specks of loose black tealeaf float atop the murky pale brown in the shared enamel cups.

The last time I ate peanut butter on white wonder bread was in the 1960s, before the North American swing to natural food caught up with my mother. Of course, today, I accept a piece of the lightweight mass-produced loaf with a sincere nod of thanks. Reliance on inexpensive starch is how the villagers survive; besides, it's thought to provide strength and stamina. I don't think so, but it's not my place to be critical or even to make constructive suggestions when I've just been welcomed as a guest.

All day long, family introductions continue, interspersed with short walkabouts to meet important neighbours. Stephen is in his element—talking and laughing, catching up and telling stories, relishing his place in the fabric of his mother's life.

At dinnertime, a little protein is added to our meal; several chickens are killed, de-feathered, pulled apart and deep-fried in sunflower oil.

As the communal plates are apportioned, I think to myself with a smile and a sigh, "Would you like some macaroni with your white rice, potatoes and *sadza*?"

I imagined the non-perishable provisions we bought in town would last Mama Hambani a long time, but there is not much left when Stephen and I leave. This first evening he looks at me across the fire, and instructs, "Oriane, say blessing, please."

"We are grateful," I say, "for this food, for those who have grown and prepared our meal and for the earth that produced it. Thank you for sharing the blessing of this family with me."

Four of us kneel on the ground in the early morning light along the edges of an elongated mound of dirt beneath which lie the bones of Stephen's long-passed father. We have come with his mother and the young man who is family-best-friend-caretaker to pay our respects to the Ancestors. The profusion of the weeds on the grave is testament to the inability of the family to pay the young man for the upkeep of this plot. Stephen is ashamed, I know, that he cannot manage this for his mother. Never mind his dreams of reactivating the deep well and irrigation system for her maize field and garden.

Heads bowed, eyes closed, the three Africans sing and clap their hands in a single rhythm, communicating with the spirits of Baba Kapanga and all the departed relatives. I follow suit, though silently, and ache with the pervasion of unmet need in the village. Not just physical survival needs, but also the essentials of everyday spiritual life, like maintenance of a graveyard, traditional gifts to the invisible presence, a bride's dowry for marriage.

Where and what, then, is the best allocation of my contribution to Stephen's family? Let him choose, of course. How would I be able to discern this with my foreign perspective? I feel ashamed at not having made his family's well being a priority. With a sigh I remember that I've had my own losses and family affairs to navigate. Inside my heart, humming, the Beatles, "Let It Be." Tears water the weeds at my knees.

Stephen begins to dig into the dirt with his strong hands and pull out the thickest weeds; his mother, too, trowels with her age-gnarled fingers. The young man and I join them, and I'm grateful for something to do.

A short while later, we walk back through the spindly maize field, my eyes on the ground. Mama Sevillia, beside me, wears worn-out, formerly black, now sun-bleached canvas shoes, slip-ons, since there are no laces threaded into the metal eyelets. The baby toe of her right foot appears perfectly comfortable poking out of a hole in the outside edge of the shoe. I wonder if she tore the hole on purpose, or whether it just wore through.

Stephen, who walks in front of us, has been lost in thought. "We need cement, to make a border for my father's grave," he says out of the blue.

Yes, I will buy cement, so that the young man beside us can carry out his duty to the family.

The young man's female counterpart in the family's social web is named Farisai, Happiness. She is the *murora* to Stephen's mother—the younger woman best-friend, spiritual caretaker, who looks out for the aging great-grandmother and will organize the funeral and settle affairs when the elder woman dies. When we first arrived, Farisai's hair was a dull mat of frayed short tufts tied with worn black yarn. It must have been that way for some time because it was loose, not tight, all over her scalp. When we

*The Geography of Belonging*

return from the grave this morning, she is transformed. She wears a new-looking white t-shirt, though her clean zambia is faded and threadbare. Her now-shiny short hair is twined in an intricate labyrinth of curves that follow the contours of her shapely head, framing her beautiful face.

Farisai appears kind-natured, attentive, and hard-working with an easy sense of humour. Stephen has said, "That woman is smart and very good person." She seems to have no husband, and I also notice that she looked away when Stephen put his arm around me.

I ask him, "Have you considered asking her to marry you?"

Farisai is part of the *kumusha* community already, though not blood-related to Stephen's family. Seems suitable to me.

"Nooo," he says,

"Why not?" I ask.

"Her husband passed away and maybe he had disease. I don't want to marry her and get disease and die."

"Can you not ask her, or someone else in *kumusha*, why he died?"

"Nooo, I am minding my business. Not asking questions."

Two little girls stand in a round plastic basin of water, while one of the young mothers gives them a thorough soapy washing. After the girls are dried off, each is rubbed all over, feet to hair, with scented Vaseline, the most inexpensive and widely used grooming product, then buttoned into matching freshly-washed dresses, white with pink polka dots. The sheen of the girls' skin and the fragrance make the little beauties irresistible.

Throughout the day, a continuing procession of water is brought from the borehole and set to heat on the fire, and almost everyone has a bath. Babies and little ones in the basin, older children and adults inside a bathing enclosure—flat stone floor surrounded by a tall twined grass screen that spirals outward so the inner space is concealed from the view of anyone outside the entrance opening.

"*Gogo*, come," Stephen's niece, Shorai, motions me to go inside with her.

I've brought my own towel and travel soap and, taking my cue from her, I undress and fold my tank top and zambia over the screen. Shorai glances at my unclothed older woman body, attempting to be discreet. It's likely I'm the only white female nakedness she has ever seen. I have a little look at her myself; her lower pelvis is entirely hairless. Stephen tells me later that a wife, Shorai in this case, is shaven by her husband, so that she won't sleep with another man when the husband is away. New hair growth in the husband's absence is naturally wiry and prickly, so that physical intimacy with another would be too aggravating, and unlikely.

Shorai has been raised in *kumusha* by Stephen's mother, her grandmother. Shorai's husband's mother is the village chief. She has sent an invitation for me to use her nearby cinder-block latrine, rather than the Hambani family pit in the ground, hidden by a dried-grass screen. Apparently, these in-laws are fearsome in the power they hold; Shorai finds them intimidating and prefers to stay here in her *gogo*'s homestead across the path. This chief upholds the law and doesn't allow Indigenous trees to be cut down for firewood.

"Dead trees only for fire, and thorn trees," Stephen says. "She can call the police to come for someone who breaks this law."

Blessing hurtles cross the open yard and flings herself into my arms. I scoop her up to sit astride my hip. She's three years old and has blatantly appropriated me. The other adults keep trying to shoo her away, as if she's bothering me, but I love her fierce self-assurance. Whenever my arms get tired and I put the young one down, she stands with her hands on her own little hips grinning at me both defiantly and longingly, before she runs off with the other children. Often one of the adults has an arm crooked around Blessing's elbow to keep the little tornado from getting into mischief.

Today she's dressed in a butter yellow t-shirt and black flouncy skirt, her best, I think. She pats my head, endlessly fascinated with my hair, my necklace, my earrings, my teeth, but eventually, when I sit on an upturned bucket beside the other women who are shelling groundnuts, Blessing rests her weight against my chest. This, more than anything, causes me to feel at home, as if I belong in *kumusha*.

I think the western phrase, "It takes a whole village to raise a child," seems a little too precious for what is just a fact of life—the village raises the children. In this family homestead of Stephen's mother, at least, the babies are picked up and passed around by whoever's arms are free. Toddlers are carried and given food by whoever is nearest. School-age children are disciplined by whoever catches a misbehaviour. There is consistency; everyone acts by the same rules and values.

In Harare I'd asked Stephen's son Hambani if he loves his own children more or differently than his brother's children, his neighbour's children.

"I love all, same," he said.

Blessing's mother is Shorai, who seems atypically disinterested in the little girl, leaving her in the care of Stephen's mother for long stretches of time to accompany her husband on his money-making missions around the countryside. He is thought of as a prospector, a buyer of gold from locals who scour long-abandoned mines in the region. This is a grassroots gold-buying enterprise, not big business, one shaft at a time, nugget by nugget. A dangerous undertaking, Stephen tells me; the workers can be buried alive in a collapsed shaft. Others pan for mercury in old streambeds; toxic, hazardous in a different way. But Stephen says the men feel they have nothing to lose when the alternative is idleness and poverty in the disintegration of Zimbabwe's economy.

Stephen is disparaging of the young husbands in *Amai*'s extended family in *kumusha*. The young men are more curious about modern life than their wives, who seem content with, maybe resigned to, traditional village life and chores. Cell phones and sunglasses make the man—those, and excessive pride in their children, for whom they do not work to feed. They have no work ethic, Stephen comments wearily, and do not help his mother, the penniless matriarch, to grow a garden.

"Lazy. Just live here for free. No one keeps them in order, those young guys. No old men nowadays to tell them how to work. These guys are not my sons, I didn't raise them, so not telling them what to do now."

I didn't feel any such qualms, myself, in the lecture to Shorai's husband about her education. After all, his mother is the chief, so there is some precedent for women's empowerment, even if hereditary. As could be expected though, a year later when I ask Stephen on the phone from Canada about Shorai, he confirms that she has a second child and remains restless and trapped in *kumusha*.

Mid-afternoon and I can't stop sobbing, alone in the small *imba* where Stephen and I now sleep at night. The red packed-earth floor is swept clean and a plush polyester blanket serves as a rug to cushion the hardness. I've lain down on another thick blanket that covers the carefully made-up, thin mattress. The once white mud-plaster wall behind my head is veined with wide cracks; the worn pink mosquito net is bunched up in a knot close to a roof pole rafter. Streaks of sunlight, blurry through my tears, pierce the thatching above me. I wonder if the roof will be patched before the rainy season.

In the few years of my coming to be with Stephen in Africa, this is the only time we've had our own little home, or more truly that I've slept in a home of his. I am not the first woman to share this *imba* with him.

An hour ago, Stephen stood on the doorsill and told me, "This is my room, from when I stayed in *kumusha* between work in the

*The Geography of Belonging*

bush. My wife from before stayed here when I am away, that baby girl was borning in this room."

He pointed outside to the tall grass along one edge of the homestead's cleared grounds and said proudly, "There, there was our garden—maize, potatoes, tomatoes, onions, pumpkin, groundnuts, everything grows when rain comes."

Then he went off to sort some plans for the evening, leaving me in the *imba* to rest.

I'm flooded, as if newly awake, in the knowledge that this is the room where he shared a bed with his last wife, Emma, the one who died of malaria while he was working with the horses in the Mavuradonha bush. I am sleeping in the home where they had a baby together and lived briefly as a family. My heart is broken open in his loss, as if it's fresh. I put my arms across my eyes and weep into the comfort of their weight. Just let all this sorrow out.

A sob-ragged breath brings a painful recognition—there is more. In the happy fulfillment of being here in *kumusha*, engaged in the minutiae of family life, I have forgotten there's another loss coming for Stephen, and for me. With that, a life-size heartache, red and raw, presses my chest; this is the last time we are likely to be together in a married way. The last time I have a place of belonging in this way, with this family.

I have asked myself, many times, a question echoed by well-meaning friends in Canada and certainly by my black friends here. Why, just why, is our relationship not going to come to full term in this world. Why am I making that choice? The answer is soul-searing and simple: the small differences that when collected just won't add up to a life together, no matter how deep or fated our love for one another. I mean, a whole life together—one where each of us is able to fully engage in the others' world and find or create common ground together.

Of course, I've imagined Stephen coming to Canada, but beyond the initial love-struck fantasies I could not fathom how he'd feel at home there or be able to work, not dependent on me, when I don't have a horse farm, nor live with Mary or Michelle or their horses anymore. And it's not that I haven't made enquiries and explored options. To be honest, although I'm tenacious when faced with challenges like immigration bureaucracy and visitor visas, I haven't felt compelled to pursue this prospect with Stephen. I have trusted that the choices with the most integrity would come, hand in hand with the means to accomplish them. And thus, it seems that my prayer for Stephen, delicate as it is, holds true—a new wife.

As I stretch my back to help shift my mood, Stephen comes in carrying something, then lowers himself down beside me on the mattress, his long legs reaching over the end. I turn sideways to face him and see a baby resting against his shoulder—his tiny grandniece, Lucia. He slides her into the crook of my arm and chuckles. The babe is fussy and Stephen instructs me in how to soothe her cries in the way of the African grandmothers.

"Put like this," he says, patting the front of his shoulder. I lift Lucia to my own collarbone and gently sit up.

"Touch, like this." He places his hand over mine on the baby's back and moves up and down, gentle strokes on the swaddled bundle. "Now say soft things to the baby."

I begin to rock back and forth, ever so slightly, and after a time, the little one nods off. I lay her sleepy weight on the bed between us. Stephen smiles at me and doesn't look away while we breathe together in the silence. A thread of sunlight through the roof thatching touches baby Lucia's soft velvet head, and her chest flutters with a delicate sigh.


Mama Sevillia is some dancer. She may be creaky and methodical in her workaday chores, but tonight she swiggles her hips and flexes her shoulders front to back, eyes bright.

Stephen and I are leaving *kumusha* tomorrow, so tonight is a farewell celebration. I've given my camera over to the kids and the great-grandmother winks coyly each time her picture is snapped. Pretty soon I've joined her in a circle with Shorai, Farisai and several young mothers as the little kids run around us shaking their bodies as if possessed. I marvel at their absence of inhibition, or more accurately, the joyfulness of their free expression. Maybe they are possessed, by life.

The younger men brought a huge stereo speaker into the main *imba* where Stephen and I slept that first night. It's powered by a car battery charged by a solar panel on the roof. Now the guys position an old-fashioned box television set on top of the speaker and busily hook it up to a DVD player. I keep my fingers crossed that the DVD I burned on my MacBook will play in this machine.

Enthusiasm for DVD watching mounts as neighbours stream into the room and settle in with the family. Everyone is curious to see pictures about Stephen's work with horses in the bush and the other family homes we've visited in previous years. And now, once the videos are underway, there's laughter and clapping each time I appear in a family role—attempting to cook *sadza*, carrying a baby on my back, holding hands with Stephen's sister. The appetite for entertainment doesn't end with the specially chosen videos we've already watched, and everyone wants to see more: Theresa's elephants, horses on the beach in Mozambique, my own family in Canada.

Much later in the evening, I ask Stephen, "Do you mind if I have a minute by myself in the bath?"

We're outside, behind our sleeping *imba*, hidden from sight, and I sit with my knees up in a big oval plastic tub normally used for laundry; the rim supports my lower back and the water is blessedly cool on my thighs. The night air is still warm, dialed down from the intense afternoon heat, and fragrant with a lingering residue of wood smoke.

Stephen has laid his clothes on the ground, on top of mine, preparing to bathe together, but with my question he seems to understand that the constant attention of his family and curious visitors has caught up with me. I'm exhausted. I just need to space out.

"*Mwedzi wakazara*," Stephen points to the sky. Yes, the moon, *wakazara*, is full, *mwedzi*; white-light brilliance dusts the African savannah with fresh snow—how the mind gravitates to perception of the familiar. Shadows too, seem more pronounced, those places on the other side of light.

Stephen dips the bar of soap in a smaller bucket of water beside the tub and proceeds to lather soapsuds all over himself. I just sit still and feel the undemanding caress of the cool water. Is it my imagination that senses the ethereal presence of his lost wife and baby, as if they are here asleep with the other young mothers and children? And I can feel, too, Stephen's relationship with his long-gone father; but no one in Shona culture is ever dead and gone. I'm acutely aware of what has come before and still exists, the *mhuri*, the social and spiritual extended family; author Malidoma Somé calls it "Echoes of the Ancestors." I'm also aware of how fleeting my presence is in *kumusha*.

At midnight Stephen and I lie quietly together in the strands of moonlight that shine through the roof thatching onto the bed. A frog has made itself comfortable on a corner of the pillow. It's been in the *imba* all the time we've been here. Yesterday I had coaxed it outside with my flip flop in my hand. It, or another, turned up this morning on the doorstep, as if waiting to come in.

I ask Stephen, "What is the meaning of a frog coming?"

"*Chura*, frog, it means the spirits are visiting you, your Ancestors are visiting."

He whispers clearly, close to my ear, "You always have home in *kumusha*. You can come here, no matter what, by yourself. Is good."

He heard me say, just once, that my former husband severed all communication after we separated, and that it made my heart sore to visit my stepdaughter and grandchildren alone, without being included in their family gatherings after so many years. I wonder if Stephen has any idea how healing the inclusion in his family is for me? Yes, I'm sure he knows. Back in Canada, when I show Mary the photos of this time in *kumusha*, she will say I look transparent, pure.

"Take my hand or you will get losted," Stephen reaches out to me.

Returning from Kadoma to Harare, the bus has deposited us at the chaotic terminus in the faded mini-metropolis of Mbare Musika. For generations this legendary marketplace was the hub of Zimbabwe's commercial produce and goods trading. Nowadays, Mbare remains a source for the spiritual accoutrements of traditional Shona culture. We're here to buy essentials for the ceremony with Mavuradonha's spirit medium, the *svikiro*.

Stephen leads me through the bustling dilapidation into a warehouse, then proceeds along the congested aisles until we come upon the right-feeling family from whom to purchase the required items. He addresses the elder woman who sits beside an intriguing collection of merchandise.

"Hallo Mama." And then he looks at me.

The traditionally dressed grandmother nods her head warmly and Stephen bids me to tell her what I need. The rest of her family is surprised by my request for the traditional things I name, but under the grandmother's direction, variations of the ceremonial requirements are offered for me to choose from.

Soon, with their help, I have a tattered cardboard box with the newspaper-wrapped items carefully stowed inside: a two metre length of black cotton cloth, the same length of white cloth (a *svikiro* wears only these fabrics, which are sewn into loose garments that wrap around him), there is a red fired-clay pot for the trance-inducing brew his assistant, the *motapi*, will concoct, plus a small carved wooden spoon for sipping it; two hand-sized cones of dried tobacco leaves (Stephen pronounces it methodically, "toe-bah-go") and a tiny hollow gourd containing *bute*, snuff powder, corked with a carved wooden plug.

As well, we have three long strings of tiny glass seed beads: one all black, one all white and one mixed together—the same kind of beads, the waist beads, given to me by Stephen three years ago that have remained on my wrist all this time.

After the long day that began in Kadoma, instead of going back to the guesthouse in the crowded, music blaring, stopping-at-every-intersection kombi, I splurge and we find a taxi (which means asking around for a guy with a car) for the remainder of the journey.

A few days later, John, the Varden's driver, comes with me downtown to South Avenue to make the final purchase. Luckily, we find leopard print upholstery-weight fabric; leopard is the *svikiro*'s animal totem, and I buy heavier fabric because it's April and winter is coming.

Devon's blonde hair is easy to spot in the distant crowd of passengers magnetized to the baggage carousel in the international arrivals hall of Harare airport. My heart leaps ahead of me—a burst of longing, seeing the familiarity of home in him—when he turns around and spots me pressed against the heavy glass window in the waiting area. Stephen stands near my shoulder with a light hand on the back of my waist.

My god, it's good to see my boy, I mean, my adult son—the first of anyone I know in Canada to venture into my life in Africa. As he comes through the doorway I don't rush forward, but rather wait for him with the warmth of the mother. Smiling sheepishly after his thirty-six hour journey, he puts his gear down on the floor and we start to laugh.

"Are you hungry?" I ask, as he lifts me up in a bear hug. A minute later he sets me down and reaches out to Stephen who steps forward, and the two of them meet with that elegant wrist-upright handshake and clap on the back, that men do when they recognize one another.

# The Spirit House

The *svikiro*'s wife shakes out a large mat composed of synthetic maize meal sacks sewn together in a slippery quilt. She lays it on the ground under the msasa tree and motions Douglas, Devon and me to sit down. As the three of us sit and wait in the veiled light of dawn, with the two young men on either side of me, a faint flower fragrance softens my nervous anticipation; I want to participate in this ceremony in the proper, respectful way, to observe a protocol, one which is impossible for me to calculate ahead of time.

I pat the flower print zambia wrapped around my head, borrowed from Stella, hoping it stays in place. My fingernails are shiny, buffed satin for the occasion and the ever-present string of waist beads are a glistening comfort wound around my left wrist. I've worn the treasured strand this way since receiving them from Stephen three years ago.

Devon gives my hand a little squeeze and lets his breath out. He is still jet-lagged, his red-blonde beard a little ragged, and I can hear his stomach rumble because he declined the tea and s*adza* porridge I offered a few hours ago in the dark. Still, I know he wouldn't miss this morning for anything—his city life at home in Vancouver has been exhausting for one brought up in the rain forest world of Cortes Island. He believes that returning to nature, whole body immersion, is the best restorative. Here we are.

Douglas, just a few years older than my son, is smaller in physical stature. The barely discernable pencil moustache outlining the fullness of his upper lip gives the appearance of a man matured by the reversals of life, and indeed, Douglas has three sons from his wife who passed away a few years ago. His new wife, Rachel, pregnant, has two children of her own.

He surveys our surroundings intently, leans over to me and says, "When my homestead is like this one, I will be very happy. Lots of trees for shade, bring out mats to sit on the ground, for teaching people about the environment."

After a long while, the *motapi* comes to fetch us. Douglas knows him; the *motapi* is the *svikiro*'s younger assistant and translator of the ancestral voice that comes through the *svikiro*. He will do this in Shona for Douglas who will then rephrase the Shona into English for me.

The *motapi*, Devon says later, looks like a trickster—magician—in a dark, mid-thigh length threadbare overcoat with collar turned up. Light on his feet, he certainly has the air of a sorcerer's apprentice. His very baggy trousers are worn through at the knees; underneath he wears faded black softer pants that are rolled up at the ankles over top of the outer trouser cuffs. Could he truly have no other pants? Is this an intentional display of poverty, I wonder?

This man, our host, picks up the ragged carton of prescribed offerings we have brought, and we follow him along a sand path, eastward, into the rising sun. I hadn't noticed the circular *banya*, spirit house, just as I hadn't in the homestead of Saki's guide, Samaita, two years ago; this one is much smaller. The direct sunlight in front of us is blinding, too bright for my eyes, so I squint and look down at Douglas' bare feet just ahead of me. Pretty soon they disappear into darkness, through the spirit house doorway. I feel my barefooted way across the threshold and sit down just inside the entrance and settle myself, folding my skirt around my legs. I can hear Devon clear his throat at my shoulder as he sits somewhat awkwardly in the doorway.

When my eyes begin to adjust in the half-light, the ceremonial space appears dense with cultural artifacts and objects from nature. Bundles of foot-long porcupine quills rest on the floor; a wealth of

*The Geography of Belonging*

red clay plates and pots are stacked according to size and shape; a collection of carved walking sticks leans against the curved wall. Lengths of black fabric and white fabric are strung across twine lines above us.

Then I see the *svikiro*.

He is already seated on my left, the north, with his back to the Mavuradonha Mountains. His stunning headdress flings me into the actuality of his role; a leopard skin headband supports a crown of pointed reeds, while multiple strands of black and white beads fall over his forehead and face, the tiny tendrils shimmy with the slightest movement of his body. Chabvuta sits cross-legged on a thick leopard skin laid upon the packed-earth floor. He wears a black cloth, with small white polka dots, draped over one shoulder. Many strings of beads and medallions decorate his bare chest as before. The voice that comes through him is low and gravelly as he leans forward and addresses Douglas.

The first order of business is negotiating payment, Douglas tells me—an entrance fee to the spirit house and a second amount for the *motapi*'s services as assistant and tailor; he will sew the fabric we've brought into garments for his *svikiro*.

"Please advise me, Douglas. What is the usual or expected amount for entrance fee and the *motapi*?"

He tells me the customary payment given by people in the community and I agree to these token fees.

Then Douglas asks me, "What amount do you offer Chabvuta, him self, for making this ceremony for your purpose?"

A brief gust of skepticism, mine, blows through the *banya*. When I was received in Samaita's spirit house the day after my mother died, Saki had said, "No, you do not need to offer any money."

On the other hand, I heard from James that two tourists, Frenchmen, were charged $200 because they were looking for an entertaining photo op, not for revelation. I would have preferred these financial considerations be sorted ahead of time, but it's clear this transaction is a necessary formality in the ceremonial proceedings, and a prelude to the deeper dialogue with the ancestral spirits.

Oh, of course—coming to agreement about payment is part of the protocol, I suddenly understand, remembering that I, too, charge for divinations in Canada, maps of guidance using tarot cards. How else would Chabvuta support his family, supplement their food crops? But I have no idea what amount is fitting and fair to both of us.

What comes to mind is the drawn out negotiation between two families for a bride price, the *labola* that is often paid in installments over time. According to Shona custom, Douglas, for example, cannot meet Rachel's mother or father in person until he has made the first *labola* payment to them and stated his intention to pay the agreed upon sum for the marriage, whether cash or cattle or household goods. In the same way that a young man pays a bride price, in the *banya* there is a price for healing and divination services.

Again, I defer to Douglas, "How much do you think is correct in this case?"

I show him the cash I have in my pocket, not extravagant. He is also aware of the money I've already invested for the ceremonial gifts from Mbare market.

Devon shifts his weight behind me.

"Mum," he says quietly with authority, "It's fine, say yes."

With a slow nod of his head and a handclap of thanks Chabvuta accepts the small amount of cash I have today, the promise of more, and our gifts. The *motapi* folds the currency into one of the clay pots we brought and puts the cardboard box aside. We now have credit with the *svikiro*, even though he won't be paid in full until next time I make a visit to him—even if that's not until I return again to Zimbabwe, it doesn't matter.

This time when the *svikiro* speaks he turns and faces me, though I can't exactly see his expression through the cascade of beads. But Douglas' patient translation is clear.

"The Ancestors know you are here, your gifts are received. They welcome your respect and accept the offerings you have made before, the soil and water from your home on continent of North America. You are a friend of the people and the Ancestor spirits."

Chabvuta's body shudders momentarily and I feel as if my parents are present, here, in the *banya*, with the Ancestors. As if the secular shell they shed when leaving this world has fallen away from me, too.

I feel compelled to be transparent, hide nothing, in this newly-forged spirit friendship, so I ask about the ethics of collecting a bit of sparkling earth and river water from Mavuradonha to take back to Canada.

I confess, "I have done this each time I return to the northern hemisphere—offer something tangible of Africa to the earth in the bioregion where I live."

I feel compelled to explain, "You know, between our homelands? Between one place of falling water and another—Mavuradonha, Zimbabwe and Ocean Falls, Canada. Is it okay?"

Douglas, of course, understands the response that the *svikiro* makes in Shona on behalf of the Ancestors, but he must follow protocol and wait until the *motapi* has spoken it aloud as well. Then my friend turns to me.

"Yes, Chabvuta says it's fine to take a pinch of soil from our land, *ivhu*, and water, *mvura*, from the river." Douglas says.

"You are the bridge who carries the gifts across the world. Then Canada knows us, too. The *svikiro* says you keep the traditional ways alive with your interest and your writing. That is what you can give us."

With this stunning affirmation, my physical body seems to dissolve and I'm no different from the porcupine quills and the *banya* walls. Something pleasing and aromatic fills the space, yet I'm not aware of inhaling—the atmosphere in the spirit house itself is doing the breathing. At the same time, I wonder if Chabvuta is wearing spiced herbal hair pomade.

As the Ancestral voice intensifies and goes on at length, the pith of his discourse begins to come clear:

"All people must respect and help one another and stay together with the spirit world. Every human is Indigenous to the earth. One world and one people unified in spirit."

Then, silence.

Douglas sits straighter, coughs, and looks at me. Time to present the final query, so I ask, "How do the Ancestors, the spirits of this sacred land, feel about me bringing sincere visitors, friends from Canada, to Mavuradonha?"

Chabvuta puts a hand to his chin, rubs thoughtfully, and returns again to the theme of unity.

"Human beings are one people. One humanity," he states. "The Ancestor's message is not aimed only at white people—but also black people's prejudice against white, rich people's prejudice against poor.

"The new rich black people don't do the spiritual ceremonies any more. They do not respect every person," he admonishes with a fervent shrug. In Harare I have seen these ostentatious ones treat their servants with not a speck of kindness.

"They are not passing the traditional values to their children. The children go to school abroad and become lost. They come home and ask to learn their grandparents' ways.

"Rich blacks go to church," he continues, beads and bells aflurry. "But do not communicate with the spiritual Ancestral presence. They go to church and appear to pray, but they are only asking for the material things. Never saying thank you, just asking, asking for more. Many white people who come to visit in Zimbabwe are more observant and respectful of the traditional ways."

After a time, Chabvuta's tone begins to calm as he talks and he gestures towards us, his small audience. Douglas makes the *svikiro*'s pronouncement to me, in translation:

"You, Oriane, and you, Devon, and your friends are one hundred percent protected from danger, from people, animals and spirits, here in Mavuradonha—and everywhere in this land."

Devon, who has been silent, takes a slow breath and gathers a question along with his excitement.

"Does that mean even on the Zambezi River canoe safari that Mum and I are going on, with those perilous hippo encounters I've heard about? "

"Yes. Everywhere."

A stomp of Chabvuta's stick, a shake of his shoulders, and the rattling of his headdress let us know the ceremony with the Ancestors has been accepted and is finished. As if tutoring me in the traditional ways of Shona culture, he also wants me to know that a grander spiritual ceremony—held for specific individuals and families, community situations and concerns—will happen at a later time when all the *svikiros* in the wider area gather together with fire, drums, mbira and the potent brew.

As we stretch our bodies outside after the long time sitting still, a duvet of shadow-white clouds rolls away from the mountains in the north; the sky along the undulating horizon shows the clear blue of late morning.


"Mum! Keep moving!" Devon commands from behind me. I'm walking in shorts and flip flops along a path near Kopje Tops Camp.

"Now, stop and stay where you are," he says firmly, then, "Turn around and have a look at this!"

He's pointing to the ground, to the path, about six feet from me and I can't see anything but a large, grey, dead leaf attached to a small branch sticking up on the path.

"Mum—it's a baby cobra," he announces, "You walked right over it."

I feel sleazily sick, unnerved by the hooded reptile head that's swiveling in the direction of Devon and Janine as they skirt very widely around it. Janine says she has never seen a cobra anywhere around here, baby or otherwise.

A few minutes later, at the stable, Douglas says to Devon and me after hearing the story, "Normally, it would strike you, close range, if you go right on top of it."

I shudder in my shorts and bare flip-flopped feet.

"Mum, I think it's an affirmation of the protection the *svikiro* told us about yesterday. Remember he said we're protected from danger in the wilderness and the hazards of any animals now?"

Douglas nods, "Yes, a sign, to assure you that you are now protected."

I do know there is always a sign—a signal from the invisible world—after a sincere spiritual ceremony, that shows us our offering has been accepted. It's curious, as the days go by, that instead of feeling entitled now, with this protection, to be less cautious in the wilderness, I become more aware than ever of what's around me and inside me: the flutter of a leaf, a slight acceleration of my breathing, changes in the sound of the river after rainfall, cloud shadows on the hillside, the imminent arrival of zebras in camp. Is this, awareness, an aspect of the protection?

MANA POOLS, ZIMBABWE

# Zambezi Paradise

If you've been in Africa, that numinous glow of first light—before sunshine's golden syrup pours itself over the land—is forever impressed upon your psyche. One's relationship with morning is full of possibility, fresh, as with a new romance and at the same time deeply intimate, comforting and familiar as a longtime marriage.

In the blush of this particular morning, I just intended to walk back a bit from our overnight camp on the Zambezi River sandbar, to have a pee, out of sight if I crouch down. After three days of canoeing in the company of six lively young adults, including Devon plus our two Tonga guides, a few minutes to myself are a treat. But once beyond range of voices and canoe-packing activity, I can't override the urge to remain alone, unencumbered, away from other humans.

I stand up, rearrange my zambia, and keep walking across the flat land, one barefoot step after another, following a trail of elephant footprints in the moist earth leafed over with flattened grass. Each depression is wider than my waist, and as deep as my mid-calf; of course, I have to take a step or two between each pachyderm imprint. The spaciousness of a little walkabout on my own is immense, a chance to catch up with myself.

I'm exhausted with exhilaration in the very real danger of disturbing the territorial hippopotamuses on the river these last few days—just like horseback riding in lion country. I miss James, and Janine, and Stephen, and Douglas, the trusted ones who have been the carriers of my safety in the wild. Then I remember the *svikiro*'s declaration of protection—is it true I do not need the company of my friends in order to be safe?

Stand still, sigh, and dare to close my eyes. Feel the contact of feet on ground, of warmth and resilience in the dampness underfoot. At rest like this, my body feels fluid, like the flowing river water. An electricity comes up from the ground; my chest opens and opens, dissolves into the dual scents of dry insect-arced aerosphere and riverine organic earth. I wonder if Eve felt like this in the Garden of Eden.

What else? Lie down on the earth—feel the Hum in Everything.

"Mum, don't wander away by yourself. We couldn't see you. I thought you got lost. Or snapped up by a hippo."

Devon sounds distressed, unusual for him.

"Everyone is ready to go, and we have a lot of river to paddle this morning. Besides, you slept through the elephant who came into camp in the night. She stood right behind our tent and you didn't even wake up. I could see her trunk through the mesh roof. Awesome."

As my son and I walk toward the readied canoes, Také and Norman, our guides, stand on the sand at the river's edge surveying the minefield of hippos submerged in the water beyond the shore, roof-top eyes spooky like periscopes. More than daunting: how on earth will we navigate our way past them, or—gulp—through them? I remember the latin roots of the word hippopotamus: river horse. It doesn't help.

In perils like this one, and when I'm a novice, the best thing to do is focus on the next small action, nothing more. Help Devon push the heavy packed canoe into the water, lift my zambia and hold on to the side of the boat, step in sideways and sit down on the bench seat in front. Okay, good. Keep my eye on the canoe ahead of us as we begin to move forward, soft peripheral vision, trust Devon on the rear seat behind me to steer with his own paddle.

I'm never doing this again I promise myself when the canoes glide into the grand expanse of slow-moving water that is the middle Zambezi River. On the far shore, the Zambia side, a few local bathers are enclosed by a semi-circle of wooden stakes and wire that supposedly creates safety from crocodile attacks. I can see tiny specks of laundry laid over bushes behind the beach. In the farthest distance across the river valley floor, the muted mountain escarpment brings a familiar feeling to the topography—very much like the mountain-ocean seascape around Cortes Island, our home in Canada. I lean back on the canvas-covered pile of gear, still wary of telltale bubble trails on top of the water.

In these days and nights on the river we've encountered no other tourists, only the occasional dugout canoe with fishermen paddling arduously in the opposite, upstream, direction. Although our Natureways safari is the economy pitch-in and make-camp-ourselves option on the website menu, nature herself doesn't discriminate. Gliding downstream in this hand-powered vessel I feel ancient and regal, in a journey of timeless opulence, my son at the helm. Humans have always traveled in handmade boats—on the Nile River and the Ganges, on the Amazon, the Irrawaddy and six of the seven seas. Tomorrow we'll reach Mana Pools, our destination, a protected World Heritage site. I know from James that it's one of the less-developed wilderness parks in southern Africa.

"Hey, Mum?" Devon says from his seat behind me. "Being out here on the river like this, full-blown nature; I'm done with living in the city. I want to come back to Cortes Island, where I belong, and go back to ocean kayak guiding. Can I stay with you this summer?"

Of course, he can. "It's our home," I turn around to him, "Our family home."

My generation, and demographic, was raised to be independent, to leave home as early as we could and at all costs, disregarding the communities we grew up in. Africa has taught me there is no shame in staying close to home and family.

How could I know, that a few years down the road Devon will, indeed, be living on the land where he grew up, *kumusha*—enthusiastically occupied as a mussel farmer, out on the ocean rafts in summer heat and in winter storms—on the wild coast of Cortes.

Mid-afternoon, our convoy of five canoes hugs the left edge of a narrow channel, about ten metres wide, in the labyrinth of lush-green flat islets—an intriguing and welcome diversion from the open space of the main river with its platoons of submerged hippos at irregular intervals.

A new sound—a sweeping rustle of grass on the opposite bank. Také, our guide, slips his cargo canoe out from the back of our line and skims into the middle of the channel. I look beyond him just in time to see a smooth gray mass lunge-slide from the bank into the water, then, submerge.

Some kind of alarm clangs in my head. Can I concentrate with all my might and quell the amygdala, my reptilian reactive brain? Okay, try to keep quiet instead of turning around to Devon in panic. Bubbles creep across the water surface toward us.

All of a sudden, Také stands up in his canoe, bends over, and violently slaps the water with his paddle broadside down. From above, the sound of an airborne whwoosh—a startled black and white saddle-bill stork sails past us downriver, not far overhead, its red and yellow noseband a beacon against the pure blue sky.

Norman, from his position first in line, raises his arm in the air and motions the rest of us, in three canoes, to keep moving calmly and methodically forward into a smaller tributary waterway.

All my instincts scream, "Paddle hard and fast, get out of here!" But, fortunately, I am paralyzed, frozen.

"Mum. Put your paddle in the boat, stay still, and let me get through this," Devon says.

Looking down at my feet, I notice my gold toenail polish is chipped; then I fold my arms across my knees and lean forward, just to rest my head for a few minutes. The gunwales of our canoe brush the grass roots of the islet riverbank.

*The Geography of Belonging*

"Mum, slowly, slowly. Sit up." I must have fallen asleep.

Something odd, just ahead on the river. I squint in the sun to see. Could it really be a caravan of elephants, five of them, walking on water? Two are little ones, scampering between the adults to keep up with their mothers. As we paddle-drift quietly closer, smooth waves skim a sandbar, barely visible under the river surface.

The elephant matriarch swings her trunk and slowly turns to face us. Her ears, like ancient wings, fan the sky. She stands before us, tusks gleaming, cooling herself. A snowy egret lands and settles on her shoulder. Something settles in our human herd, too. An elephant heart beats less than half as fast as the human heart—we've been found by the true pulse of the wild.

Two days and a case of Zambezi beer later, Devon and I arrive by bus in the township of Magunje, still wrapped in the afterglow of our experience on the river. Mbira music is our purpose. Welcomed into the home of Tafadzwa Matamba's brother, Japhet, we meet their village friend Gift, who is an esteemed mbira maker.

After a shared meal, the shy, shiny-shoed elder presents Devon and I with our own brand-new instruments that he has just finished tuning. Everyone moves outside, each with mbira in hand, to sit on wooden crates under the jacaranda tree. As the pink-gold sky turns amethyst, Devon and I learn the beginner's song *Kariga Mombe*. Japhet and Gift patiently teach us the fingering of the tine keys and by the time night falls, we can't see our hands, only feel our way, note by note, in the dark.

The next morning, we wave goodbye to Japhet and Gift through the open bus window. In a few hours we'll arrive in Chinhoyi to rendezvous with Stephen and stay with his sister Taffy. Her husband, Robert, is a well-educated long-distance truck driver, and they now have a fourth daughter, just two weeks old. My first visit with them was three years ago, en route to Chiwiti *kumusha*. This time, my heart is full in a different way, Devon is part of the family affair.

# The Ethics of Generosity

Sometime before coming back to Zimbabwe, with the hope of visiting Jonathan Mazulu's family who also live in Chinhoyi, I imagined making a photo album for them, in remembrance of him. In fact, I didn't make a photo album—when I arrived in Harare, on the shaded verandah of my cottage I made a DVD movie of my photos from Mozambique Horse Safari. Pictures of Jonathan, and of Pat and Mandy, of our favourite volunteers, the horses and the stables, and the gorgeous scenery in Vilanculos.

Stephen came one afternoon and helped choose a track of soulful music by Snatam Kaur, a sacred chant, "I'm Coming Home."

I've texted Mandy, but don't yet have any phone number or address for the Mazulu family.

Just as our bus arrives into Chinhoyi, a message finally arrives from Mandy with a phone number for Portia Mazulu. Stephen is waiting at the bus station with his niece, Priscilla, who is suddenly shy when I introduce Devon. Stephen hoists my duffle bag to his shoulder and takes my hand.

Later, in the evening, I ask Robert to call Mrs. Mazulu; he will be the most diplomatic and communicative. Robert disappears outside and returns within two minutes. That was quick—we'll go to her home in the morning, Robert, Stephen, Devon, and six-year-old Ellen, Taffy and Robert's daughter who has adopted me. This is a spontaneous, in the moment, do-it-now way of life. Robert is more thoughtful however, about my desire to respect the custom of arriving with the gift of a sack of mealie meal for the family.

"It's harvest season," he says. "I think she will have enough maize meal of her own. Let's stop at the grocery store for other staples."

In the morning in the back seat of Robert's car, I have a little conversation with my mother and my father; I feel them in the spirit world with the Ancestors.

Okay mum and dad, you've got to be with me right now (though I know "they" are ever-present). We're making a family visit together, the occasion calls for the presence of your generation. Oh! Jonathan is in heaven too, with you both! (Though I don't exactly believe in a heaven place). Come with me, please, to Portia Mazulu's house and make this a valuable occasion full of grace.

We're here. A new-looking brick house in the middle of a recently cut golden maize field. Tall wildflowers mark the pathway to the front door. I had been prepared to make the customary Shona greeting for a new acquaintance, *"Makadii?"* with a handclap and slight curtsey. But Portia Mazulu is waiting on the path and walks straight up to me with her arms outstretched and folds me into her welcome. She is absolutely lovely—familiar feeling, quietly radiant, articulate. Being in her home feels natural, and a privilege, as I meet the Mazulu family. Portia introduces me to their second-born son, Shepherd. His resemblance to Jonathan disrupts my composure, and I have to stay silent and focus on breathing for a few minutes to avoid fainting in the sweltering enormity of their loss. Of course, other family relations are assembled as well, young granddaughters, Portia's sister and a very pregnant daughter-in-law. We hear that their maize crop was harvested with a two tonne yield. Their workday in the fields will recommence as soon as we leave.

Settled on the couch beside Portia I share stories of conversations and interactions with Jonathan at Mozambique Horse Safari, showing how we all valued him.

Hands folded in her lap, Portia quietly talks about the last weeks they had together and the date he died. About the scarf and handmade soap Mandy had sent along as a gift. Jonathan had been in the Chinhoyi hospital but came home for his final days, and though in otherwise unbearable pain, remained concerned for his loved ones, uncomplaining and kind.

"He was a very good husband," says Mrs. Mazulu.

I look at Portia's hand with the wedding ring on her finger. Jonathan passed away right here, in their new cottage, in the bedroom. Portia shows me around the house; the inside walls are not plastered yet, but each room has its essential furniture. She is most pleased with the kitchen with its propane stove and big wooden table surrounded by chairs—though the house is small the entire extended family will live here with her.

"Oh, I would be lonely by myself," she says. "The family wants to be all together."

The rooms fill with downy presence. When we return to the sitting room, the handmade lace doilies on the back of each upholstered chair draw my eye.

"I have one of those at home in Canada. Lisa, a Mozambique horse volunteer and friend, sent it to me when Jonathan passed away. It's one he gave her as a farewell gift when she left Mozambique." Portia nods, smiling, gets up and reappears in a moment with an armful of placemat-sized cream-coloured finely crocheted circles.

"Here, for you. Traditionally they are made in sets of three, like this."

The supple, cottony thickness folded into my arms is pleasing on my bare skin. I marvel at the craftswomanship in each design and Portia says, "I don't want to sell them, only for gifts." Of these four sets, one I will send to Lisa, and one I will save for Devon's trousseau (never mind that he will one day be a groom not a bride).

Shepherd, just graduated as a schoolteacher, has a laptop and asks if we may watch the DVD now. My companions, Stephen, Devon and Robert, excuse themselves and go outside.

Devon whispers to me as he leaves, "I've already cried my way through it."

Ellen hops onto my lap and leans her weight against my belly and chest. The curtains are drawn to shield the bright sun as Shepherd inserts the DVD and clicks the play button. Portia, still beside me on the couch, allows my hand to find hers, warm, firm, soft. Somehow my voice doesn't break, quietly commenting on people and places, horses and history. Both radiant and teary, Portia marvels at the blue ocean, Shepherd laughs at the horses swimming, the family have never been out of Zimbabwe. Their faces soften with pictures of Jonathan, husband and father, smiling on the screen. We are distracted momentarily by something shimmering on the curtain behind the laptop. A dragonfly in a stray trace of sunlight. A blue emperor dragonfly, a little early for this time of year.

The emailed comment of an expat Zimbabwean comes to mind: "It is a lovely idea, your photos, but not much appreciated in African cultures. They are not brought up with our sentiments. The family would appreciate money far more than photos as their main breadwinner has died. Their cultures are so far removed from ours."

How can a white person who lives here actually say this in the 21st century? How could anyone with a heart have ever believed this? By the same token, though, I've heard for myself on occasion, the black nouveau riche and power-holders, even the well-educated, disparage their fellow citizens who live in the villages and rural areas. I never get over it, and am humbled to the ground whenever I become conscious of a prejudice in myself; any harbouring at all, however faint, here or in Canada, of an attitude of "them" and "us," or of superiority in me. It's a life-long practice, this vigilant uncovering.

*The Geography of Belonging*

In the evening, we reassemble in Robert and Taffy's house, relaxing on the overstuffed crushed velvet couch and armchairs. Their eldest daughter brings amber glass plates of *sadza* and chicken, which warm our laps. Hearing me sigh, Robert looks over and says, "What you did this morning was one hundred percent."

After dinner Stephen's thirty-year old daughter Diana joins us in the sitting room, new baby held snug against her back by a towel wrapped around her torso.

"Is there anything else the baby needs?" I ask.

"Yes, a warm blanket for winter," Diana answers.

Stephen and Robert both shake their heads, "No!"

Robert says, "The baby's father is working, it is his job to provide for his family. You have given enough, Oriane." He proceeds to enumerate the contributions I've made to Stephen's extended family. I haven't been keeping track and am startled that he has.

"First you bought the school clothes for Teneyi. You took food for the whole family for the days of your visit in Kadoma *kumusha*, Stephen's mother's village, and brought gifts from Canada for everyone. You brought more farrier tools for Stephen's work. You went out this morning to buy food for my family's breakfast. And you paid for those groceries for Portia Mazulu. I'm sure there is more. You are a kind and generous person. You have done enough."

I haven't stood back and looked at my place in the scheme of things. This giving is just what my own mother and grandmother did when they would visit family or friends. My maternal lineage also says that I need to pay my own way and make sure my hosts are not put out by my presence. Robert's words of acknowledgement are piercing, though, and I can only say quietly: "Thank you, Robert. It is my pleasure."

On my way out of the room I pick up the dinner plates and carry them to the cold-water tap outside. Leaning over the cement basin, tap turned on full, I splash water up to my face till the ache in my throat disappears and the sink is full.

Robert's reflection sparks a curiosity in me and I begin to wonder, soul-search really—what are the ethics of generosity? One morning back in Harare, in conversation with my dear friend and confidante, Mel, it becomes clear that I haven't identified a weariness behind my fairly constant elation, something she calls "donor fatigue."

Have I been assuming need everywhere, without discernment, even with those who are self-reliant? Have I overdone it, simply by following the precedent set by my mother, who always arrived to stay with my sister or me with bags of groceries in her arms?

No, I think not. My situation is different from Mel's. She's involved with an organization—always politics and the expectation of accountability in both the benefactors and the recipients. I, on the other hand, have been blessed with inclusion in Stephen's family, with living in the wild with horses, with beauty, acceptance and love in the eyes of my friends here. The contributions I've made—whether informal fundraising in Canada for the Mozambique horses and preserving Mavuradonah Wilderness or shopping for groceries here in Zimbabwe—feel to me no more than gestures of appreciation, the natural reciprocity between kindred spirits. The fatigue Mel observes in me, beyond her own projection, is, I think, just what comes with adjusting to immersion in the unfamiliar.

Still, it won't be until I find myself weeping early one morning when I'm back in my own garden on Cortes Island in Canada, that Robert's recognition sinks in. On my knees, pressing manure-fragrant compost around tender green pumpkin plants, his words return, "You have done enough."

Somewhere deep inside, myself, or the earth, I hear the *vadzimu*:

"You are worthy of these life-altering experiences that Africa offers up to you." And "Yes, you have given in return."

Taking up my notebook in the shade of the honeysuckle trellis, I wonder: how can I write about this giving, without self-aggrandizement? I remember the wisdom of Saki's spirit guide Samaita as if I am sitting again in his spirit house. I can write by understanding that it's not about me.

I think of Stella, effervescent in her magnificent hard-worked market garden near Siya Lima Farm, on the outskirts of Mavuradonha Wilderness. I often stopped by to see her, either to buy vegetables or simply to enjoy a woman's chat. Stella reminded me, in a good-natured way, each time I visited, about her need for a hosepipe to bring water from the lake to the top reaches of her garden near the road. She had a diesel-powered pump but no plastic pipe, so she carried the water in buckets to her one thousand tomato plants.

However, I had been advised by the Vardens not to give anything to individuals or else everyone in the community would expect something of foreign visitors. This had been their experience and perhaps the genesis of Stella's request. In the past it would have been easy for me to shut off from Stella, to feel uncomfortable with the disparity in our financial circumstances. But my engagement with the people of Zimbabwe has opened me beyond that kind of measured boundary. Nonetheless, I didn't give Stella the money she asked for, initially to respect the Varden's trust in me as their guest. Also because it felt so good to be in her warm-hearted company and I didn't want to feel that I'd bought her friendship. So Stella and I continued to enjoy one another's company, marveling at her crops, taking walks together, and sharing stories of our children and grandchildren. And I gave the funds raised from my presentations in Canada, as intended, to the Vardens in support of securing heritage status for Mavuradonah, the wilderness.

One day, though, while Douglas and I were cleaning saddles I asked him about the Varden's directive to me, since I was here under their auspices. Janine and James had made many contributions to the Siya Lima community toward self-sufficiency: funding a rabbit-breeding program for food at the primary school, the

Honey for Money project for families, procuring donated medicines for the health clinic, and more. I noticed too, that when Douglas and I were out riding and came upon a homestead, he would often receive a pumpkin, some greens or tomatoes in return for a favour he himself had done; putting someone's son to work, taking a pregnant woman to the health clinic in the donkey cart. These gifts would be tucked into a saddlebag and later cooked for our dinner. I queried Douglas about Stella's request—of course I wanted to support her livelihood—so wanted to know, truly, the best course of action for me as a foreign white woman who was in this Shona community for a temporary time.

"Do what you feel," he replied.

One afternoon I couldn't help myself and started to cry at Stella's. No longer the ever-cheerful guest, I was leaving Zimbabwe soon and overcome with sadness.

"Don't cry Oriane, there are so many difficulties," she said. "They will press on your heart and you get heart pain. Just give your everything to God."

The day before my departure from Siya Lima, I found just the amount of cash Stella needed, tucked away in a zip pocket of my backpack, given to me by a friend in Canada whose business is clean water. So, I made my way through the tall grass along the sandy path to Stella's homestead with this gift. We hugged a last good-bye. She held on to my shoulders and looked at me.

"I have never met such a woman as you, with so big kindness in your heart.

"When you come next year," she added, "you will have all the vegetables for yourself and your guests from my garden, yes!"

A host of snowy white egrets lofted into the sky. And looking upward, Stella exclaimed, "God has blessed us!"

As I consider the meaning of reciprocity, I think about John, the Varden Safaris driver and property caretaker in Harare, who arrived that same day to fetch me. We were having a last communal dinner at Siya Lima farmhouse when he stopped over for the night. John sat down beside Douglas on the low bench against the charred wall of the courtyard where the cooking fire is always kept burning. Shepherd and I sat on the opposite bench, the four of us enveloped in orange glowing firelight, eating *sadza* together. The three African men were talking about the paddock fence repair and where best to graze the horses the next day. Wait a minute, I'd thought: they're talking in Shona. I didn't know the words exactly, but the gist of their conversation was clear to me.

Just then, casually, between mouthfuls of pumpkin leaf relish, John looked over and said in English, "Oriane, you are one with the people."

# *Ziva:* Wisdom

Chipunza sits down on the cushioned rattan chair and accepts the glass of coke I offer him. He has come to the Dairy Cottage this Sunday afternoon, our first encounter since my mother's passing two years ago. We're outdoors on the cottage veranda, a warm breeze shuffles the tall fronds of the potted palms. His finger-length dreadlocks are tinged with grey at the roots, and the top button is undone on the yellow plaid shirt covering his husky frame. The sleeves are buttoned at the wrist, not rolled up. He enquires about my family.

"My son is here in Zimbabwe, leaving soon," I say. "Everything has gone perfectly for his visit. He's in Chimanimani this week helping with a youth leadership group. Outdoor sports, canoeing, rock climbing, ropes course."

"That's very good," Chipunza says. I ask about his family, as well, and then a different question, thinking about Devon's grandparents, my mum and dad.

"How does your Shona culture address and express grief?" I ask. "First of all, personal loss when someone passes away, and more importantly, loss of biodiversity, the extinction of habitat and species?"

He begins to tell me exactly how grief is welcomed when someone dies. The deceased person is honoured with a funeral arranged immediately, within a day or two, allowing the family to grieve unrestrained while being fed and cared for by the community. Endless hours, even days, of singing, prayers for the departed and for the still-living, consultation with the Ancestor spirits, and the distribution of all the person's belongings into the community. For some weeks the family are left free to do nothing but mourn their loss. I remember Douglas describing the passage of his first wife Sheila, and the one personal belonging his son wanted to keep of his mother's, the nature necklace I'd made for her.

After that grace period for grieving, over the timeline of a year, the one who has passed away is helped to transition into the realm of the Ancestors with a series of ceremonies, and to perhaps return as the spirit of an animal totem in a surviving family member. Not surprisingly, I realize, the ritual process parallels the practices in Tibetan Buddhist tradition.

Chipunza leans back in the chair and stretches his arms overhead. In the far-off distance, cowbells jangle in their afternoon procession homeward. In silence, Chipunza and I eat a few handfuls of ground-nuts and some peeled *nanje*, orange, and then he continues.

"We have a good story about protecting habitat for the plant and animal kingdoms. It is necessary to stand up for the spirits in a place and for the value of making a ceremony. When a Chinese mining company received the rights to the diamond mine site in eastern Zimbabwe, the very area they proposed to dig with their big machinery was the home for twenty-three baobab trees. The mining company requires a permit from me, from NMMZ, to dig and I said 'No, you cannot do this. Baobab trees are spiritual beings, sacred to us, and cannot be sacrificed.' The company asked about moving the trees and I said very very expensive to do that. They don't care how much money it costs, so we allowed them to move the trees with their big machinery, an experiment. First we consulted the spirits of the trees to ask their permission and did a ceremony to assure their protection. The baobabs were taken on huge flatbed trucks to the same location where the villagers from that land were re-settled. The new habitat is unsuitable for baobabs, but the trees are thriving now, six years later, with the villagers."

Chipunza goes on to tell me about Great Zimbabwe, one of the country's most significant archeological sites, a UNESCO World Heritage site on the scale of Machu Pichu in Peru and the great pyramids in Egypt. The entire historical complex was constructed in a "dry stone" masonry technique that uses no mortar or binding material to hold the intricate patterns of cut stone in place. He describes some very precarious sections of Great Zimbabwe, saying that his engineers want to reinforce the segments that by all measure of logic should have crumbled down by now.

"I cannot allow them to do that," he says. "They must not tamper with the stones. It is the spirit of the ancestors that hold the walls in place. The spiritualism in these monuments, and so many others in Zimbabwe, is ignored nowadays.

"These are actually not monuments at all," he sighs and sits taller in the chair. "Each one is a shrine—*rushanga*—a place where serious spiritual matters are dealt with."

He has recently written an article entitled "Conservation of Dry Stone Walled Monuments in Zimbabwe." He tells me how the traditional craft has survived. "Dry stone masons are called by their ancestors in a dream to work on the restorations, without being previously trained. Just "knowing" how to do the work. These are the stone masons who come to us now, the ones who keep to the original ways."

Chipunza finishes his by-now-warm coke and I venture to respond. "You know, this is valuable information for visitors, maybe the most valuable of all the information about Great Zimbabwe and other sites, the spiritual significance. Educating visitors about the real purpose of your sacred sites, *rushanga*, could be a great service to modern ways of thinking, to recognize the ancient wisdom in historical locations."

"Oh, good idea," he replies. "We are soon going to update the walking-tour brochures for Great Zimbabwe. Let us include this aspect. Good also for Zimbabweans to learn these things."

After a quiet pause, Chipunza grows wistful as he recalls out loud his early mentor at the University of Zimbabwe, David Collette.

"He believed that education removes the soul, that it undoes the spiritual upbringing."

Chipunza laughs, "The Director of NMMZ knows if I 'am involved there will be a ceremony at the site."

Chipunza's stories are deeply resonant, reassuring, grounding, even. Yet the agnostic impulse in me wants to assert its sovereignty, wants to debunk Indigenous spiritual cosmology. Ridiculous as it sounds, I'm aware that my rational mind automatically diminishes whatever I hold sacred and true.

Agnostic impulse: the disbelief in invisibles, enculcated since birth in the Western mind. Named first by Henri Corbin and referenced by Stephen Harrod Buhner in his book *Ensouling Language: On the Art of Non-Fiction and the Writers' Life.*

What is the source of this agnostic impulse, in me specifically, I wonder—beyond 20th century science of reason and the burgeoning materialism of North American society in the 1950s and 60s? My parents come to mind.

My mother, who when asked about God or prayer or spiritual life, responded, irritated, "How would I know? Don't ask me that!"

And my father, who as a youngster felt the dissonance in his mother's devoted churchgoing with her overbearing concern about keeping up appearances, especially his, as she projected her unfulfilled ambition onto him. So my father professed no religious inclination, in fact a patent aversion; end of conversation. But I've come to see his orientation to life as deeply spiritual, one of integrity, acceptance and faith, though he did not name or claim it to spare me the taint of his mother.

"Don't worry about the future," he'd say, "Do your best and things will work out. They always do."

"Chipunza, what do you think of inviting other people, kindred-spirited visitors, to experience the spiritual atmosphere of Mavuradonha, not just the historical sites and artifacts? I could ask the Vardens about organizing the logistics, running it through them."

"Yes, it's a good idea. We can do that."

"But first," I query him, "one must go see the *svikiro* for Mavu-radonha, so he can create a ceremony and ask for permission of the Ancestor spirits on our behalf. Right?"

"Yes, that is the most important thing to do."

"Well, Douglas has taken me to see that *svikiro*. I went to pay my respects, and to offer the traditional gifts in thanks for the priv-ilege of being welcomed by the landscape and the Ancestor spirits of that place. And to ask what contribution I can make in return."

"All right, that's good."

By coincidence, a few days later, when Saki comes to the Dairy Cottage for a tarot reading to chart the way forward for his art school, the guidance in the cards will direct him to return to the spiritual practices of his culture. I'll mention the prospect of going into Mavuradonha with Chipunza, and though they haven't met, Saki is enthusiastic—after all, *Ziva*, the name of his art school, means wisdom, knowledge, in Shona language. The artist and the archeologist, both spirit guides.

Back to this afternoon with Chipunza, the air cools down under the shaded veranda, the conversation seems to have passed so quickly.

"Chipunza, may I ask how goes your project to obtain heritage status for Mavuradonha? Where are you now in that process?"

"Documentation of the area is complete," he replies, "and we are now at a problematic stage. The key players, the stakeholders, need to meet and come to agreement on the boundaries, responsi-bilities and benefits of the proposed national heritage site, so that when status is given there will be no conflicts."

He tells me that the key players include the rural councils, the traditional tribal chiefs, the safari tourism, the camp lease-holders, and an NGO community group that has been inactive.

"I am dreading this roundtable in three months time. It will be a bruising meeting, with a crisis of expectations."

Something twinges in my gut. A musical friend in England comes to mind and I mention her to Chipunza. Chloe Goodchild uses singing for conflict resolution; she has worked with international policy makers in her "Singing Fields." Chloe has sung for the Dalai Lama, and created the music for Eve Ensler's Vagina Monologues in Madison Square Gardens, New York. This last one I don't say to Chipunza.

"That would work," Chipunza muses, "People in Zimbabwe do a lot of spiritual singing. During the war (of liberation, 1978-80) spiritual singing is what pulled us through. I think we just have to go ahead and do it, regardless of which stakeholders accept it. If the heritage status is not blessed it may well fail."

Chipunza puts a broad hand on his chin and rubs his jaw. After a short silence, I return to our conversation about going to Mavuradonha with a visiting group next year. I ask what he imagines we would do with the visitors who come to experience the cultural landscape and the deeper spiritual eco-system. First though, I suggest accommodation at Ann's guesthouse for a few days, where we can all meet in Harare. Chipunza agrees it's a perfect location with the peaceful gardens, and that he will give an orientation to the wilderness' archeological history, an academic audio-visual presentation. And he agrees that I should guide some Meditating With The Body practices to help people relax and acclimatize to being in Zimbabwe. After that we will make the half-day drive up to the wilderness bush camp in the Mavuradonha Mountains.

"Then what?" I ask.

He says matter-of-factly, "I play mbira and have a group of mbira musicians who play only for the spiritual ceremonies."

"Mbira?" The electric fan on the desk swivels and a warm wind passes across my face.

Chipunza continues. "The other mbira players wanted to go commercial, to play weddings, parties, any events to make money. But I said no, they cannot do that, mbira is not for that. We must respect the purpose of mbira and the traditional ways."

He pauses and grins to himself. "The group is busy every week-end in the year with spiritual rituals, now. The people want to know our traditional culture in this lost modern world. The mbira players are making more money, too, than if they were doing what they wanted to last year. So we can go together to Mavuradonha, build a big bonfire and play mbira all night, until sunrise. When daylight comes, we walk with everyone to the *rushanga*."

However, it turns out that Janine is not in the mood for looking ahead to next year, nor for planning an itinerary on speculation. The cancellation, due to no clients, of our long-planned horse safari into the Cultural Landscape of Mavuradonha next month has been discouraging. On the practical side of things, I understand and respect Janine's position; it makes more sense for me to gather a group together first of all, and then approach her about booking dates with payment ready. That's easy to do, based on my Hollyhock program development experience, and I feel a resurgence of purpose imagining returning to Zimbabwe with kindred spirits in hand.

It's been almost two months since Munhondo's injury and a month since his surgery. A few days ago, I took him for a little grazing walk on the grounds of the veterinary hospital; his spirits were bright with the fresh green grass, although the infected bone had crumbled significantly, allowing no weight bearing at all. Janine went to see him last evening when she got back from bush camp and more heart-rending signs of suffering are showing—his other hind hoof has developed laminitis due to overload fatigue. She called this morning in tears, to tell me they have let him go.

The mighty Munhondo, strong resilient leader of the safari endurance horses, is gone. He, who climbs rock mountains, fords rainy-season rivers, and fearlessly faces lions, is no longer of this world. Remembering too, Bhura, trusted lead mare of the herd on that first safari in Hwange, who died two years ago without warn-ing, a few months after giving birth to a lively filly who survived.

Choosing a life with horses anywhere in the world means vivid awareness of impermanence, the seasons of life and death. Horses cycle through this life on earth in a shorter time span than humans. Foals are born, fillies and colts grow up, treasured equine friends pass away. They seem so enduring, yet at twenty-five or thirty years old a horse is elderly, and even before then, injury and affliction can take their lives.

Back home in Canada, Mary has lived on her farm sanctuary in Goldstream all her adult life. The horses buried over the years in the 20-acre rolling field are called "the Spirit Herd." At times we feel their presence, especially during Equine Guided Learning programs. And Michelle at Spirit Gate Farm lost one of her three magnificent black Trakehner geldings on Good Friday last year, his head resting in her lap as he passed on. Two days later, Easter Sunday, a beautiful filly, baby Sheema, was born to Michelle's Arabian paint mare.

Here in Africa, the Vardens donate the body of their horses who pass away to a wildlife sanctuary just outside Harare, as food for the rescued and orphaned animals. And that's why the horses are not euthanized by injection, but rather, the very veterinarian who has cared for them has to shoot his patient. With kind words and close range, in the forehead, so the horse's body is toxin free for the sanctuary animals who will become the beneficiaries. The cycle of life—compassion, sorrow, and resurrection—carries on.

A few days before my departure for Canada, Emeesh's five-year-old daughter Tsungi stands on the back seat of the taxi clinging to the headrest, hollering, and sobbing with all her heart. I've been visiting the family in their village home by Lake Chivero, near Harare. Tsungi remembers our times together in the past—now, she is inconsolable in my leaving her and wants to come with me.

I slide onto the seat, hold her close, and forcefully, tenderly, try to lift her out, feeling villainous with this action. But I'm not strong enough, and neither is MaiTsungi, her mother, so she and I now stand a few feet away, beside each other, bewildered. Emeesh comes out of their *imba*, leans into the car, sits down and begins to speak quietly to his young daughter. After a time, her tantrum gives way to tear-choked hiccups; then, at last, by Emeesh's gestures, and Tsungi's smile, I can see he is promising her I will return. Tsungi climbs over her father and stretches her thin legs to the ground. She walks toward me, head up, her little skirt swirling with each footstep. She slides her hand into mine and leads me to the taxi driver who stands behind the car.

*"Chengeta gogo vangu,"* she says resolutely to the burly man, who bends down to hear her.

Take good care of my grandmother.

Very early in the morning, before my evening plane flight begins the journey back to Canada, Stephen comes by the Dairy Cottage, as planned, to say good morning before he goes to work at the stable.

*"Mangwanani,"* he calls. I'm waiting in the cottage doorway and move to sit down beside him on the still dewy grass, our blue-jeaned legs stretched out in front. A wisp of elm tree fluff alights on Stephen's eyelash.

I want to read aloud stories I've written about him, an integrity check to make sure I have his permission to write the real story. Stephen listens as an audio editor would, objectively, as if he personally is not the subject of the story. I'm amazed he isn't roused by the description of those first nights together in Harare, a lifetime ago it seems.

He simply nods, "Yes, it was like that."

Mid-way through reading the scene of our bath in Chiwiti *kumusha*, I ask, "Can you really gentle a sable antelope doe? I mean, walk up to the *mharapara* and she wouldn't run away? Is it correct if I write this?"

"Yes," he says solemnly. Next question.

"My editor thinks that describing you as a 'black' beauty of a horse is too obvious, too racial. What do you think?"

"I am black. Write black. I am African. We are proud of our black skin, shows our culture, our strength."

When I finish reading, he responds, "Yes, everything, you can say it.

How does one describe a friendship founded in the genus of divine intimacy? *Hushamwari*, sacred friendship. *Mudiwa*, the beloved.

My heart pulses into my throat.

"I want to say, *maita basa, Baba*." I begin. "Thank you. Thank you for your *muti* to me, the good medicine of being with you. You know your medicine makes me well. And thank you, too, for the gift of Africa from your body—the land, the trees, the water, the birds, the animals, always."

Stephen turns to look in my eyes, "*Zvakanaka, Amai.*"

He is saying "You are welcome, mama."

I go on, "First we have a love affair, only you and only me. Now we have a family affair; my son has come to Zimbabwe and met your sons, and I know all your family now—sisters, mother, everyone. And we are business partners, too. Now, you are free. Free to find a wife, a full-time permanent wife.

"A woman who will cook your *sadza* and make you fat again. Who will keep your *imba*, your house, nicely-nicely. Who will grow your crops on your land in *kumusha* and keep your money. And talk-talk-talk with you in Shona, and listen, and make plans for the future."

There is a long silence. Birds hush, a green cricket pauses on the step. The gardener keeps his distance cutting grass with a long-handled scythe. The elm leaves rustle softly. The slight pulsing of Stephen's left temple is so familiar.

He clears his throat and says, "When I get a new wife—yes, older woman, not young one—and when you come back to Zimbabwe, she will meet you. She can say to you, *Makadii, maiguru?* What she can say is, 'Hello, to Stephen's wife before.' "

# Impermanence

Five weeks after returning to Canada I receive an urgent phone call, with grim news from Zimbabwe. The nearest white neighbours of the farm at Siya Lima, a farmer and his adult daughter, were brutally attacked on an afternoon walkabout with their dogs. Both of them died in hospital a week or so later. The perpetrators are still at large, reportedly hiding out in the Mavuradonha bush. As the crow flies that farm isn't far from Siya Lima—isn't far from where I walked alone in the shimmer and shadow of Nyambare Mountain.

I can clearly picture coils of black plastic plumbing pipe stacked in the Siya Lima farmhouse courtyard. That same farmer was about to begin work replacing the waterworks in the farmhouse. I try not to picture a field and a ditch, a scene of barbarity.

The horses have been moved from Siya Lima farm to a safer, less isolated location closer to Harare. The Vardens stay away, not wanting to inflame tension in the community. Only Shepherd, the one groom who lives beside the farm and is safe as a local, remains to caretake the empty farmhouse and stable for the time being.

My mind ricochets with questions that have shadowed my time in Zimbabwe: What leads impotence to seek power in brutal ways? How do the widowed and orphaned, of every ethnicity, survive the murder of their families? What determines the resilience in one human being in the aftermath of tragedy and trauma?

I walk outside, into my garden on Canadian soil. Everything is still, no breeze, no birdsong, and I lie down, gut on the ground. Enormous rhubarb leaves shade my eyes from the brightness of high noon. The earth is soft under my cheek, a shiny black ant is busily dragging a dead insect casing over gleaming mica particles and tiny shreds of composted horse manure. A faraway seaplane purrs its way north. The sun burns hot on the back of my bare legs.

In early July, Douglas texts that Rachel has given birth to their first child together, Douglas' fourth son. They have named the baby Devon Chinhamo, to honour their friendship with my son Devon.

With Douglas' celebratory text message, I wake up to a distressingly personal consequence of the atrocity in the Siya Lima community—the evaporation of my hoped-for home in the farmhouse and my joy in the prospect of Douglas, Chipunza and Saki guiding my Canadian friends into the spiritual eco-system of Mavuradonha next year.

My sense of purpose and place drains in the shadow-truth of living in Zimbabwe. To imagine making a plan at this point would be wrongly-founded and irresponsible.

As the summer progresses on Cortes Island, seasonal visitors who know her charms take up residence and gush enthusiastically about the warm ocean water. They set off in their kayaks at sunrise, host dinners of fresh salmon and oysters, report sightings of dolphins and orca whales. Devon returns to our island *kumusha*, to live, and is kayak guiding as he did in the summers through high school and university.

But this year, my new lawn hasn't seeded properly, it looks thin and bare; the usually welcome heat is enervating, and I can barely muster the energy to bike to the lake for a swim after working with the horses. I take a mattress outside so I can sleep under the stars, while the moon is dark, hoping for deliverance.

In the throes of feeling so gutted with loss, mine and the collective, still, one tiny tendril sprouts—one that matters more than anything—and that is being able to know, inside myself, a miniscule fraction of the suffering of those displaced and homeless, both human and animal, in Zimbabwe, and everywhere else on this planet.

By the end of the year Mel and Charlie give up their residence in Harare, before conditions in the country worsen, and move to live full time in their home on the south coast of Spain. My dear Ann has finally found a buyer for her Borrowdale Country Manor and relocates to a much smaller and easier to manage guesthouse in town near the Harare Botanical Gardens. And Stephen is no longer working in Harare—nor even in nearby Chegutu with his shop.

It turns out, as might be expected, that running the shop in Chegutu was more complicated than Stephen had imagined and being indoors all day didn't suit him at all, once the novelty wore off. So he quit that and invested instead in a maize grinding mill, something he had actually wanted all along and an easier source of daily revenue, "money in the pocket." Householders bring a bucket of maize kernels, stripped from the cobs they have grown, and pay one dollar to have it ground into mealie meal for *sadza*. The grinding machine is now in the care of the sister who lives in Chegutu. Stephen himself is back, after a four-year absence, building paddocks and training horses with a new riding outfit in the wilderness nearby Hwange National Park—where I was first bitten by the Africa bug.

Twelve months have gone by without returning to Zimbabwe. Late one summer evening, I sit with my laptop open, outside on the patio. I'm checking Facebook posts, mostly of friends in Africa, to see their most recent photos and news. Theresa posts new pictures of the elephants just about every day, probably as a means of staying sane and connected with a world of caring supporters beyond the Chiredzi lowveld. I've drafted an email to her, asking about staying at Wasara over the coming (Canadian) winter to finish the book.

Suddenly I can't breathe and tears are spilling onto the keyboard. The posts are referring to Theresa in the past tense. Let me get a tissue and wipe my glasses. Take a deep breath and look again. Yes, the date is from yesterday. Theresa just collapsed, in Harare. She died. That's the only information posted. The most poignant picture shows Mellie, her Swiss niece, from behind, sitting on the ground at Wasara with Chitora standing beside her, heads down low.

"Missing Mum," the caption says.

The on-line journal Voices for Biodiversity, for whom I have written several articles based on my field notes in Africa, publishes a tribute to Theresa that I send them. A few months ago, she met her heroine Jane Goodall at a conservation conference in South Africa. James Varden now posts a photo of Theresa arm-in-arm with Jane, the caption reads: "Two of a Kind."

Within the month, social media around the globe is lit up with news of the killing of Cecil the lion, one of the most majestic pride patriarchs in Hwange National Park. Zimbabwe. And then another headline story—the oldest and biggest living elephant in the country, perhaps all of southern Africa, is gone from this earth, killed by legal hunters just outside the boundary of Gonarezhou National Park. Zimbabwe. His magnificent ivory tusks had reached almost to the ground. I will come to hear first-hand the repercussions of these two deaths in the social order of their leonine and pachyderm communities and the eco-systems they inhabit.

When one's own heart has been stirred to courage by wild lions in Hwange and one's own soul has been roused to action by elephants in Gonarezhou, the only decent thing to do is lie down, on the ground, and weep your guts out. Watering the garden of grief. Once again.

As I lie here in my garden, face to the earth, beneath the pink blooming day lilies, an image of Jonathan Mazulu comes—doing just this when Patrick Retzlaff's favourite horse, Shere Khan, succumbed to the toxic weed that killed half their Mozambique safari herd. The magnificent Arabian lay lifeless at the bottom of a pit dug by hand in the dirt. Mandy wrote that Jonathan had dropped to the ground above, beside the open grave, and sobbed his heart out.

Working on a memoir is such an exercise in patience, along with marvel in the unfolding of one's own life. The deep attunement of imagining myself "back there," in time, in Africa, until it is alive in me now, so that I can write in the present tense—details and specifics, evocations of colour, sound, taste, landscapes, touch. And, smell.

I remember before I went back to Zimbabwe a year after the first horse safari, in part to meet up with Stephen, that my wondering, my curiosity, was about the fragrance of his skin, the smell of his neck...and everywhere.

And I remember surprising myself that first night. Being able, with him, my real-life-dream lover, to open...and open...and open. To feel thresholds of my own contraction and closure, and then to say "yes" in the innermost, and melt...go with...rather than resist.

What happened with that laying down of arms?

I got over myself, the one who defined herself by parameters of the familiar. I found... I found myself initiated, brought into the resonance of earth Africa through Stephen's body. Through his body—Africa, earth, body—in mine.

I thanked him for that when we parted company last year in May, for bringing me into the earth of Africa through his body—a tree, a flower, a river, a horse. He listened, as if this is normal—which it is, in the geography of belonging.

I stay in touch with Stephen, hoping to keep our friendship and having no idea if that's possible in his culture or his character, after untying the strings. And for months, I steadily and open-handedly bear witness to the stream of change in the country I have come to love. And I wonder when and where will come an opening for my return to Africa, presumably to complete this book and to ride in the wilderness again, or at least be in smelling range of horses.

Where on earth will the guidance of the Ancestors lead me, if I am meant to go at all?

Standing up from my desk this morning to stretch and make a cup of tea, a sudden longing arises for contact with Africa, in real-time, to inspire this morning's writing and to assuage my heart. The phone rings. It's Stephen.

Without preamble, he says, "You can come to Hwange. Help with the horses. Eight horses I am training for riding in the bush. I made a plan for accommodation discount in the safari camp, or you can sleep in a tent by the stables. Yes, it's all right with the woman, owner for Hwange Horseback Safaris. You will like the horses; Sanali, Bongoro, Lily, all of them. Everything good for you."

# DETE, ZIMBABWE

The Nissan pick-up truck, weathered-red in the twilight, rolls up to the stable with me in the front passenger seat. Stephen pulls on the hand brake to stop the vehicle and turns toward me.

"Someone is cooking *sadza* for you."

I can see the silhouette of a woman bending over a fire.

Stephen waits a minute before opening the truck door, his hand on the chipped plastic door handle.

"You pray me to get a new wife," he says. "So, now. I am not throwing you out of my heart, because I have got new wife. I am not chasing the wife away, because you are here. We are relatives, all same—my mother, my sisters, my wife's mother, her sisters. And you."

I take a deep breath before we walk to the fireside.

"What is her name?"

"Faith," he says. "Her name is Faith."

*To speak, and to write, is to assert who we are, what we think. The necessary other side is to surrender these things—to stand humbled and stunned and silent before the wild and inexplicable beauties and mysteries of being.*

Jane Hirshfield
"Writing and the Threshold Life"
from *Nine Gates: Entering the Mind of Poetry*

# Epilogue

Two months into my stay at Miombo Safari Camp, where the Hwange Horseback Safari horses are in Stephen's care, exceedingly good news comes from Canada. An unprecedented coalition of First Nations, environmentalists, forest companies and the provincial government signs The Great Bear Rainforest Preservation Agreement. February, 2016. One of the largest intact coastal temperate rainforests left on the planet is now protected in perpetuity.

A year later, in January 2017, the Mavuradonha Wilderness is designated a National Heritage site by the Zimbabwean government. Mission accomplished. Wildlife is reintroduced by the new lease-holder—zebra, giraffe, impala, sable, elephant and more—with an area of perimeter fencing and active anti-poaching scouts to keep them safe. Predator species may be brought in beyond that, deeper into the wild mountains.

I return to Zimbabwe again, and again. Stephen remains a central figure, trusted soul friend. During the time when I finished transcribing the final edits in the marked-up print copy of this manuscript, onto my solar-powered laptop, we are in the wilderness once more. The Ngamo Plains of southeast Hwange National Park. Lions are coming near to the camp at night, lured by the horses.

I tell Stephen the manuscript pages are to be burned, to stay here in the African wilderness where the story came from. It's twilight, my last evening in camp, and I imagine offering the pages, small handfuls at a time, to the cooking fire after dinner.

Stephen says, "Give to me" and reaches for the heavy bundle of paper. Picking up a metal shovel he single-handedly scoops it full of glowing coals from the fire and strides to a huge pile of branches at the edge of the stable clearing, ready to be lit to keep the lions at bay in the night. He drops the paper bundle onto the wood. He looks at me, then, pours the orange-red coals on top. A rocket-burst of flame spires to the tree tops, alive against the dark violet sky.

By the new year of 2020, the beautiful country of Zimbabwe has fallen prey, once again, to what the South African Daily Maverick newspaper calls the "predator elite." The abrupt removal of Robert Mugabe from presidential office in late 2017, by his own party rivals, brought a celebratory optimism in the people that continued through the national election in 2018 and kept ZANU-PF in power. But the promise of positive change with a new president fell short, abysmally short. A woman friend in a stricken high-density suburb of Bulawayo sends me a Whatsapp message: "I don't know how we left behind our cultures as humans. There's no love, anymore."

As I reflect on the decade of traveling between Canada and Africa, a second book, true sequel to this one, is taking shape.

*Scent of the Earth* begins with a divination by African elder, Malidoma Somé—confirming horses as the portal to the healing and wisdom found in the spirit world. I enter more deeply into Shona spiritual culture, through the music and ceremony of mbira. And, indeed, find myself at the gates of Healing-with-Horses-Zimbabwe, a therapeutic farm, a refuge of love and inclusion for special children and the volunteers who serve them. My seventieth birthday is quietly celebrated, there, in a field with children and horses. At home in Canada, two white horses await.

# Acknowledgments

Firstly, Mandy and Pat Retzlaff of Mozambique Horse Safari, and James and Janine Varden of Ride Zimbabwe, who opened the way to Africa, with their horse stewards, Jonathan Mazulu and Stephen Hambani, respectively. And each wise person in Africa who is woven into this story, especially Tafadzwa Mupfawa and Simon Mbomba.

Frances Guthrie, on Cortes Island, introduced me to natural horsemanship and has been a faithful mentor in my journey with horses. Ann Dewar entrusted her horses to me for long periods of time. Michelle Atterby first offered a home with horses. Mary Rostad Robinson gave me the opportunity to practice the "manure meditation" through many seasons of change. Jonathan Field opened the barn door to competence and confidence on horseback.

Deborah Marshall translated Linda Kohanov's book *The Tao of Equus* into hands-on learning for me with her own herd. Linda-Ann Bowling models "know thyself" through horses. Lauren Fraser lives her horse dream in the most practical ways. Sandra Wallin lives and breathes the archetypal world of horses with her own equine quartet and others in far-off places. Most recently, Güliz Ünlü and Kera Willis' magical kinship with the natural world inspires our work, "Earth Wisdom, Horse Wisdom."

All the horses who have been my medicine, friends and teachers, here on earth, and those now with the Ancestors' spirit herd. Most especially Cosun, Sid, Nepenthe, Tsunami, Munhondo and Prince.

Kristen Scholfield-Sweet, longtime spiritual friend and mentor—for the ground that underlies everything I know and write about. Likewise, Atum O'Kane, in his own language. Julie Kramer and

Tami Simon for their spirited friendship, generosity and wisdom along the path.

First reader, Erin Skye Robinsong, read what started out as a travelogue during my first trip to Africa and said: *You need to put the love story in.* She wouldn't stand for my reticence. Nancy Flight, then of Greystone Books, pointed out that the human love story *is* the narrative arc of the book. Then again, the love story is with the motherland, herself.

Priya Huffman for her unfailing early encouragement to keep writing the story while I lived it. In the same vein, Heather Read, Chloe Goodchild, Kolin Lymworth and Margie Gillis have been seminal supporters all along. So, too, have Heather Read, Naomi Hayter, Indrus Piché, Norm Gib-bons, Lizanne Fisher and Siobhan Robinsong.

A deep bow to the writers—writing workshop teachers—who offered their literary wherewithal and helped me breathe life into the manuscript. Notably, Sharon Butala, whose books I have re-read till they're ragged. Mark Matousek, a most generous listener of the human heart. Shaena Lambert, for a hand up, after the deep dive.

My most profound thanks must go to the editor of my original manuscript, Cynthia Woodman Kerkham. When I'd barely begun the writing, Canadian Horse Journals invited me to publish a personal story about Horses-in-Africa. I had no idea if my writing was up to standard. I called upon Cynthia, who proceeded to teach, mentor and counsel me, not only about writing, but also about truly digesting life experience over our time of working together in *The Geography of Belonging*.

To be welcomed by Salmonberry Arts & Publishing with generosity and trust fulfills my writing odyssey. And to the *vadzimu*, blessings abound. *Ndatenda*.

# About the Cover

*The Geography of Belonging* brings the reader into the radiant sun, the smell of the earth and the smile of our people. The story carries my sense of *home* when I am away from Afrika.

When Oriane Lee asked me to design the cover of her book, I rummaged through my late father's things and found the rough cut-out of a heart and decided it would be the canvas of a painting. I also found a box of colorful inks in my things. My 6-year old daughter – a budding artist – was delighted and we laid out some newsprint on our long dining table.

"I don't know what you're painting but I love it!" she gushed as we began. I call the painting *Moyo we Rudo*: heart of love. I placed the Nguni symbol for love/passion inside the heart. Having focused professionally on graphic design, I haven't painted since MFA years at Yale in the eighties; it was pure joy to find myself now painting alongside my young daughter, Rumbi.

The heart sits on a carved wooden stool, a head-rest for Shona royalty in ancient times. Blue is the sky of Zimbabwe and the water of west coast Canada. The front cover is framed, top and bottom, with *retso* patterns from ceremonial cloth worn by Shona *svikiros* – spirit mediums. On the back cover, a Zebra appears from an ancient cave drawing. Oriane Lee rides toward the sacred Nyambare Mountain, where spirits dwell. Photographed by Douglas Chinhamo, the two of them respectfully skirt around the mountain into the Mavuradonha Wilderness beyond.

Saki Mafundikwa, graphic designer and author of *Afrikan Alphabets, The Story of Writing in Afrika*

*Stephen Hambani on Apache, in Kopje Tops Camp*

# About the Author

Oriane Lee Johnston lives on Cortes Island, in the west coast temperate rain forest of BC, Canada.

Horses have taken her riding in the sacred mountains of Ecuador, swimming in the Indian Ocean, on safari into the Okavango Delta of Botswana, and to the legendary wild herds of the Nemaiah Valley in BC's Chilcotin Country. Former program director for Hollyhock Leadership Centre, Oriane Lee initiated and produced Compassion in Action retreats for environmental and social justice advocates and activists.

Her writing has appeared in The Zambezi Traveler, Harare Magazine and Canadian Horse Journals, and in the online journals Ecology.com, Voicesforbiodiversity.com, Equitrekking.com and Lifeasahuman.org.

Find photos and music playlist companion to the story.
www.orianelee.com